BORGES' CLASSICS

T0372717

In *Borges' Classics*, Laura Jansen reads the oeuvre of the Argentine author Jorge Luis Borges as a radically globalized model for reimagining our relationship with the classical past. This major study reveals how Borges constructs a new 'physics of reading' the classics, which privileges a paradoxical vision of the canon as universal yet centreless, and eschews fixed ideas about the cultural history of the West. Borges' unique approach transforms classical antiquity into a simultaneously familiar and remote world, whose legacy is both urgent and unstable. In the process, Borges repositions the classical tradition at the intersection of the traditional Western canon and modernist literature of the peripheral West. Jansen's study traces Borges' encounters with the classics through appeal to themes central to Borges' thought, such as history and fiction, memory and forgetfulness, the data of the senses, and the vectors that connect cultures and countries.

LAURA JANSEN is Lecturer in Latin Language and Literature at the University of Bristol.

CLASSICS AFTER ANTIQUITY

Editors
Alastair Blanshard
University of Queensland
Shane Butler
Johns Hopkins University
Emily Greenwood
Yale University

Classics after Antiquity presents innovative contributions in the field of Classical Reception Studies. Each volume explores the methods and motives of those who, coming after and going after antiquity, have entered into a contest with and for the legacies of the ancient world. The series aims to unsettle, provoke debate, and to stimulate a re-evaluation of assumptions about the relationship between Greek and Roman classical pasts and modern histories.

Other titles in the series

Classical Victorians: Scholars, Scoundrels and Generals in Pursuit of Antiquity

Edmund Richardson

ISBN: 978-1-107-02677-3

Modernism and Homer: The Odysseys of H.D., James Joyce, Osip Mandelstam, and Ezra Pound

Leah Culligan Flack

ISBN: 978-1-107-10803-5

Argentinian writer Jorge Luis Borges at the ruins of the temple at Selinunte, 1984.
Photo: Ferdinando Scianna / Magnum Images Ltd.

BORGES' CLASSICS

Global Encounters with the Graeco-Roman Past

LAURA JANSEN

University of Bristol

Shaftesbury Road, Cambridge CB2 8EA, United Kingdom

One Liberty Plaza, 20th Floor, New York, NY 10006, USA

477 Williamstown Road, Port Melbourne, VIC 3207, Australia

314–321, 3rd Floor, Plot 3, Splendor Forum, Jasola District Centre, New Delhi – 110025, India

103 Penang Road, #05–06/07, Visioncrest Commercial, Singapore 238467

Cambridge University Press is part of Cambridge University Press & Assessment, a department of the University of Cambridge.

We share the University's mission to contribute to society through the pursuit of education, learning and research at the highest international levels of excellence.

www.cambridge.org
Information on this title: www.cambridge.org/9781108406024

DOI: 10.1017/9781108289979

First published 2018
First paperback edition 2024

A catalogue record for this publication is available from the British Library

ISBN   978-1-108-41840-9   Hardback
ISBN   978-1-108-40602-4   Paperback

To my sister, Perla

Primera cuestión: la lectura es un arte de la microscopía, del espacio (no sólo los pintores se ocupan de esas cosas). Segunda cuestión: la lectura es un asunto de óptica, de luz, una dimensión de la física.

First point: reading is a microscopic art, an art of space (not only painters are concerned with these things). Second point: reading is a matter of optics, of light, a dimension of physics.

Ricardo Piglia, *El último lector*, 2005 [on Borges as a reader]

Escribir sobre un escritor puede ser una manera extraordinaria de leerlo.

To write about a writer can be a remarkable way to read one.

Alan Pauls, *Interview with Rodrigo Fresan* [on writing about Borges] Casa América, 2011

Contents

Preface

Jorge Luis Borges (1899, Buenos Aires – 1986, Geneva) is nothing less than a titanic figure in the history of literature and criticism. As one of the most significant and influential Latin American writers of the twentieth century and a colossus of global letters, he looms large in the literary imaginations of every language into which he has been translated, including English. His importance for Anglophone thought about books, libraries, poetry, the practice of reading and the art of writing was confirmed by his famous Charles Eliot Norton Lectures at Harvard in 1967–68 (published in 2000 as *This Craft of Verse*); few scholars of such matters go very far without invoking him. It would be no exaggeration to say that Borges has shaped not only how we think about the humanities, but even how we dream about them.

Nevertheless, Borges remains somewhat underserved by English-language scholarship, and he lacks any major study of his relationship to Graeco-Roman antiquity, which remained throughout his career an Ariadne's thread to his labyrinthine thought about the literatures and cultures of the entire world. With *Borges' Classics*, Laura Jansen steps boldly into that scholarly breach. Her timely volume addresses a range of audiences: those interested in Borges in his own right; those similarly interested in Argentinian or Latin-American or Hispanophone literatures; scholars of comparative and world literatures; scholars of what has come to be called 'global Classics'; other scholars of classical reception; and classicists looking for creative perspectives on classical literature itself. To read Jansen reading Borges reading Classics is nothing short of a rediscovery of what it means to read – with wit, imagination and humanity.

Jansen deftly conjures Borges as he negotiates his complex relationships to such major figures of the classical canon as Homer, Vergil and Lucretius. Not stopping there, however, she follows him through somewhat less celebrated terrain, like that of the Pre-Socratic philosophers, and farther still, into the broken bits and pieces that comprise much of what lingers, often anonymously, from the ancient past. So too does she track his engagement with his more immediate predecessors, like Franz Kafka, as well as his influence on contemporaries and successors, including Italo Calvino, Umberto Eco and Derek Walcott (each of these, of course, is famous in his own right as a 'receiver' of the classical past). The resulting portrait of literary influence is breathtaking in its sweep, with Jansen attentive to both continuities and discontinuities – as Borges himself was, ever-mindful of the lessons of Heraclitus (the subject of Jansen's second chapter). And one of the many things that this portrait reveals is the truth of the lesson Borges derives from his reading of Kafka: 'The fact is that each writer *creates* his precursors. His work modifies our conception of the past, as it will modify the future.' In other words, Borges provides us not only with an especially complex and dynamic example of tradition and reception at work; rather, he confounds the very temporalities by which literary history is generally thought to play out, troubling, in the end, our conceptual hold on time itself.

Arguably, the most remarkable achievement of *Borges' Classics* is that, by its conclusion, it has reduced its title subject to the status of a pleonasm. That is to say, the reader comes away no longer able to imagine – indeed, unable to remember having ever imagined – any 'Classics' that was not always already 'Borges''. This, to be clear, is not the same as concluding that Borges belongs, at least partly, to Classics. Laura Jansen does unfold, by and by, a compelling argument to this effect. But she knows full well that to limit herself to this would be to claim yet another extraterritorial writer for an imperious (and imperial) West. Her more important argument is instead a converse one that unites the sharpest insights of classical reception studies, global Classics and planetary modernisms. Adding Borges' supra-Western, cosmic conception of classical antiquity to the bookshelf of the classical tradition brushes centuries of dust off the tomes already sitting there. Making the classics strange and wonderful again, Borges frees even the most familiar works to address us in almost forgotten ways, once again opening vast and thrilling vistas onto human experience and its place in the cosmos.

SHANE BUTLER
EMILY GREENWOOD
ALASTAIR BLANSHARD

Acknowledgements

I cannot recall with precision when the idea of this book came to me because I have been reading Borges and the classics for so long. Yet the first tangible memory takes me to the island of Sifnos in July a few years ago. I spent that happy summer rereading a bilingual edition of *The Book of Sand* in Greek and Spanish that reinvigorated my passion for Borges' oeuvre in more ways than I could then imagine. Thank you, Nikolas, for filling my bookshelves with Borges and countless other authors for so many years. This book also has a beginning in Bristol, in late 2014, when I co-organized "Two Nights with Borges" with Shane Butler, then Director of Bristol's Institute for Greece, Rome and the Classical Tradition (IGRCT). I am grateful to Shane for his genuine support, and for encouraging me to write on Borges and the classical past. Warmest thanks also to the editors of *Classics After Antiquity*, Alastair Blanshard, Shane Butler and Emily Greenwood for their enthusiasm about this book and their careful feedback, to Michael Sharp, who offered constant guidance and support, and to Richard Hallas for his terrific work during copy-editing. The anonymous readers were outstanding. I am fortunate to have benefitted from their vast knowledge and expertise.

I would not have been able to complete this book without the generous financial support of a Leverhulme Trust Research Fellowship during 2015–16 and three awards from Bristol's Faculty of Arts' Research Fund in 2014, 2015 and 2016. The project was also greatly enhanced by a Visiting Fellowship at Princeton University in 2015–16, a Scholar Grant at the Centre of Hellenic Studies, Harvard in 2016, a long stay in Paris consulting the National Library of France and numerous visits to the wonderful Fondation Hardt in Geneva, a city much beloved by Borges. I am grateful for the opportunity to speak about Borges and classical antiquity at Bristol, Brown, Cambridge, Johns Hopkins, Princeton, Reading, the Boghossian Foundation, Brussels, The Virgil Society, London, the Society of Classical Studies at San Francisco and Yale. I feel privileged to have been able to discuss my work with such prestigious audiences. Throughout the entire project, I travelled widely to undertake research in the UK, continental Europe, the United States and my own Buenos Aires. This has given me the unique opportunity to meet and exchange communications with writers, translators, biographers, photographers and expert readers of Borges, who either knew him or have extraordinary knowledge of him. Amongst them, I would like to mention Alberto Manguel, Ricardo Piglia (†), Celia Milstein, Fernando Scianna, Daniel Balderston, Evelyn Fishburn, Francisco García Jurado, Edwin Williamson, Jason Wilson and James Woodall.

I would like to express my gratitude to Andrew Laird, who supported this project from its early beginnings, when it was no more than a vague paragraph, to its full expression. Throughout this process, we discussed a lot of Borges in Oxford, Princeton and Brown, while co-translating several pieces from Spanish and French into English for the book. Evi Fishburn, Charles Martindale and James Porter read the entire book and improved it with incisive and erudite comments. Warm thanks for their intellectual generosity, encouragement and time. I am also grateful to Richard Cole for proofreading different parts of the book, and to my dear friend Vasileia Kouliouri for her help with the bibliography. Amongst numerous friends, colleagues and postgraduate students who have shown enthusiasm for this project, I would like to acknowledge (in alphabetical order): Rosa Andújar; Francisco Barrenechea; Pablo de León; Al Duncan; Andrew Feldherr; Tristan Franklinos; Moira Fradinger; Bob Fowler; Bruce Gibson; Roy Gibson; Lorna Hardwick; Brooke Holmes; Kathi Iuanyi; George Kazantzidis; Duncan Kennedy; Dimitris Kousouri; Marina Kousouri; Lisa Kraege; Vassilis Lambropoulos; Miriam Leonard; Justine McConnell; Pantelis Michelakis; Irini Michali; Neville Morley; Ellen O'Gorman; Alex Purves; Ed Richardson; Connie and Ron Stroud; Polina Tambakaki; James Uden; Georgios Vassiliades; and Phiroze Vasunia. My undergraduate students at Bristol took up the challenge of rereading Lucretius' *De rerum natura* alongside Borges' *Fictions* and Calvino's *Invisible Cities*. I learned a lot from our class discussions, their stunning essays (even exam responses!), as well as their exercises in creative writing and performance. A similarly wonderful experience was IGRCT's Borges Postgraduate Reading Group, which offered me the chance to think about material for this book with a group of brilliant and imaginative postgraduates.

Luke Roman read the entire manuscript and improved it with rare intelligence and vision. I owe him many observations made in this book, and I am deeply grateful to him not only for his time and generosity of mind, but also for his warmth and constant encouragement. My nephews and brother-in-law were keen on this project from its beginning. They offered help when I was not in Buenos Aires, going to exhibitions for the commemoration of the 30 years of Borges' death in 2016, and sending me articles on Borges from local literary magazines and newspapers. I would like to express my gratitude to them for being there for me during the past two years. This book is dedicated to my wonderful sister, who continues to show me like no other that there is inherent beauty in laughter and sophisticated simplicity.

Chronology of Borges' Life and Works

[Adapted from Williamson, E. (2013)]

1899   Born on August 24 in Calle Tucumán 840, in the centre of Buenos Aires, to Jorge Guillermo Borges, a half-English lawyer and aspiring writer, and Leonor Acevedo Suárez.

1900   Family moves to Palermo, then a poor district bordering the pampas, inhabited by immigrants and once notorious for knife-fighters and brothels.

1914   Family goes to Europe and settles in Geneva until end of World War I. Attends secondary school, and learns French, Latin and German.

1919–21   Family spends time in Majorca, Seville and Madrid. Joins an avant-garde group of poets known as the Ultra.

1921   Returns to Buenos Aires. Forms a group of *ultraístas* and introduces avant-garde ideas through "mural magazine" *Prisma* and little review *Proa* (*Prow*).

1923   *Fervor de Buenos Aires* (poems).

1923–24   Second visit to Europe. Becomes disillusioned with Spanish *ultraísmo*. On return to Buenos Aires, relaunches *Proa* with a group of young writers and develops a left-of-centre cultural nationalism called *criollismo*.

1925   *Moon Across the Way* (*Luna de enfrente*) (poems) and *Inquisitions* (essays). Frequent clashes between Borges' *criollista* group around *Proa* and an avant-garde group associated with the "cosmopolitan" review *Martín Fierro*.

1926   *The Extent of My Hope* (*El tamaño de mi esperanza*) (essays, many on *criollismo*).

1927   Creates a "Committee of Young Intellectuals" with a group of *criollistas* to campaign for the re-election to the presidency of the Radical party candidate, the populist Hipólito Yrigoyen. Increasingly opposed by right-wing nationalists.

1928   *The Language of the Argentines* (essays). Yrigoyen elected president.

1929   *San Martín Copybook* (*Cuaderno San Martín*) (poems). Meets Nicolás Paredes, a former Palermo gang boss, who will inspire his first story, 'Man on Pink Corner'.

1930   *Evaristo Carriego* (biography of a Palermo poet, plus essays on folk themes). President Yrigoyen overthrown in military coup d'état by right-wing nationalists. Disillusioned, Borges abandons *criollismo*.

1931   Invited by Victoria Ocampo to join board of new cultural journal *Sur*.

1932   *Discusión* (essays). Contributes to various literary magazines.

1933   Co-editor of the Saturday colour supplement of mass daily newspaper *Crítica*, where he publishes stories, essays, reviews and sketches until 1934. Becomes a leading opponent of right-wing Argentine nationalism and repeatedly denounces fascism and Nazism in Europe.

1935   *A Universal History of Iniquity* (fictionalized biographical sketches).

1936   *A History of Eternity* (essays). Edits fortnightly books section of popular weekly magazine *El Hogar* (*The Home*), for which he writes reviews and capsule biographies of writers.

1938   Employed as library assistant in a municipal library, his first full-time job. Father dies. Accident on Christmas Eve leads to life-threatening septicaemia.

1939   Writes 'Pierre Menard, Author of the *Quixote*' while recuperating. Loses job at *El Hogar*. Publicly supports the Allies in World War II, and will condemn Nazism and its many sympathizers amongst Argentine nationalists throughout the conflict. Joins *Unión Democrática*, a coalition of Radicals, socialists and communists opposing the pro-Axis nationalists.

1940   Begins collaboration with Adolfo Bioy Casares, which will produce stories, film scripts and translations over the years. They compile, together with Silvina Ocampo, an *Anthology of Fantasy Literature* and an *Anthology of Argentine Poetry*. Begins contributing regularly to *Sur*, where he will first publish many of his famous texts.

1941	*The Garden of Forking Paths* (fiction).
1942	*Six Problems for Don Isidro Parodi* (detective stories), with Bioy Casares under common pseudonym H. Bustos Domecq.
1943	*Poemas (1922–43)*. First edition of his collected poems, but the three collections of the 1920s considerably revised, a process continued until tenth edition in 1978. Military coup by nationalist officers sympathetic to Mussolini, including Colonel Juan Domingo Perón.
1944	*Fictions* (*Ficciones*), consisting of *The Garden of Forking Paths* (above), and *Artifices*, comprising six new stories.
1946	Perón elected president of Argentina. Borges resigns post as library assistant when offered dubious promotion by Peronist authorities. Becomes an implacable opponent of the Peronist regime. Earns living by giving lectures on literature. Editor of *Los Anales de Buenos Aires* but resigns in 1947.
1948	Mother and sister arrested and latter briefly imprisoned for demonstrating against Perón.
1949	*The Aleph* (fiction).
1950	Elected president of SADE, the Society of Argentine Writers, a focus of opposition to Perón.
1951	French edition of *Fictions*, first book to be translated into a foreign language.
1952	*Other Inquisitions* (essays). Death of Perón's wife, Eva. SADE closed down after Borges refuses to comply with official mourning decreed by Peronist authorities. In Paris, Roger Caillois publishes *Labyrinthes*, an anthology.
1954	Accident damages his congenitally weak eyesight and can no longer read or write.
1955	Perón overthrown in a military coup and goes into exile. Borges strongly supports the new junta in its campaign to root out Peronism from public life. Appointed Director of the National Library. Elected to the Argentine Academy of Letters. Jean-Paul Sartre publishes eight essays by Borges in *Les Temps modernes*. *La biblioteca di Babele*, a collection of his *ficciones*, appears in Italian.
1956	Appointed to a professorship of English and American Literature at the University of Buenos Aires. Receives

	honorary doctorate from the University of Cuyo, Mendoza, the first of many. Awarded the National Prize for Literature.
1957	*Manual de zoología fantástica* (sketches of fantastic animals), with Margarita Guerrero. *Book of Imaginary Beings* is an expanded version published in 1967. *Other Inquisitions* published in French as *Enquêtes*.
1960	*The Maker* (*El hacedor*) (prose and poems).
1961	Awarded International Publishers' Prize, jointly with Samuel Beckett.
1961–62	Semester at the University of Texas at Austin. Innumerable trips abroad henceforward until the end of his life. *Ficciones* (1962), first book translated into English.
1963	First lecture tour of Britain.
1964	*Obra poética 1923–64* (new title for collected poems). Includes new poems in a section called *The Self and the Other* (*El otro el mismo*), later published as separate volume in 1969.
1965	*For Six Strings* (lyrics for *milongas*).
1967	Marries Elsa Astete Millán. *Chronicles of Bustos Domecq* (spoof essays), with Bioy Casares.
1967–68	Nine months at Harvard as Charles Eliot Norton Professor of Poetry.
1969	*Brodie's Report* (fiction). *In Praise of Darkness* (poems).
1970	Legal separation from Elsa Astete.
1971	*The Congress* (novella), later included in *The Book of Sand*. Begins relationship with Japanese-Argentine María Kodama. Peronist guerrillas start campaign of bombings and kidnapping against the ruling military junta.
1972	*The Gold of the Tigers* (poems).
1973–74	Resigns as Director of National Library after a Peronist wins the presidency. Borges calls those who voted for him 'six million idiots'. In September Perón himself elected president but dies in office in July 1974 and succeeded by wife, María Estela. Guerrillas escalate violence in face of counter-terror by death squads.
1974	First edition of *Obras Completas*.
1975	*The Book of Sand* (fiction). *The Unending Rose* (*La rosa profunda*) (poems). Mother dies at the age of 99. Returns to Geneva for the first time since 1923, and visits frequently thereafter.

1976	*The Iron Coin* (poems). María Estela Perón's government overthrown by military coup. Borges makes controversial statements in the media supporting the new Argentine junta as well as General Pinochet in Chile. Armed forces pursue a 'Dirty War' against the guerrillas through torture and 'disappearances' of opponents.
1977	*The History of the Night* (poems). *New Stories by Bustos Domecq* (fiction), with Bioy Casares.
1977–78	Borges criticizes Argentine military junta for nationalistic sabre-rattling against Chile over islands in the Beagle Channel.
1979	*Borges oral* (lectures given at the Universidad de Belgrano). Dispute with sister and a nephew over joint bank account. María Kodama named his sole heir in new will.
1980	*Seven Nights* (lectures at Teatro Coliseo, Buenos Aires). 'Shakespeare's Memory' (story) published in *Clarín* newspaper; subsequently the title story of a collection incorporated in *Obras Completas*, 1989. Supports 'Mothers of the Plaza de Mayo' and calls on junta to provide information on the 'disappeared'.
1981	*The Limit* (*La cifra*) (poems).
1982	*Nine Dantesque Essays on Dante* (five previously published in 1948, one in 1951). Argentine invasion of the Falkland Islands/Malvinas. Publishes poems regretting the ensuing war with Britain. Calls himself a pacifist and an 'inoffensive anarchist'.
1982–83	Fall of military junta. Denounces torture and 'disappearances'. Calls for investigation into crimes by both sides during the "Dirty War" and for punishment of military officers. Writes the poem 'Los conjurados' ('The Confederates'), praising Swiss Confederation for enabling citizens to 'forget their differences and accentuate their affinities', and claiming Geneva as 'one of my *patrias*'.
1983	*'August 25, 1983' and Other Stories* (fiction). Welcomes return of democracy. Celebrates election of Radical candidate Raúl Alfonsín as president.
1984	*Atlas* (travel pieces), with María Kodama.
1985	*Los Conjurados* (*The Confederates*), (poems and prose). In September diagnosed with cancer. In November secretly leaves Buenos Aires with María Kodama.

1986   Receives medical treatment in Geneva. Dispute with nephews and housekeeper over property and remuneration, respectively. In April marries María Kodama in Geneva, after obtaining divorce from Elsa Astete and marriage license by proxy in Paraguay, as divorce illegal in Argentina. Dies June 14. Buried in the Plainpalais cemetery in Geneva.

Abbreviations

Authors and works are abbreviated following the practice of the *Oxford Classical Dictionary*, 4th edition, ed. S. Hornblower, A. Spawforth and E. Eidinow (Oxford 2012), and journals according to that of *L'Année philologique*. The following abbreviations are offered for the convenience of the reader.

CF   Jorge Luis Borges, *Collected Fictions*, translated by A. Hurley. New York, 1998.

EDG   R. Beekes, *Etymological Dictionary of Greek*, 2 vols. Leiden, 2010.

EDL   M. de Vaan, *Etymological Dictionary of Latin and Other Italic Languages*. Leiden, 2008.

HE   M. Finkelberg (ed.), *The Homer Encyclopedia*. 3 vols. (Wiley-Blackwell 2011).

L&S⁹   H. G. Liddell and R. Scott (eds.), *Greek-English Lexicon*, 9th rev. edition. Oxford, 1996.

OC   Jorge Luis Borges, *Obras Completas* I–IV (1923–49; 1952–72; 1975–85; 1975–88), Edición crítica anotada por Rolando Costa Picazo e Irma Zangara. Buenos Aires, 2009.

OCD⁴   S. Hornblower, A. Spawforth and E. Eidinow (eds.), *Oxford Classical Dictionary*, 4th rev. edition. Oxford, 2012.

ŒC   Jorge Luis Borges, *Oeuvres complètes I-II*, Préface de L'Auteur et edition établie, présentée et annotée par J. P. B. (Gallimard 2010).

OLD   *Oxford Latin Dictionary SNF* Jorge Luis Borges, *Selected Non-Fictions*, edited by E. Weinberger. New York, 1999.

SP   Jorge Luis Borges, *Selected Poems*, edited by A. Coleman. New York, 1999.

CHAPTER I

Borges' Classical Revisions

That intellectual sphere, whose centre is everywhere and whose circumference is nowhere.

J. L. Borges, 'Pascal's Sphere' (1951: *SNF* 352)[1]

In the summer of 1984, two years before his death in Geneva, Jorge Luis Borges went on his last tour around Southern Europe. The itinerary included Rome, Sicily, Athens and Crete.[2] In Sicily, he visited the ruins of Selinunte, the ancient Greek city that had been part of Magna Graecia from the sixth century BCE and had thrived on the south-west coast of the peninsula until its destruction by the Carthaginians around three centuries later.[3] Photographers, journalists and fans followed Borges during this visit as he walked around the ancient acropolis with his common-law wife, María Kodama.[4] He was nearly 85, almost blind, and by then regarded as one of the most extraordinary literary minds of the twentieth century. He had captivated generations of readers with a kaleidoscopic oeuvre whose subject matter spans over two thousand years of Western and Eastern literature, culture and thought, including those of ancient Greece and Rome. In recognition for his outstanding contribution to world literature, France granted him the *Ordre national de la Légion d'honneur* in 1983. He held honorary doctorates from the world's most prestigious universities, as well as numerous prizes in literature, including the Cervantes Prize (1980) and the Prix International (1961), which he shared with Samuel Beckett.[5] His lectures on topics such as metaphor, blindness, the craft of poetry and translation mesmerized audiences both in Argentina and abroad. By 1984,

---

[1] For all citations of Borges' works, I give the date of publication in *SNF*, *CF* and *SP*. For the original place and date of publication of Borges' oeuvre, see the relevant entries in *OC* I–IV and *Œ* I–II. Unless otherwise stated, all translations are mine alone or in collaboration with Andrew Laird.

[2] Borges and Ferrari (2014: 8–10).   [3] Stefania de Vido in Bagnall et al. (2013) s.v. 'Selinous'.

[4] Scianna (1999: 9–10).

[5] On Borges' failure to win the Nobel Prize, see Williamson (2004: 397 and 425–26).

I

he had become a 'global classic' on a par with Marcel Proust, Frank Kafka and James Joyce. His profile as a blind author placed him within a Western tradition that dates back to Homer. Furthermore, he was deeply admired by a generation of writers such as Italo Calvino and Derek Walcott, (post)modern thinkers such as Gérard Genette, Michel Foucault and Harold Bloom, and filmmakers in Latin America and continental Europe.[6] That day in Selinunte, therefore, was for many a rare, and possibly last, chance to see the celebrated author uniquely surrounded by the cultural heritage of the classical world, a world whose presence is ubiquitous, if indeed idiosyncratic, in his oeuvre.

Ferdinando Scianna, the Italian photographer chosen by Editorial Novecento to portray Borges' visit to Sicily, took magnificent photographs of the day. In the morning, Borges and Kodama visited the Regional Archaeological Museum in Palermo. Scianna's thematic focus was the blind author's sensory experience. After the loss of sight during the mid-1950s, the world at large had become for Borges a site to be reimagined. Several images show Borges' hand as it encounters classical objects and Kodama describes them to him (for an example see image on page 158). In the introduction to his album, Scianna describes Borges' excitement. Both the author's touch and María Kodama's voice become the means to experience the material culture exhibited before them:

> At the museum she describes the statues and metopes to him, the light that bathes them, she guides his hand as it discovers the grooves of a sarcophagus, a bust of Caesar, the smooth perfection of the ephebe of Selinus or Hercules slaughtering a deer. Borges' faces lights up: 'Look, María, look!' His hands see what María's eyes see. Later he will walk around the magnificent acropolis of Selinunte, under the shining sun. (Scianna (1999: 10) (my translation))

Perhaps the best image that Scianna took on that acropolis is titled 'Borges at the ruins of Selinunte, Sicily 1984' (frontispiece). The image continues to explore Scianna's interest in Borges' experience of the cultural past through blindness. It shows the author wearing a suit, as was his lifetime habit, with silver-grey hair worn slightly long, disarrayed by a Mediterranean sea-wind. He stands facing the Temple of Hera at a distance.[7] To his left and right there are vestiges of the ancient Greek city scattered about the natural

---

[6] For a comprehensive study of the influence of Borges on (post)modern theory and the visual arts, see the essays in Aizenberg (ed.) (1990). This volume was published four years after Borges' death. For more recent discussions, especially on Borges influence on (post)modern fiction, see Chapter 7 ('Successors of Borges' Classicism').

[7] For a description of the archaeology of the Temple of Hera in Selinunte, identified as Temple E, see Neer (2012: 230–31). The structure one can see nowadays was re-erected from existing material between 1956–59.

landscape. Above his head, a side of the temple can be seen in almost all its past glory: six Doric columns supporting a fragmentary metope. The focus on the author is well defined, whereas the temple before him is somewhat blurred: a contrast that seems to dramatize a simultaneous sense of distance and closeness in Borges' encounter with the classical past. Standing behind Borges, Scianna captures the back of his subject's head, neck and shoulders, as the author faces the ruin. What we, the viewers, don't see is Borges' face. Details of his facial expression and sensory experience have been left to our vast curiosity and imagination, and deliberately so. With this experimental shot, Scianna wants to convey the unique vision with which Borges plots our world and its cultural history.[8] As we shall see throughout this book, full disclosures of the past, in this case the classical past, never interest Borges as a mode of interpreting its identity, status and tradition. Instead, what intrigues him are the stances that we adopt to experience – and, above all, the way we reimagine – that past as it reveals itself successively in space and time before us. Such is the intrinsic character of Borges' classicism.

Examples of this mode of encountering ancient Greece and Rome abound in Borges' writings, and amount to pioneering rereadings of the classical canon in twentieth-century world literature.[9] Borges presents us with intriguing revisions of antiquity that point to experimental ways of recalling our cultural memory, replotting the temporal mechanisms with which Western literature and thought orders its cultural history and tradition, while also helping us to rethink the dialogue between antiquity and modernity. As in Scianna's photograph of Borges' encounter with the Temple of Hera, the interplay of distance and closeness to the classical object is crucial to the classical forms that we find in Borges' writings. As we shall soon see, Borges pictures the classics that we know so well in ways we have never imagined them before.

A Rumour of Homer

One way to begin thinking about this issue is to consider Borges' presenta-tion of 'classics as a rumour'. Take, for instance, the manner in which the

---

[8] Scianna understands well the significance of capturing Borges and the Temple of Hera in the way that he did. 'Borges always saw the whole world like this, through an alternative perspective, and with mind and intelligence. For me, this was a necessary shot [to capture this idea].' Warm thanks to Ferdinando Scianna for discussing this image – as well as his time and conversations with Borges during his visit to Palermo in 1984 – with me.

[9] In this sense, my study of Borges' classicism is in close dialogue with the collection edited by Graziosi and Greenwood (2007) on the reception of Homer in the twentieth century. I discuss this dialogue in the closing section of Chapter 3 ('The Idea of Homer').

Argentine author envisages an afterlife for Homer in 'The Maker' (1960),[10] as the ancient Greek poet forgets the memory of his own authorship and his canonicity dissipates in the course of time. This short story functions as a biographical riddle for the reader. The narrator relates the life experiences and recollections of a man whose name is never revealed. We only know from the title that he is a – or, more precisely, *the* – maker. The narrative carefully weaves allusions and clues that may be understood as classical (e.g. red-figure pottery; astronomy and myth; marble sculpture; wild boar as a staple food; the sea; women; and wine), but which first-time readers are meant to plot gradually as they follow the story to the end. From the outset, the man strikes us as oddly familiar: he could be a figure of cultural importance, even perhaps an ancient Greek, although we cannot yet ascertain his identity. In the opening paragraph, we learn about his character. For the maker, life experiences are not events to be recollected from memory, but ones that make up the very essence and spirit of his being:

> He had never lingered amongst the pleasures of memory. Impressions, momentary and vivid would wash over him: a potter's vermilion glaze; the sky-vault filled with stars that were also gods; the moon, from which a lion had fallen; the smoothness of marble under his sensitive, slow fingertips; the taste of wild boar meat, which he liked to tear at with brusque, white bites; a Phoenician word; the black shadow cast by a spear on the yellow sand; the nearness of the sea or women; heavy wine, its harsh edge tempered by honey—these things could flood the entire circuit of his soul. ('The Maker' (1960: *CF* 292))

We next follow the maker's endless wanderings around the world, all of which begin to add a spatially global quality to his character and experience. Now overcome by blindness, and mysteriously older by what appear to be centuries, '[g]radually, the splendid universe began drawing away from him', and '[e]verything grew distant, and indistinct' (*CF* 292). The world of sensory experience, specifically that illuminated by vision, abandons him, and he perceives that all he has left are his recollections. Then he begins to descend into a labyrinth of forgotten childhood and manhood memories. These come to him 'the way one might feel upon recognizing a melody of a voice', but also as a kind of déjà vu: he senses 'that all this had happened to him before' (*CF* 292–93). Two memories, adventure and love, are the most acute, and finally lead him – and Borges'

---

[10] Borges published most of his prose and verse first in separate form, either in newspaper literary sections or journals. The dates of publication given in this book correspond to those given in *OC* I–IV, *ŒC* I–II and *SNF, CF* and *SP.*

readers – to the revelation of whom he once was and what his destiny had been. It is at this last point in the narrative that Borges gives us concrete classical references that identify the man, the maker whom we had encountered in the title, with Homer, the author of the *Iliad* and the *Odyssey*:

> With grave wonder, he understood. In this night of his mortal eyes in which he was descending love and adventure were also awaiting him. Ares and Aphrodite – because now he began to sense a rumour of glory and hexameters, a rumour of men who defend a temple that the gods will not save, a rumour of black ships that set sail from his beloved isle, the rumour of the *Odysseys* and *Iliads* that it was his fate to sing and to leave echoing in the cupped hands of human memory. (J. L. Borges, 'The Maker' (1960: *CF* 293))

The importance of 'The Maker' in Borges' construction of his own public and private authorship and autobiography will be discussed at length in Chapter 3, together with 'The Immortal' and a series of texts in which Borges explores the Homeric tradition. Here, I wish to draw attention to the manner in which Borges reimagines Homer for his readers. By appealing to a riddle that takes us from what seems strangely familiar to something we realize we already know, Borges invites us to recall the Greek poet and the texts that we attribute to him, while simultaneously creating a new memory of a Homeric postclassical life, or of a 'Homer after Homer'. On one level, 'The Maker' works as a supplementary narrative which, fictionally speaking, adds an unexplored biographical dimension to the post-Homeric life. On another level, it invites us to rediscover Homer and his poetry by bringing back their memory in the shape of a rumour that comes from his classical past. Arguably, the innovative aspect of this story is not the past memory it ultimately recollects – after all, we don't need Borges' story to remember that Homer is the author of the *Iliad* and the *Odyssey*. What shows great innovation is the experimental narrative through which the story takes us to recall the Homeric life and afterlife: 'The Maker' first stages a cognitive distance between us and the Greek poet by imagining a facet of his post-Homeric life that we, naturally, don't know and have to plot, then narrows that gap by appeal to a whisper that reminds us of the Homeric past we know well.

The motif of classics as a whispering memory that puts antiquity and modernity into an experimental dialogue forms a significant part of Borges' approach to reading the classics. As we shall see in more theoretical detail below and throughout this book, this unique perspective of reading has the effect of destabilizing the 'normal' directionality with which the Western tradition tends to plot classical memory in historical time and cultural space.

Pierre Menard's *Odyssey* and *Aeneid*

The classical canon partakes of an equally intriguing journey in Borges' 'Pierre Menard: Author of the Quixote', published in *Fictions* in 1944. While in 'The Maker' Borges explores the interplay of temporal and spatial distance and closeness to recall the memory of Homer, 'Pierre Menard' opens new routes to rereading the *Odyssey* and *Aeneid*, and the classics more generally, by disrupting the logic of original and imitation that dominates Western literary history. This fiction relates the story of Pierre Menard, an early twentieth-century author who sets himself the task of rewriting Cervantes' novel verbatim, while claiming that his version of the Quixote is as original as Cervantes'. The two texts, or at least the lines that Menard technically reproduces from Part I, Chapter IX of Cervantes' *Quixote*, are identical but their meanings turn out to be markedly different.[11] As Menard explains:

> I have assumed the mysterious obligation to reconstruct, word by word, the novel that for him (Cervantes) was spontaneous . . . Composing the Quixote in the early seventeenth century was a reasonable, necessary, perhaps even inevitable undertaking: in the early twentieth, it is virtually impossible. Not for nothing have three hundred years elapsed, freighted with the most complex events. Amongst those events, to mention but one, is the *Quixote* itself. (J. L. Borges, 'Pierre Menard, Author of the Quixote' (1944: *CF* 92–3))

Borges' 'Menard' articulates a paradox: two exact same texts of the *Quixote* turn out to mean different things when produced and read in different centuries.[12] This notion may appear to recall the premises of (new) historicism, which, despite its many revisions, continues to stress the importance of interpreting texts according to the contexts in which they are produced. Yet Borges is not a standard-issue historicist (old or new). By its central paradox, 'Menard' undermines any view of the primacy of original meaning: the same words mean differently, and that is not just a question of how one contextualizes them (in fact, could a corollary be that 'different' might mean 'the same'?). It is important to remember that, above all, Menard's project is a project of translation, which gets one inevitably into a dialect of sameness and difference, and the paradoxes engendered thereby.[13] The paradox could also be seen to foreshadow what would become one of the most enduring

---

[11] The Borgesian narrator cites the line: '. . . truth, whose mother is history, rival of time, depository of deeds, witness of the past, exemplar and adviser to the present, and the future's counselor'.

[12] See Sarlo (1993: 31–3) for the implications of this paradox in Borgesian poetics.

[13] I am grateful to Charles Martindale for discussing the complexity at the heart of Borges' paradox with me.

theories of reception to date, where the meaning of a text is realized at the moment of its reception.[14] However, Borges' concern is not exactly who or what guarantees the meaning of the text. His interest is in the question of the status and identity that texts acquire in the course of cultural history, a history that tends to operate chronologically and categorize texts in the canon in terms of original and adaptation. For Borges, Menard's *Quixote* can claim to be as original as Cervantes'. Or, put differently, Cevantes' *Quixote* can equally be understood as a version of the Quixote de La Mancha just as Menard's is. This is because, Borges argues, neither of these texts are definitive stories of the fictional Quixote. It does not matter who wrote it first. Each of the stories is a rendition of a fictional idea that already exists, as all knowledge exists and can be discovered, rather than originally invented and subsequently copied, by us. Hence, we have the story of a knight called Quixote who comes from La Mancha, a story that can be told differently, even when the same words are used, in the seventeenth, twentieth or any century in between and after. 'Fate enjoys repetitions, variations, symmetries', Borges argues in 'The Plot' (1981), a short fiction that explores the cyclical repetition of Caesar's assassination in the murder of a gaucho from the Argentine Pampas (discussed in Chapter 2). Despite the fact that we know that Cervantes' version appears before Menard's, we can still read both of them as variations of an ongoing theme that exists, regardless of who relates it first or last. This premise can equally be applied, as the Borgesian narrator concludes in 'Menard', to our reading of classical themes, such as Odysseus' and Aeneas' travels in Homer's *Odyssey* and Virgil's *Aeneid*, the latter of which is typically plotted as a reworking of the former. Thus, the story concludes:

> Menard has (perhaps unwittingly) enriched the slow and rudimentary art of reading by means of a new technique—the technique, requiring infinite patience and concentration, encourages us to read the *Odyssey* as though it came after the *Aeneid* … This technique fills the calmest books with adventure. Attributing the *Imitatio Christi* to Louis Ferdinand Céline or James Joyce—is that not sufficient renovation of those faint spiritual admonitions? (J. L. Borges, 'Pierre Menard, Author of the Quixote' (1944: *CF* 95))

Menard's remarkable reading technique throws into disarray the pervasive structure and temporal order that organize our interpretation of canonical texts, like the *Odyssey* and the *Aeneid*, into original and copy by introducing

---

[14] For a seminal study of this notion in classical literature that has influenced subsequent, worldwide discussion, see Martindale (1993).

the liberating idea of the *version* as an alternative exegetical paradigm. This paradigm becomes a guiding force in Borges' encounters with the Graeco-Roman past, and presents us with groundbreaking re-readings of Homer, the Greek lyric poets, the historic and fictional Caesar, and Virgil, amongst other authors and themes from the classical canon discussed in the present book.

Zeno after Kafka

The disarticulation of traditional forms of plotting the classics and their transmission takes on a further reconfiguration in Borges' 'Kafka and his Precursors'. This fictional essay, one of Borges' outstanding discussions of the mechanisms of literary influence, focuses on a series of texts that the Argentine author sees as informing the narrative structure of Kafka's last, unfinished novel *The Castle* (1926). The first text that Borges identifies is Zeno's paradox against motion, retold by Aristotle in *Physics* 6.9.239b, and appealing to the figures of the arrow and Achilles as illustrations:

> At one time I considered writing a study of Kafka's precursors. I had thought at first that he was as unique as the phoenix of rhetorical praise; after spending a little time with him, I felt I could recognize his voice, or his habits, in the texts of various literatures and various ages. I will note a few of them here, in chronological order. The first is Zeno's paradox against motion. A moving body at point A (Aristotle states) will not be able to reach point B, because it must first cover half of the distance between the two, and before that, half of the half, and before that, half of the half of the half, and so on to infinity; the form of this famous problem is precisely that of the *The Castle*, and the moving body and the arrow and Achilles are the first Kafkaesque characters in literature. (J. L. Borges, 'Kafka and his Precursors' (1951: *CF* 363))

Studies in Borgesian poetics and theory generally read this fictional essay as a text that anticipates the perennial question of the ontology of the author and reader vis-à-vis the text that has preoccupied thinkers before and since Barthes.[15] What has received little or no attention is the unique manner in which Borges reimagines a classical theme in this fiction. In 'Kafka', we unexpectedly find Zeno of Elea's familiar reference to the flying arrow and Achilles racing against the tortoise in a light we have never seen them in before. With Borges, they cease to be mere examples of Greek analytical philosophy to become no less than 'the first Kafkaesque characters in

---

[15] Wood (2013: 36–7).

literature'. This, Borges maintains, is what makes them the very precursors of Kafka. Yet this innovative recasting of Zeno's illustrations into dramatic, influential figures of early twentieth-century world literature is not without a further sense of paradox:

> If I am not mistaken, the heterogeneous pieces I have listed resemble Kafka; if I am not mistaken, not all of them resemble each other. This last fact is most significant. Kafka's idiosyncrasy is present in each of these writings, to a greater or lesser degree, but if Kafka had not written, we would not have perceived it; that is to say, it would not exist . . . The word 'precursor' is indispensable to the vocabulary of criticism, but one must not try to purify it from connotation of polemic or rivalry. The fact is that each writer *creates* his precursors. His work modifies our conception of the past, as it will modify the future. (J. L. Borges, 'Kafka and his Precursors' (1951: *CF* 365))

Here, Borges calls for a redefinition of the word 'precursor', which, he argues, is a critical tool for plotting a competitive relation between source and target texts. Yet his search for a redefinition of this critical idiom is even more far-reaching. We have seen that Borges presents Achilles and the ancient Greek arrow as the precursors of the narrative structure of Kafka's *The Castle*. Paradoxically, however, these classical figures become precursors of Kafka only after *The Castle* implicitly points to their literary influence on its narrative structure. As 'the first Kafkaesque characters in literature', they can therefore be plotted as such only *after* we read Kafka. Zeno's familiar examples then become bizarre successors of a twentieth-century novel by virtue of a later writer's ability to modify, as Borges concludes, 'our conception of the past, as it will modify the future'. As with the question of literary succession in Borges' 'Menard', the notion of literary influence we find in 'Kafka' further disrupts long-established orders of plotting the classical past. In Borges, this crucial reconfiguration is intimately connected to the author's conception of time and its volatile flux in literary history, a theme that receives special attention in this book.

Classical Memory and Forgetfulness

The interplay of memory and forgetfulness is intrinsic to Borges' plotting of the classics and their tradition. This feature is particularly apparent in Borges' innovative approach to reading 'classical absences' (discussed in the next section), by which Borges principally means the Greek and Roman classics that we have forgotten once existed, either because they are lost to us, or because they have been 'eclipsed' from our memory as a result of the cultural impact of other

surviving canonical texts. Borges elaborates on the makings of his
own literary memory in a dialogue with Osvaldo Ferrari in 1984:

> My memory is rather a memory of quotations from pages of poetry I have
> read . . . these quotations are from texts that imposed themselves on my memory;
> they have moved me to such a point that they have become unforgettable . . .
> Now, I think that memory requires forgetting. The justification of this thought
> can be found in my story 'Funes the Memorious'. ('On Memory',
> *Conversations* I (2014) 265–66 (trans. J. Wilson))

'Memory requires forgetting': indeed, 'Funes the Memorious' is arguably
one of the most thought-provoking representations of this notion in
twentieth-century fiction. In this story, we encounter the prodigious yet
monstrous memory of Ireneo Funes, a barely educated Uruguayan with
a bizarre passion for both the Latin language and Pliny the Elder's *Historia
Naturalis*. After two meetings with Funes, the Borgesian narrator (presented in this story as an erudite reader of Latin and connoisseur of the
classics) describes Funes' unprecedented condition:

> [Funes] is virtually incapable of general, platonic ideas. Not only is it
> difficult for him to see that the generic symbol 'dog' took all the dissimilar
> individuals of all shapes and sizes . . . [his] own face in the mirror, his own
> hands surprised him every time he saw them . . . He saw – he *noticed* – the
> progress of death, of humidity. He was a solitary, lucid spectator of
> a multiform, momentaneous, and almost unbearably precise world . . .
> To think is to ignore (or forget) differences, to generalize, to abstract.
> In the teeming world of Ireneo Funes there was nothing but particulars –
> and they were virtually *immediate* particulars. (J. L. Borges, 'Funes and his
> Memory' (1944: *CF* 136–7))

'Funes the Memorious' is a rich text that been analysed in multiple ways by
scholars of different disciplines, from the Arts and Humanities to the
Neurosciences.[16] Yet little has been said about Funes as a reader, or plotter,
of reality. As the Borgesian narrator describes him, Funes is not a close
reader of the empirical world, since he cannot identify particulars and use
those identifications to generate abstract thought. This is because he recalls
every single thing that he sees, feels, hears or touches anew, to the point
that his mind becomes a collector of unprocessed data (as Funes explains to
his interlocutor, 'My mind is like a garbage heap', *CF*, 135). Funes therefore
cannot grasp the concept of 'a dog', as Borges points out. Instead, he
remembers every single instance that he has seen, without being able to
process these instances into the abstract figure or notion that we identify as

---

[16] See Bär (2010: www.lanacion.com.ar/1229225-borges-se-anticipo-medio-siglo-a-las-neurociencias).

'dog'. The same occurs with his own facial identity: every time he sees his face in the mirror, he does not see 'Funes' but a face of someone called Funes, which he will repeatedly discover anew until his death. By contrast, through his lifespan, Funes is able to picture *detailed totalities* in a way that our selective memory, one guided by reason and abstraction, does not allow us to do. Conceived this way, one can argue that Funes is a *universal reader of reality* by virtue of his ability to capture every single instance of everything in quantifiable detail, as if he were recording sequences for a universal, rather than a specific, film. In fact, the film metaphor seems apt: while most of us are able to follow a story in a film because each particular shot is shown in fast motion, Funes instead sees each particular shot in the slowest of motions, without grasping the story. He can plot the *whole* through its essential components, but not its possible logic or meaning.

As will be shown in the present book, these contrasting, indeed extreme, modes of apprehending reality, arising from Borges' formulation of the interplay of memory and oblivion, become crucial in his approach to our recollection of the Graeco-Roman past. The classics both form and inform this approach, as they do in 'Funes the Memorious'. Particularly impressive in this story is Funes' word-for-word recitation in Latin of lines in Pliny the Elder's *Historia Naturalis* Chapter 24 on the topic of memory, one that amazes the erudite classicism of the Borgesian bourgeois narrator. Furthermore, the second part of the narrative is centred around Pliny's catalogue of classical figures with outstanding mnemonic skills, such as Cyrus, King of Persia, Mithridates Eupator and Simonides of Ceos, and closes with an intertext to Horace's *monumentum* at the beginning of *Odes* 3.30 (*exegi monumentum aere perennius | regalique situ pyramidum altius* 1–2), which monumentalizes Funes' inexhaustible memory ('[Funes] seemed as monumental as bronze, more ancient than Egypt, anterior to the prophecies and the pyramids' *CF* 137).[17] In his innovative engagement with an Uruguayan gaucho, Pliny, Horace and classical erudition in general, Borges offers perceptive comments not only on the interaction of memory and abstract thought, but also on two contrasting ways of recalling the classical past. With the narrative of Funes, Borges implicitly prompts us to reconsider the part that memory plays in our modes of acquiring knowledge of classical antiquity: in our modern engagement with antiquity, should we attempt to recollect each possible

[17] On the significance of Pliny the Elder and Horace in Borges' conceptualization of memory and monumentalization of the past in 'Funes', see Zonana (2006: 207–33).

instance of its totality in the manner of Funes? What would that look like? Or should we perhaps accept that the distant past can never be fully recalled, and that our cultural memory is necessarily the result of a form of forgetfulness? Furthermore, how does our manner of building the memory of the classical past compare to that of Funes' monumental recollection of the classics? Borges' recollection of Horace, who attempts to build the *Odes* as a literary monument by selecting and concentrating a wealth of available *materia* into a poetic collection, further complicates this series of reflections: the 'monument' we build out of the classical past is marked simultaneously by impulses towards totality and distillation, by obsessive memorization and formative forgetting.[18] Borges' problematization of our (Western) mode of recollecting the past underpins the various theoretical and methodological considerations of the interplay of classics and cultural memory developed in this book.

Classical Absences and Desires

One further dimension of Borges' classicism worth exploring here is the unique manner in which our author discloses levels of presence of classical texts that are either temporarily eclipsed or permanently lost to us. We find an important example of this phenomenon in Borges' references to Tacitus, whose presence in the Borgesian oeuvre receives dramatic levels of focalization. In 'The Garden of Forking Paths', one of Borges' most labyrinthine fictions, the main character, called Tsun, gets in a train to the south-west of England. As Tsun looks for a seat in the empty train, he particularly notices a young passenger fervently reading the *Annals* ('There was almost no one ... I walked through the cars ... I recall ... a young man fervently reading Tacitus' *Annals*', *CF* 121). The reference to Tacitus' text amounts to no more than a few words. Yet, the fact that Tacitus is unexpectedly mentioned at a highly focalized moment in Borges' multiple-level narrative, as well as the manner in which Tacitus is being read – 'con fervor' – by an absorbed reader, advertises this classical author as a highly desirable text for readers of Borges' own fiction. Something similar, yet more dramatic, occurs in a brief citation of Tacitus in 'The Library of Babel'. Babel is a metaphor for the eternal character of the universe and our inability to grasp its immense totality, whether this is conceived in terms of space or time. It also represents the extraordinary concept of what would be

---

[18] Warm thanks to Luke Roman for discussing these issues with me and helping me think the question of memory and totality in Borges' classicism further.

known in Borges' Spanish as 'la literatura completa' – the 'Universe of Letters' – that exists in and outside the world of human letters, as well as in and outside human time, and where nothing remains unwritten and therefore unread:

> The Library is 'total' – perfect, complete, and whole ... its bookshelves contain all ... all that is able to be expressed, in every language. *All* – the detailed history of the future, the autobiographies of archangels, the faithful catalogue of the Library, thousands and thousands of false catalogues, the proof of the falsity of those catalogues, the proof of the falsity of the true catalogue, the Gnostic gospel of Basilides, the commentary upon that gospel, the commentary on the commentary on that gospel, the true story of your death, the translation of every book in every language, the inter-polations of every book in all books, the treatise Bede could have written (but did not) on the mythology of the Saxon people, *the lost books of Tacitus*. ('The Library of Babel' (1944: *CF* 115) (emphasis added))

The citation of Tacitus' lost books at the close of this catalogue of unknown literatures and histories should not escape us. Here, not only do Tacitus' lost *Histories* and *Annals* of Caligula, Vespasian, Titus and Domitian emerge as the incomplete text *par excellence*, but also as a highly desirable text because it is well outside our reach. As we are told in Borges' story, generations of librarians dwelling in the hexagons of Babel have struggled unsuccessfully to discover the mysterious 'Total Book', *the* index of all indices, which records all knowledge unavailable to us, including 'the lost books of Tacitus'. Borges' engagement with Tacitus taps a central issue that preoccupies those in the field of reception and its most recent rethinking:[19] how do we approach our reading of the fragmentary, and especially the lost, literary past? Do we attempt to reconstruct its textuality in full, despite knowing that not all of it can be recovered, or do we experience it as we have inherited it: in parts? At first sight, Borges seems to offer a therapeutic approach to our reading of Tacitus' fragmentary text. He seems to be telling us that reading a classic like Tacitus necessarily involves that we recall – and accept – the incompleteness of the Tacitean text. Yet, his therapeutic readings of fragmentary antiquity are not without a sense of paradox. For, while Borges calls attention to incompleteness as an inevitable condition we must accept, the librarians of the Library of Babel clearly do not accept this condition, and are obsessed with finding the 'Total Book', which, amongst all things lost to us, contains the missing part of Tacitus' text. One might therefore equally argue that Borges' story

---

[19] Butler (2016) and Jansen (2016).

demonstrates that we must accept our own inevitable, if unfulfillable, desire for completeness; i.e. that we must accept that we will be driven by a desire we can never fulfil. Borges' exploration of classical absences implicitly reveals the motives behind our desire for recuperating the past, while pointing to a radical philosophy of reading human letters. His allusion to classical presences also discloses the complex texture that past culture acquires in our cultural memory, as will be shown in his revisions of Lucretius' *De rerum natura*, the Virgilian corpus, and his encounters with the Greek Anthology in the following chapters.

The examples explored thus far are suggestive of the provocative dimensions and directions of Borges' classicism. Each of the cases outlined points to the ways in which the Argentine author reconfigures the traditional paradigms by which we tend to plot the classical canon and its tradition, particularly at the heart of the West. We have seen that Borges places concepts such as sound, forgetfulness and absences at the centre of his thinking of the classical past. Borges' classical revisions moreover innovatively re-familiarize us with Graeco-Roman antiquity. They do so by staging a sense of temporal and spatial distance and closeness between us and the past, which reinvigorates aspects of our classical memory and presents us with unique perspectives on how antiquity renews itself in modernity, without losing sight of the classics as fascinating objects of study. As we shall see throughout this book, the effects of this reconfiguration of antiquity are numerous, not only in Borges' corpus, but also in classical receptions after Borges (Chapter 7). Borges' revisions furthermore give a distinct texture to the classical canon, as the author resituates this literary culture in the remote, non-canonical scenarios and landscapes of his avant-garde fiction. At the core of this procedure, we find an author whose vision emerges somewhere at the crossroads of two contrasting cultures of the West, and who exhibits increasingly global aims and ambitions.

Classics at the Crossroads: Towards a Global Vision

Born in Argentina at the turn of the twentieth century to an Anglo-Spanish family, and educated both in his country and Geneva, Borges' upbringing was culturally diverse. To begin with, his authorial identity is neither fully Argentine nor precisely 'international'. On the one hand, he is an instantly recognizable name worldwide, as is the case with Proust, Kafka and Joyce. On the other hand, Borges remains a quintessentially Argentine writer, especially for the Argentine and Latin American reader more used to thinking of his writings as belonging to the traditions of New World literature. In other words, Borges' authorial identity emerges somewhere at the crossroads where the European tradition meets the cultural developments of postcolonial Argentina.[20] In fact, this is what Borges himself argues is the character of the Argentine writer producing literature in the Argentina and South America of the late nineteenth and early twentieth centuries.

In an essay titled 'The Argentine Writer and Tradition', Borges explores a series of definitions on the question of Argentine literature. One of these is by his near-contemporary, Leopoldo Lugones (1874–1938), who in *El payador*[21] makes a passionate case for José Hernández's *Martín Fierro*, a 2,316-line epic work of gauchesque literature typically compared with the Homeric epics, and considered *the* classic Argentine poem. Here, Borges' concern is with how literary works are understood as canonical by virtue of their predominantly national characteristics:

> There [in *El payador*] we read that the Argentines possess a classic poem, *Martín Fierro*, and that this poem should be for us what the Homeric poems were to the Greeks . . . I believe that *Martín Fierro* is the most lasting work we Argentines have written; I also believe, with equal intensity, that we cannot take *Martín Fierro* to be, as has sometimes been said, our Bible, our canonical book. ('The Argentine Writer and Tradition' (1951: *SNF* 420))

Borges follows this statement with a further elaboration on and refutation of attempts to define Argentine canonical literature by its local colour, its relation to Spanish culture or a desire to break away from European literary influence. He concludes by offering a definition that reclaims Western culture as a fundamental aspect of the Argentine tradition:[22]

> What is the Argentine tradition? . . . I believe that our tradition is the whole of Western culture, and I also believe that we have a right to this tradition, a greater right than that which the inhabitants of one Western nation or another may have . . . I believe that Argentines, and South Americans in general, . . . can take on all the European subjects, take them on without superstition and with an irreverence that can have, and already has had, fortunate consequences. ('The Argentine Writer and Tradition' (1951: *SNF* 425–26))

---

[20] Sarlo (1993).

[21] A 'payador' is a gaucho minstrel who improvises 'payadas', that is, competitive songs about the countryside life. *Mutatis mutandi*, the payador, can be understood as a modern version of the pastoral *cantores* one finds in Virgil's *Eclogues*.

[22] Borges here belongs to a strand of Latin American 'nationalist' (including pan-regional) appropriations of classical antiquity against the counter-claims of Europe (and America) of the kind one finds in Rubén Darío's 'El Triunfo de Calibán' (1898).

One of these 'fortunate consequences' is, of course, Borges' own oeuvre, which blends with utmost creativity a variety of Western elements, while remaining simultaneously local and European. Yet the cultural blend of two branches of the West that we find in Borges is equally informed by antiquity itself, and more specifically by the further cultural fusions of East and West that Borges finds at the very heart of the peripheral communities of ancient Greece. Note, for instance, his understanding of what Rome and Magna Graecia represent in terms of Western identity in an interview held just before his trip to Italy in 1984:

> I know Rome clearly, I could even say, like all Westerners, 'ciuis romanus sum'—I am a citizen of Rome. But now I will know the South, Greater Greece. You could say that the West began to think in Greater Greece—in parts of Asia Minor and the South of Italy. ('The Eternal Traveller', *Conversations* I (2014: 8) (trans. J. Wilson))

Here, Borges makes an implicit, if perhaps over-generalized, contrast between Magna Graecia and ancient Rome. For him, Rome represents one meaning of the West: a meaning that we (and *he*) tend to assume to be the homogenous cultural formation that we identify as 'Western Europe' and its tradition. By contrast, he understands the culture of Greater Greece to have emerged from a diverse fusion of East and West, which Rome later inherited. This conception of the ancient Greek world is beautifully articulated in Borges' prologue to his *Conversations* with Ferrari, where he plots the makings of Western culture in a manner that the Lucretius of *De rerum natura* would certainly have enjoyed:

> The best event recorded in universal history happened in Ancient Greece some 500 years before the Christian era, namely, the discovery of dialogue. Faith, certainty, dogmas, anathemas, prayers, prohibitions, orders, taboos, tyrannies, wars and glory overwhelmed the world while some Greeks to the East and West of their mainland acquired the peculiar habit of conversation— how, we'll never know. They doubted, persuaded, dissented, changed their minds, postponed. Perhaps their mythology helped them, which was, as with the Shinto, an accumulation of vague fables and variable cosmologies. These scattered conjectures were the first root of what we call today, perhaps pretentiously, metaphysics. Western culture is inconceivable without these few Greeks. Remote in space and time, this volume [the *Conversations with Ferrari*] is a muffled echo of those ancient conversations. ('Prologue', *Conversations* I (2014: ix) (trans. J. Wilson with minor alterations))

In this passage, Western culture is an 'event' that emerges 2500 years ago as a result of an interconnectivity occurring on two sides of ancient Greece, the East and West, by which Borges means Magna Graecia, Asia Minor and Sicily, as well as the ancient Greek mainland. This event, this cultural form, turns out to be the notion of *dialogos*, of conversation, which the ancients mastered, and which Borges now interprets as a 'muffled echo' from antiquity, just as the blind and timeless Homer of 'The Maker' finally hears the 'distant rumour' of his prior authorship and works. Like remote atoms, the cross-cultural conversations of those Greeks now take new forms in Borges' own conversations with Ferrari in the Argentina of 1984–85, also the product of profound fusions of the European and peripheral West. The connection is distant, but the sense of classical antiquity's renewal in Borges' modern Buenos Aires is most palpable.

A close study of Borges' cross-cultural classicism furthermore reveals something more complex in his authorial development: his growing interest in the cultures of the East and Far East in his middle and late period. This interest gives the increasing impression that his authorship, and hence his classicism, are global.[23] When it comes to Borges' appeal to the East in classical literature, his vision remains predominantly that of an erudite Western reader. For instance, he tends to consider the Greek and Roman epic as a genre that includes some elements from Eastern literature and culture, rather than as one that is constituted by a dynamic fusion of Eastern and Western influences.[24] It is not until his late period that he problematizes his geopoetical perceptions of Graeco-Roman antiquity. For instance, in a poem called 'Elegy', published in the last decade of his life, and dealing with the sensuous power of poetry, Borges envisions Virgil's *Aeneid* as a 'world classic' that reaches audiences well beyond Europe, even where there is little or no classical tradition. This reading emerges in contrast with, for example, that of T. S. Eliot, a near contemporary of Borges, who argues fervently for the quintessentially European character of Virgil's epic (Chapter 4).[25] In *Atlas* (1984), a collection of poems that includes descriptions of dreams and world tours, Borges displaces the classics further from the classical tradition in Western Europe. As he travels from Buenos Aires through the Mediterranean to the Far East, he recasts classical themes, such as the nightingale of Theocritus, the Minotaur in the labyrinth and Odysseus' return to Ithaca, in remote geographies and

---

[23] While Borges' 'global' approach to literature extends to other traditions and cultures, such as those in the far North (e.g. Scandinavian and Icelandic), his classicism engages more directly with the interplay between Western Europe and Argentina, and between the West and the East, as broadly defined by Borges. For a discussion of the term 'global' as I explore it in this book, see the section that follows.

[24] E.g. *Seven Nights* (1984), the 1967–68 Norton Lectures at Harvard, Borges and Ferrari 'Epic Flavour' (2015).

[25] T. S. Eliot, address to the Virgil Society (1944).

cultures with a high level of experimentation and innovation (Chapter 5). Borges' cross-cultural classics can also be traced in his celebrated interviews with Osvaldo Ferrari (1982–84), mentioned above,[26] in which he offers sharp insights into how the West has received (and often misconceived) the cultures of the East and the exchanges between East and West in ancient multicultural regions, such as Magna Graecia, Roman Egypt and Asia Minor (Chapters 3, 4 and 5).[27]

At the heart of this brand of classicism are the movements to which Borges belonged and which he helped forge in avant-garde Argentina in the early- and mid-twentieth century. These movements blended aspects of nineteenth-century Existentialism and late-nineteenth-century Symbolism, along with ideas from the Surrealist movement that unfolded during the 1920s in Buenos Aires.[28] Borges' own education furthermore influenced foundational aspects of his classicism. As a young boy, he spent his formative years reading the Graeco-Roman classics intensively, both in English and Spanish, in his father's library in the Palermo neighbourhood of Buenos Aires. During his teenage years, the family settled in Switzerland. There, he completed his secondary education at the prestigious Collège de Genève, which at the time placed a great emphasis on classical antiquity in its curriculum.[29] It is at this point that Borges began to read classical texts in Latin and French, though, as he often reminds us, he never learnt Greek.[30] By the time Borges begins his professional literary career, the classics are already an intrinsic aspect of his cross-cultural writings and understanding of the part Argentine literature and its tradition play in Western and non-Western culture and literature. Finally, and as will be explored in detail in subsequent chapters, Borges' brand of classics also betrays global tendencies and ambitions, especially in his aim to situate ancient Greece and Rome in relation to the East and beyond.[31] This development responds to a turning point in the history of classical reception outside Europe and North

---

[26] Recently translated into English by Wilson (2014) and Boll (2015).

[27] E.g. 'Argentine Identity' and 'The Eternal Traveller' in Borges and Ferrari (2014). On Borges' engagement with Eastern culture, see Forero and Garabieta (2013).

[28] For the interplay of philosophical and artistic movements in Borges' fiction, see Griffin (2013).

[29] I am grateful to the Collège Calvin (formerly the Collège de Genève) for information about this issue.

[30] Mentioned in interviews and lectures, *passim*. In theory, Borges had no Greek although, in practice, he had command of an extensive vocabulary, as well as knowledge of etymologies. See, for instance, his 'Epidaurus' in *Atlas*.

[31] By 'beyond', I refer to some classical traces in Borges' engagement with Scandinavian, Nordic and German literatures, a subject which I am currently researching. I also mean 'universal', since Borges often locates literature, including classical literature (e.g. the lost books of Tacitus), outside our world, as we shall see in the following chapters.

America, when modernist South America became postmodern, and began to find syncretic points of contact with other peripheral and non-peripheral cultures.[32] It also emerged when artists in the postcolonial New World begin to cite the Graeco-Roman classics, not specifically to question or reject their tradition of Western Europe, but rather to articulate the ways in which the classics embody these artists' own modernity.[33] This aspect of Borges' poetics informs his decentred vision of classical literature, a literature that, for him, can be transported to any geography or point in time.

Borges' modality of reading the classics coheres with his own position at a cultural crossroads: he constantly shifts between a cultural marginality that strives towards a universalizing vision of the classics and a vision of a classical universe that seems radically eccentric.[34] This approach to the classical world and to the history of ideas in general is encapsulated in 'Pascal's Sphere' (1951), a fictional essay that traces the cultural history of the metaphor of the circle as an analogue for divinity, the universe and infinity. In this fiction, Borges reworks a memorable line by the seventeenth-century French philosopher Blaise Pascal, which I offer as the epigraph of this introductory chapter: 'That intellectual sphere, whose centre is everywhere and whose circumference is nowhere' (*SNF* 352). Pascal's metaphor opens up a theoretical and methodological framework for exploring the modus operandi of Borges' classicism, especially when it comes to his experimental ambition to re-situate the classical canon in the often un-classical realms of world literature. If one were pressed to reduce Borges' classical vision to its very essence, this would be its *centrelessness*. His vision of the classics tends to circumvent the enduring paradigm that characterizes the gravitational plots of Western intellectual history; a history that tends to regard the classics as the very origin and centre of its cultural identity and tradition. While Borges does not deny the fundamental importance of the classics in the formation of the Western canon and intellectual thought, he equally conceives of a classical canon whose stage is the cultural world at large. Thus, his Homer is a classic that coexists between the rumour of his Greek preclassical past and the bizarre landscapes of twentieth-century fiction, just as his Tacitus coexists between the established canon and Babel's eternity. This is a form of classicism born 'at the crossroads' of the two versions of the West – centre and periphery – but whose horizons are 'global'.

---

[32] On this issue, see Calvino's essay on Borges (2009). For a discussion of the (post)modern syncretist aesthetics of Argentine and Modern Greek literature, see Kefala (2007).

[33] Fiddian (2013: 96–7).

[34] On Borges' peripherality, see de Toro (1995: 11–43); on Borges' cultural 'edge', see Sarlo (1993).

Key Terms and Concepts

'Global', 'World' and 'Universal' in Borges' Classicism

The discussion thus far has framed Borges' engagement with the literature and culture of ancient Greece and Rome in terms of a 'global' model of reading the classical past. This chapter and the following ones also refer to Borges' 'globalizing vision' of the classics, a vision that involves a series of radical strategies for plotting antiquity and its legacy in space and time. Furthermore, 'world' and 'universal' are also regularly invoked in relation to Borges and literature, categories that acquire a specific – even uniquely untranslatable – semantics in Borges, but that also are uppermost in the mind of many scholars of comparative literature. In this section, I would like to address the question of how Borges' encounter with the classical past may be understood as 'global' in preparation for the discussions that will emerge in Chapters 1–5. Chapter 6 will return to this discussion, and will deal with the question of whether Borges' 'global classics', or a form of classics that, in Borges' understanding, enters 'world' and 'universal' categories, recuperates or manages to transcend some of the negative, parochial dimensions that many critics have attributed to 'global' and 'world literature'.

The terms 'global' and 'world' (French *'mondial'* and Spanish *'mundial'*) have undergone intensive critique and scrutiny in recent scholarship in comparative literature. Views on what the terms mean vary widely[35] and ultimately are concerned with debates about: (1) the extent to which the cultural capital and hegemony of Western Europe and North America dictate what constitutes the notion of literature at the national and international levels; (2) the degree to which literary cultures outside the hegemonic 'centre' welcome, reject or attempt to overcome the label of 'peripheral';[36] and (3) the future of Comparative Literature as a discipline, procedure and institutionalized body of knowledge where 'world literature' is studied and promoted.[37] Even the manner in which one presents the idea of world literature is problematic. Some scholars find the concept of 'world-literature' with a hyphen[38] restrictive. They prefer to think about 'the literatures of the world' in 'transcultural'[39] or, as has recently been proposed, 'ecological' terms,[40] in an attempt to map out the notion of literature as a constellation of interacting cultural systems.

---

[35] Cheah (2008 and 2016) and Damrosh (2013).
[36] Mostly as a critical response to Casanova (2004) and Moretti (2004).   [37] Huggan (2011).
[38] Beecroft (2008).   [39] Pettersson (2008).   [40] Beecroft (2015).

Furthermore, one of the most radical propositions to date denies the idea that 'world literature' can exist, since the terms 'world' and 'global' are 'untranslatable', especially as one moves from one culture to another.[41] Despite this palpable lack of consensus on what and how literature means and does not mean at the global level, recent scholarship nevertheless more fruitfully agrees on the criticism that certain privileged European and Euro-American cultures have annexed the term 'global' for themselves, rather than employing it as an umbrella notion for exploring the interconnectivity that exists between literary cultures of the world at large, as the idea of globalization suggests.[42] Borges has provocative things to say about this topic – ones that are not out of place in the debates about world literature discussed above – especially when it comes to the way early postcolonial nations, such as the Argentina of the early- and mid-twentieth century, relate to the literatures of Europe. I expand on this issue at various points of discussion in this book, especially in the conclusions of each chapter. In using the terms 'global' and 'world' in connection with Borges' classicism, I therefore consistently bear in mind this complex debate in comparative literature, while attempting to define what and how the concepts mean in the specific context of both Borges' modernist fiction and his distinctive approach to antiquity and literature more broadly.

When one moves to Borges, terms like 'global', 'globalizing', 'world' and 'universe' acquire distinct meanings. These meanings at times overlap with those of recent comparative literature debates, while at times they preclude them and/or even transcend them. Throughout Chapters 2–7, I primarily use 'global' and 'globalizing' when referring to Borges' *ever-expansive* and *atopic* vision of classical antiquity, a vision that revolves around the axis of place and time, as conceived by Borges. Perhaps the

---

[41] E.g. the French term *mondialisation* does not have an exact semantic correspondence with the term 'globalization' in English, which tends to be associated with economic interconnectivity. For this argument, see Apter (2013: 175–90), who derives her interests of untranslatables from Cassin (2004). Additionally, *mondialisation* can be contrasted with Glissant's *mondialité*, which builds on the archipelagos of the Antilles as a network and metaphor for cultural connectivity and interrelation. Amongst a wealth of essays and televised interviews on the topic, see Glissant (1997) and Obrist and Raza (2017: 12–42).

[42] Most recent work on the question of 'world' and 'global' literature builds on a criticism of Casanova (1999, translated in English in 2004) and her now seminal study of 'the world republic of letters', as well as on Moretti (2004) and his conjectures on the question of world literature. This criticism typically revolves around assumptions about the order and value that peripheral literatures have for 'core' cultures (Casanova, 2004) and 'core specialists in the field of literary study'. See Beecroft (2008: 54).

most comprehensive example of this vision can be found in Chapter 3, which explores Borges' large-scale recasting of Homer from the Greek poet's multiple identities in preclassical Greece, through the multiple geographies and landscapes that he occupies in the postclassical world, to the realm of oblivion, an atemporal or more precisely post-temporal location that Borges' Homer shares with Borges' Shakespeare. Borges' global vision of Homer, however, is temporarily and spatially non-linear, as exemplified by the Greek poet's erratic and labyrinthine journeys back and forth through times and geographies, from twentieth-century London and late Imperial Rome, through humanist Europe, to Roman Egypt and precolonial America. Furthermore, topographically speaking, Borges' Homer does not betray the 'imperialistic' features one finds in the expansive structures of Virgil's *Aeneid* or Ovid's *Metamorphoses*. Rather, the global Homer that Borges presents has points of contact with the kind of 'universal' form that one finds in Lucretius' Epicurus in Book 1 of *De rerum natura*, where the Roman poet sketches the philosopher's cosmological journey from Greece, though the edges of our world, to the vastness of the atomic cosmos (*Graius homo . . . | processit longe flammatia moenia mundi | atque omne immensum peragrauit*, 'a man of Greece . . . marched far beyond the flaming walls of the world as he traversed the immeasurable universe' 66, 73–4). Borges' expansive visions of Homer and the classics are nevertheless more complex than those Lucretius stages for Epicurus. In Borges, Graeco-Roman antiquity becomes a cultural body whose roots and tradition have no specifically demarcated geographical or temporal borders. Indeed, it is not exactly that Borges situates the classics in an omnipresent form of universality. Rather, it is that his classics can *potentially* emerge *anywhere* for him, in any context or form, and at any point in space and time, whether this occurs in the makings of history, or in the extra-temporal zones that Borges so enjoys exploring in his experimental genre of fiction. For Borges, classical antiquity (like any other moment in our deep history)[43] has no designated homeland, either spatial or temporal – no clear-cut origins or roots, no precise tradition or status, no foretold beginning or end and, above all, no gravitating cultural centre. In this sense, Borges offers a vision of antiquity (and past literature in general) that is intensely *atopic*, not only because he plots classical culture in dynamic and ever-shifting geographies and landscapes, as we shall see, but also because he does not acknowledge the 'territorial' claims

---

[43] Butler (2016) and Jansen (2016).

of one authoritative tradition, such as the Western tradition and its common ground in Europe and its (post)colonial worlds.[44]

Borges' globally atopic classicism nevertheless features some moments of focalization. On occasion, I call these 'pan-globalisms'. Often, Borges' readings globalize ancient Greece and Rome to a certain extent and level of concentration. For instance, in Chapter 4, he amplifies our vision of Virgil as the Roman poet's cultural memory has significant impacts on certain literary cultures and nations, such as the Scandinavian, which as a group represent a 'regional globality'. On other occasions, Borges' global classicism betrays signs of syncretism, especially with the Far East. We have seen how, in his dialogue with Osvaldo Ferrari, Borges is keen to liken the eclectic mythologies that inform Magna Graecia's dialogical phenomena in his conversation to the 'vague fables' and 'variable mythologies' of the Shinto.[45] More examples of this form of syncretism in Borges' global classics will be discussed in connection with Borges' configuration of classical time and Buddhism (Chapter 2).

Space and Time in Borges' 'Physics of Reading'

A central point in this introductory discussion is that Borges' classical revisions have the effect of eliminating, or destabilizing, the 'normal' directionality in (a) historical Time and (b) geopolitical/cultural Space. The first sections of this chapter, which were concerned with how Borges' ideas subvert the categories of successor and precursor, imitator and model, and before and after, drew attention to the effects of a Borgesian perspective on our conventional understanding of time. In the discussions of Borges' revisions of Homer, the *Odyssey* and the *Aeneid*, Zeno's paradoxes and the Tacitean text, it was moreover argued that Borges' approach to hermeneutics potentially undermines the priority of the whole over the fragmentary, i.e.

---

[44] The term 'atopic' is nevertheless complex when applied to Borges' classicism. If one appeals to ancient Greek semantics, Borges' classical vision could be understood as 'strange', 'out of the ordinary', even 'illicit' and 'out of physical space', as one finds in Plato's, Aristotle's, Plutarch's and Plotinus' use of the adjective ἄτοπος, ον, s.v. *DGS* ἄτοπος, ον. Moreover, it combines the modern understanding of atopia as 'placeless', 'uprootedness' and 'migration', to name a few etymologically based semantics of the term. Furthermore, classical atopia in Borges features a set of overlapping relations that makes it equally 'heterotopian', in the sense developed by Foucault, himself a keen admirer of the Argentine author. For Foucault as an admirer of Borges, see Wood (2013) 30–1. For Foucault on Borges and heterotopia, see Foucault (1970), xv–xix. For Foucault and the six principles of external space, see Foucault (1984).

[45] The Shinto is the ethnic religion of Japan, whose ritual practices and observations are based on a collection of native beliefs that connect modern Japan with its multiple ancient traditions. For Borges and the Shinto, see Forero and Garabieta (2013) and Fiddian (2013: 104–5).

the notion that the fragmentary past must be constantly supplemented in order to progress towards ever greater proximity to the whole. This too can perhaps be read on the axis of 'time', since it concerns the very idea of our role as readers of the Graeco-Roman past. The latter part of this introduction, which discussed Borges' cross-cultural and globalizing approach to the classics, concerned the way in which the 'normal' directionality and hierarchy of space (e.g. the established spatial notions of the Western classics), along with the geopolitics those hierarchies imply, are dissolved in a Borgesian perspective. There is a political dimension, clearly, to what Borges is doing, yet not in the sense of simply opposing the cultural authority of the Classics and the West to which he ultimately belongs. Instead, he does something more profound: he submerges 'classical' past and 'modern' present, East and West, colonial cultural authority and peripheral epigoni, within a universalizing and encyclopaedic perspective that destroys the very premise of cultural priority, either temporal or geographical. Borges does not attack the bastions of cultural authority so much as create a universe in which the very notions on which cultural hierarchy is based are unable to establish themselves properly because a different 'physics of reading' is in operation. Borges seems to create, or simply describe, a world in which the principle of gravity that gave objects their different weights is absent.[46] My appeal to the term 'physics' in relation to Borges' reading strategies is significant for the present argument and discussions in the chapters that follow. By 'physics', I mean to convey a concept close to the notions of Greek *phusis* (φύσις) and Latin *natura*, as one finds them in, for instance, Lucretius *De rerum natura*, in which the Roman poet is concerned with describing the *qualities* that render the universe as a *system* of knowledge. Borges' approach to reading the classics also distinctively points to the emergence of a system of cultural knowledge displaying certain qualities or principles:

1. *centrelessness*: centrelessness, as has already been noted, is a key aspect of Borges' reading of the classical past in space and time. This chapter has drawn attention to Borges' 'Pascal's Sphere' (1951) as a powerful paradigm for capturing the Argentine author's cross-cultural plotting of antiquity, one that constantly explores the interplay between centre and periphery. Chapters 2–5 examine this interplay throughout, as Borges reimagines the classical canon, as well as the lost literature of

---

[46] Warm thanks to Luke Roman for discussing the implications of this chapter with me, especially the centrality of Borges' 'physics of reading' antiquity through the axis of space and time.

the past, in multiple contexts and temporalities inside and outside human time. The effect of this aspect of Borges' physics of reading is that the classics do not gravitate towards a specific cultural centre, but instead exist in a cultural constellation that spans our world and the universe at large.

2. *memory and forgetfulness*: the interplay of remembrance and oblivion becomes crucial in Borges' reinvigoration of the question of our cultural memory of the classical past. As demonstrated in the section discussing the classical canon and the fragmentary and lost literature of antiquity, this interplay offers a fruitful revision of the processes by which both classical presences and absences are recalled. Here, the senses add a fresh dimension to Borges' mnemonics. For instance, we have encountered a partially blind Borges recalling a blind Homer who, from oblivion, remembers his classical past by means of a whispering voice. Likewise, in Chapter 4, we discover a Borges overcome by tears in 1960s Buenos Aires as he recalls the haptic quality of Virgil's poetry, a process that ultimately discloses the intensely geopoetic and sensory impact that Borges attributes to the Virgilian oeuvre in our modern memory and imagination.

3. *antiquity as a fragmentary phenomenon in time*: attempts to know the classical world in its entirety point to a modality of knowledge acquisition that, for Borges, is spectacularly doomed to fail. Borges instead offers a new paradigm for reading antiquity, which is based on the notion that all literature and material culture are phenomena in flux. Throughout this book, I illustrate the ways in which Borges offers a 'therapeutic' alternative to the problems posed by a lost and fragmentary past. Yet this therapy must begin with the acceptance that antiquity emerges in our modernity inevitably as a version of a former past that we do not and cannot ever know fully.

4. *antiquity and modernity*: antiquity and modernity are not concrete historical categories for Borges. Instead, they are parts of a deeply layered history of our culture that must be observed laterally, rather than as a palimpsest from the present 'above' to the 'past' hidden underneath. This 'layered' history spans human time, and even reaches into the realms of eternity, where Borges contends all knowledge exists in its complete form. From this perspective, Borges shows us how our understanding of the past will always be partial and subject to revisions, just as our own modernity will be so for future generations. Thus Borges' solution to our cognitive desires and frustrations is his 'physics of reading' the cultural past, an approach that offers a way into

making sense of the complex emergence of antiquity in our modernity. As will be demonstrated in the chapters that follow, these four categories, often interrelated and irreducible to a single principle of Borgesian reading, present us with a radically new paradigm of plotting modernity's engagement with the Graeco-Roman past. This paradigm furthermore raises important questions about the interplay of the classical canon and 'world' literature, as well as the interdisciplinary dialogue between Classical Reception and Comparative Literature, in which the field of 'global Classics' emerges (Chapter 6).

Aims and Scope of the Book

The present book has two interrelated aims: to illustrate and thematize, as fully as possible, the cultural influences and fusions at play in Borges's global classicism, and to consider how these inform his encounters with antiquity, as well as the texture of his own work (Chapters 1–6). Chapters 1–5 collectively examine the various ways in which Borges incorporates and enters into dialogue with classical material. These chapters concentrate on key topics in Borgesian thought: the flux and volatility of socially constructed time (Chapter 2); constructions of identity in and beyond cultural history (Chapter 3); geopolitical space and the senses (Chapter 4); and world and cosmos (Chapter 5). Drawing on the findings of Chapters 1–5, the discussion then returns to the question of Borges' classics with a special focus on its theoretical and practical implications for the field of global Classics (Chapter 6). The study finally considers the question of the successors of Borges' classics. It examines the responses to Borges' global vision of the Graeco-Roman past by three authors and critics: Italo Calvino, Umberto Eco and Derek Walcott (Chapter 7).

Chapter 2 ('The Flow of Heraclitus') primarily explores Borges' engagement with the pre-Socratic thinker Heraclitus of Ephesus. It considers how Heraclitus and his river metaphor underpin Borges' reading of antiquity and inform his understanding of the re-emergence of the classics in time. The discussion focuses on a series of fictions and poems in which Heraclitean time emerges as the very logic of Borges' thinking about the literary tradition and its reception. In these texts, Borges elaborates on the complex fluidity that marks antiquity's renewal in modernity within the larger structure of what Borges conceives as our world's cultural history, a history that, for him, does not follow a strictly sequential narrative, and owes as much to fiction as it does to fact. The first part of the chapter investigates how the classics partake in Borges' conception of time. It deals with the conceptual question of how Borges' complex temporalities shape his thinking about infinity, eternity and cyclicality, and in turn how these concepts interplay with his classical presences. The second part explores Borges' artful appeal to Heraclitus to articulate one of the most provocative and insightful readings of the classical tradition in modernist literature. The third and last part of the chapter examines another facet of Borges' engagement with Heraclitean flux: the recurring, yet volatile, processes which characterize the disclosures and eclipses of the ancient past. This chapter prepares the reader for the discussions in Chapters 2–5, since the topic of time, like that of space, is central to Borges' aim to expand the dimensions and structures of our reading of the classics in his work.

Chapter 3 ('The Idea of Homer') examines the ubiquitous appearance of Homer in Borges' writings, including his published lectures and interviews. As with his reading of highly canonical authors such as Dante, Shakespeare, Cervantes and Kafka, Borges' Homer is a complex figure, who blends aspects of the history of the Western literary canon with themes in Borgesian fiction that universalize that canon, such as dreams, visions and the labyrinth. This chapter first focuses on 'The Immortal' to examine how Borges reads Homer from the viewpoint of the Greek poet's authorship and the transmission of his text. This fiction, considerably more challenging than 'The Maker', introduced above, invites us to rediscover Homer both inside and outside his tradition, by appeal to a narrative that not only disrupts a received Western understanding of the author, but is also highly irreverent towards the question of how literary history should be approached. The chapter then considers how Borges' decentred reading of Homer is incorporated within aspects of Borges' increasingly globalizing autobiography. Homer's blindness, as well as the literary tradition of blind poets which culminates with Borges, are important components in Borges' autobiography, particularly towards the end of his life. Yet, it is in his role as 'maker', i.e. a poet, that we find Borges' most intimate dialogue with Homer, and where readers can find the most complex aspect of his connections with the author of the *Iliad* and the *Odyssey*. This aspect of Borges' engagement with Homer re-situates both Homer and Borges somewhere between the Western canon and modern world literature, and further aligns the biographical correspondence between the two, as Borges constructs it, for his readers.

Chapter 4 ('Virgil's Touch') examines how Borges' engagement with Virgil becomes a medium through which he inscribes fundamental aspects of his own cultural poetics of the classical past. Furthermore, it shows how in Borges' Virgil we find one of the most powerful examples of Borges' transcultural classicism. The chapter considers Borges' encounters with Virgil from two main interrelated points of discussion. The first of these concerns the geo-cultural spaces that Virgil occupies in Borges' memory, a memory that maps out a constellation of Virgilian presences (and Lucretian absences) across various locations and temporalities. The second part of this chapter takes stock of this discussion to investigate Borges' Virgil in a series of Borgesian poems, fictional essays and lecture material, many of which are not available in English. It examines the manner in which Borges retraces selected lines from the Virgilian corpus and transforms them into poetic ideas whose sensorial quality have the effect of 'touching' readers through time. The chapter closes with a theoretical discussion of Borges' cultural memory of Virgil as a new paradigm for reading the Roman poet in the twentieth century, and will highlight the part that geopoetics and the senses play in Borges' globalizing presentation of Virgil and his tradition.

Chapter 5 ('Antiquity in the Poetic Cosmos') explores the texture of Borges' classicism in his poetry from two specific, interrelated points. The first part of the chapter traces the presence of the classics chronologically, from Borges' early to late poetry, paying close attention to Borges' presentation of his poetic collections as 'miscellanies' or 'casual ensembles'. The central contention of this section is that it is precisely this aesthetics of randomness in Borges' poetic collections that gives the classics their specific presence and effects. The second part of the chapter explores Zeus, Oedipus, Janus and Proteus, 'threshold' figures who are granted a unique role in sketching the coordinates of Borges' complex global vision in his poetry. Here, I argue that the presence of classical myth in Borges' poetry becomes fundamental to Borges' exploration of the horizons of his own brand of world poetry (and world literature more broadly). Once more, Heraclitean time is the measure of this poetic vision, as well as the code for our own reception of Borges. The chapter closes by tracing this programmatic idea in a poem called 'Cosmogonía', first translated in English for the present book, which readers of Borges can interpret as a neat summation of his global, indeed 'deep' classicism.

Chapter 6 ('Interlude: Borges and Global Classics') is a bridge discussion between the preceding chapters and Chapter 7. It explores a dialogue between (non-)Anglophone Classical Reception Studies and questions concerning 'world' literature with a view to raising some future directions in the study of global Classics, as it unfolds in Borges' encounters with the Graeco-Roman past. Each of the sections considers the emerging field global Classics by appeal to the central metaphors and idioms that guide Borges' global thought and the mobility of classical antiquity in his work. The discussion also prepares readers for the successors of Borges' global classicism in Chapter 7, who offer further insights into Borges' global project and the character and scope of global classicism after Borges.

Chapter 7 considers the impact of Borges' classicism in (post)modern world fiction and postcolonial criticism. The chapter does not aim to provide an exhaustive survey. Rather, it discusses a selection of key post-Borgesian 'global' authors and critics who have been deeply influenced by Borges' mode of reading the cultural past, as well as Borges' relationship to antiquity, one that is informed by a global vision of literature that incorporates the classical past into itself. The chapter first offers a panoramic discussion of the vast impact of Borges' approach to past culture in literature, criticism and visual and performative art. The discussion then turns to three successors of Borges' classicism: Italo Calvino (Cuba 1923–Italy 1985), Umberto Eco (Italy 1932–2016) and Derek Walcott (Saint Lucia 1930–2017). In their own specific ways, these global authors situate Borges and his classicism at the heart of twentieth-century world literature, offering penetrating readings of his eccentric modality of reading the ancient past in tandem with their modernity. In exploring these successors, this chapter aims to introduce a model for the large impact of Borges' classicism in and outside the European tradition, as well as the subsequent conceptions of the classics as belonging to the realms of 'world literature'.

CHAPTER 2

The Flow of Heraclitus

It is also the river with no end
That flows and remains and is the mirror of one same
Inconstant Heraclitus, who is the same
And is another, like the river with no end.

'Ars Poetica', *The Maker* (1960: *SP* 137)

Perhaps the most complex aspect guiding Borges' encounters with the classical past is his conception of time and the role this has in his understanding of how antiquity is renewed and embodied in his own modernity. The question of time permeates Borges' writings, especially those delineating ideas about the self, identity, literature and human history. Here, the classical world is constantly present, although Borges tends to introduce it in the abbreviated and encyclopaedic fashion that characterizes his erudite system of citations, situated within the globalizing vision with which he regards the Graeco-Roman past. We have seen that, in his classical revisions, Borges disrupts the categories of before and after, imitator and model, and successor and precursor that emerge from a linear organization of time. Implicit in this subversion of conventional time, one finds Pascal's sphere once more (*SNF* 351–53), but this time in the shape of a circular structure whose mechanism and movement is temporal, rather than spatial.

Borges' receptions of antiquity ultimately respond to a temporality whose very character is cyclical. For Borges, the classics re-emerge at random intervals through the generations, even though this process does not involve an eternal repetition of historical and cultural sameness. Rather, the renewal of antiquity in our author's literary imagination occurs at intermittent periods of time, which often manifest themselves in a volatile manner. Examples of this understanding of the temporal workings that mark the tradition of the classical world are ubiquitous in Borges' oeuvre. This chapter focuses on two of its fullest and most powerful illustrations: the event of Caesar's murder and its cyclical re-embodiment in political history and fictional drama, and the figure of an author of *The Greek Anthology*, whose work is putatively lost to us, but whose cultural history lives on in multiple forms in our global memory and imagination. In these appeals to antiquity, Borges discloses a classical past that intermittently restores itself in historical and literary contexts across the globe necessarily as a *version* of its former self. Yet, for Borges, the events of the classical past that have an impact on subsequent historical and intellectual developments are *also* versions of other versions that predate the classical past, a past often beyond our material reach and recollection. In this sense, Borges' classics can be understood as cultural phenomena that, in theory, do not even originate in the classical world, even though they do take concrete place in the classical past, since they present a renewal of a distant time that has no beginning and will have no end. The conceptualization of antiquity as a version that recurs through the generations thus operates within a temporal structure that spans cyclically *ad infinitum*. This latter point and its effects on the receptions of antiquity in Borges' modernism will be explored in the sections that follow, as well as in Chapter 3, which considers Borges' *ad infinitum* poetics of reading Homer in space and time.

This chapter deals with these themes from three perspectives. First, it investigates how the classics partake in Borges' complex conception of time. Here, my aim is not to offer an exhaustive study of Borgesian time. There is an extensive list of monographs and articles, some of them excellent, fully dedicated to this topic in Borges, even though classical antiquity hardly makes an appearance in them.[1] My focus is instead on the question of how Borges' understanding of time informs his thinking about infinity, eternity and cyclicality, and in turn how these concepts interplay with classical presences in his work.[2] The ideas discussed in this section deal predominantly with conceptual issues that are key to the meaning of the temporal forms of Borges' classicism in the following sections and the rest of this book. The second part of this chapter considers the significance of a highly influential classical figure in Borges, that of Heraclitus of Ephesus,

---

[1] Although there are numerous critical studies in Borges and time, there is no in-depth exploration of Borgesian time dealing specifically with the question of how this informs his understanding of the classical tradition and its reception. For the subject of time in Borges' philosophical and fictional writings, I found useful the general discussions in Bossart (2003: 79–107), Johnson (2009), Griffin (2013: 5–6 and 9–10) and Wood (2013: 39–40). Amongst the extensive bibliography on specific aspects of time in Borges, I single out Mosher (1994) on atemporality, Earle (2003) on the interplay of temporal and extra-temporal structures in Borges' narrative fiction and Bartoloni (2003: 317–33) on time in Borgesian criticism.

[2] This question has received little, if any, attention, either in Borges Studies or Classical Reception Studies. My first explorations on the topic are in Jansen (2016) and (2018).

whose river metaphor underpins Borges' poetics of reading antiquity across various temporalities and geographies. Like the river of Heraclitus, the classical tradition, as envisaged by Borges, is subject to an unpredictable flux almost imperceptible at the very moment of reception yet tangible when considered in the depth of time.[3] This flux is ultimately endless, as Borges tells us in the last lines of his 'Ars Poetica' (1960: *SP* 137), quoted at the beginning of this chapter, and presents us with an inconstant vision and recollection of the classical past. This latter point is the focus of the third section of this chapter, which considers Borges' reception of the lost literature of antiquity.

Borgesian Time and the Classics

Borges' preoccupation with time, especially in his early and middle writings, is predominantly ontological. Arguably his most overtly philosophical essay on the topic is 'A New Refutation of Time' (*SNF* 317–32), published in the original Spanish in 1947. In this piece, Borges builds on the idealism of Plato and later thinkers influenced by the Greek philosopher, such as Berkeley and Hume, to negate the objective existence of time.[4] For Borges, time is a subjective notion that we construct in our minds as we perceive events and associate their duration with the length of our past memories and future expectations. Borges opens the essay with an epithet containing an epigram from the seventeenth-century German poet and dramatist Daniel von Czepko's *Sexcenta Monidisticha Sapientum* 3.2: 'Before me there was no time, after me there will be none. /With me it is born, with me it will also die' (*SNF* 317). The epithet perfectly captures a question that fascinates Borges not only in this essay, but in several of his fictional and non-fictional works: if time, as we know it, exists as the product of our perception, then no time can really exist outside this perception. In other words, there exist two contrasting worlds: the world made of time, as we construct it on a daily basis, and with which we typically organize the narratives of our history, and the world outside time, of which we have no knowledge.[5] Borges often ponders how the world outside time might work in practice. What would it be like to experience a sense of space beyond our own temporal perceptions? And, even if we could experience this space, how could we explain it in our world?

[3] For a discussion of 'deep time' and the classics, see Butler (2016: 1–15).
[4] Griffin (2013: 5–6; 9–10).   [5] Earle (2003: 1–13).

I believe that one of man's ambitions is the idea of living outside time. I do not know if it is possible, although twice in my life I have felt myself outside time. Although they could have been illusions. Twice in my long life I have felt myself outside time or, in other words, eternal. Of course, I have no idea how long each experience lasted because I was outside time. I cannot communicate the feeling either – it was something very beautiful. (*Conversations* I (2014: 16–7) (trans. J. Wilson))

While human time is a phenomenon that we can explain as a result of perception, as Borges does, our desire to gain an objective understanding of this perception remains ultimately an illusion. For it is impossible for us to communicate an experience of time, outside time, within the temporal structures that organize our human narratives. We know this goal is unattainable, yet our desire to know what time outside time might be like remains inexplicably alive.[6]

This inexplicable desire to know often leads Borges to explore the theme of temporal order, or sequence, and its interplay with the question of infinity. In an interview with Osvaldo Ferrari in 1984 on the subject of 'Order and Time', Borges expands on this topic. He claims that he is persuaded by Kant's argument that infinity is impossible for humans to grasp, just as it is impossible for us to ascertain when time, as we know it or have constructed it, began, since this presupposes knowledge of a time that comes before it, and in turn the time that comes before that, and so on *ad infinitum* (*Conversations* I, 34). Yet in his characteristically cross-cultural and globalizing manner of arguing a case in point, Borges admits that the cyclical structures we find in, for instance, the Buddhist philosophy of reincarnation do suggest that infinity exists:[7]

Now, take Buddhism. It holds that each life is determined by a karma woven by a soul in its previous life. But with that we are obliged to believe in infinite time, for each life presupposes an earlier life, that life presupposes an even earlier one and so on till infinity. That is, there never was a first time nor a first second of time. (*Conversations* I (2014: 17–8) (trans. J. Wilson))

This incidental comment in the conversations with Ferrari reveals a crucial facet of Borges' formulation of time: the possibility that there are no beginnings to mark the events and endeavours of our time. In turn, this suggests that the notion of originality that has been so pervasive in our approach to understanding human history and its development, especially

[6] Jansen (2016: 292–93 and 298–301).
[7] On Borges' interest in and engagement with Buddhism, especially in connection with time and space, see Almeida and Parodi (2005: 101–24).

in the West, lacks a solid foundation. If we agree with this radical proposition, then we could argue that every event in our world is a version that exists in flux *ad infinitum*, inside and outside time. As will be shown in the next section, Borges reinforces this idea throughout his mid and late literary career in his quasi-religious appeal to Heraclitus.

Eternity is another kind of temporal order that exists beyond our intellectual grasp; one Borges is keen to distinguish from the concept of infinity. While infinity involves a succession of beginnings and ends which, in theory, can be plotted *ad infinitum*, eternity is a different type of order impossible to conceive in practice: it represents the vision of the whole in the past, present and future all at once. This is the theme of 'A History of Eternity', a philosophical essay published in 1936, in which Borges defines eternity as 'the simultaneity of the three tenses' (*SNF* 124).[8] In the same interview with Ferrari mentioned above, Borges elaborates on this issue:

> Eternity – I have written about this in 'The Aleph' – is that very audacious hypothesis that there is an instance and that in that instant converges the past – all of our yesterdays, as Shakespeare put it – the present and the future. But that would be a divine attribute. (*Conversations* I (2014: 18) (trans. J. Wilson))

It is interesting to note that, while the existence of infinity suggests that there is no fixed instant to account for the beginnings of things, i.e. that there is no concept of originality, the idea of eternity that Borges entertains here presents us with a single instant encapsulating all universal events at once. In this sense, eternity could potentially offer a vision (or a version?) of originality itself. This idea remains well beyond our intellectual faculties, even our imagination, yet Borges attempts to conceive it with utmost creativity in his masterpiece, 'The Aleph' (*CF* 274–86), a narrative that combines classically informed erudition with speculative fiction.

The central theme of this story is man's burning desire and obsession to attain a complete image of the universe at large, inside and outside subjective time, where even one's own self is contained: a story that Italo Calvino, a self-confessed followed of Borges, brilliantly reworks in his

---

[8] Cf. the strong point of contact with T. S. Eliot in the first five lines of 'Burnt Norton' (*The Four Quartets*):

> Time present and time past
> Are both perhaps present in time future
> And time future contained in time past.
> If all time is eternally present
> All time is unredeemable.

Like Borges, Eliot shows an interest in the convergence of past, present and future in this famous passage and experiments with a chronology that becomes pivotal to Modernist experimentation.

novel *Mr Palomar*.[9] 'The Aleph' is set in Buenos Aires in the bourgeois milieu of the 1930s and '40s, and its main characters are two literary-inclined men: Carlos Argentino Daneri and a fictional Borges. Structurally speaking, the story is organized into two loosely related narrative halves. The first half relates Borges' visits to Carlos Argentino's home on the successive anniversaries of the death of his cousin, Beatriz Viterbo, with whom Borges had been madly in love.[10] The men have little in common, especially when it comes to their literary taste: Borges admires what a classicist would identify as an Alexandrian sense of brevity and erudition (indeed the story cites the classics intermittently throughout the narrative), while Carlos Argentino enjoys verbose and clichéd pieces. As the narrative unfolds, the story changes into the subject of eternal vision and the question of how each man reacts to the reception of the temporally simultaneous whole disclosed to them. It is at this point that the reader first encounters the Aleph, an object that Carlos Argentino finds in his cellar and consults as he writes a copious encyclopaedic work. The Aleph is the first letter of the Hebrew alphabet and has important theological associations with the *Kabbalah*.[11] Yet, in Borges' story, it is described as a curious optical contraption shaped like a small glass sphere through which the universe may be glimpsed all at once from within and without the confines of human history. But the Aleph is not a gadget many can handle. It requires an astute user, like the fictional Borges, able to grasp the tensions brought to bear between 'the simultaneity of the three tenses' that the Aleph reveals and the limited ability of his human mind to grasp and retain that very vision in his memory. After enumerating the exhaustive catalogue of things he has seen through the Aleph, the fictional Borges next relates a series of final totalizing visions that include the vertiginous image of the Aleph itself:

> I saw ... I saw ... I saw the Aleph from everywhere at once, saw the earth in the Aleph, and the Aleph once more in the earth and the earth in the Aleph, saw my face and my viscera, saw your face, and I felt dizzy, and I wept, because my eyes had seen that secret, hypothetical object whose name has

---

[9] Calvino (1999: 237–43). On Calvino's engagement with Borgesian modernist poetics, see Varsava (1990: 183–99).

[10] The names of Daneri and Beatriz are often read as a comic allusion to Dante's *Divine Comedy*. Other literary intertexts are suggested by the fiction's structural form. This is especially the case when the narrative reaches the cellar, where the Aleph can be found, and which appears to be a kind of labyrinth whose architectural structure could have been designed by Daedalus. For a discussion of both allusions, see González Echevarría (2013: 127).

[11] On Borges and the *Kabbalah* as an ancient tradition of mythical interpretation, see Fishburn (2013: 57–60). On the Aleph and Kabbalistic interpretation, see González Echevarría (2013: 125).

been usurped by men but which no man has ever truly looked upon: the inconceivable universe. ('The Aleph' (1949: *CF* 283-4))

Implicit in this temporally simultaneous vision of the 'inconceivable' whole that Borges calls the eternal universe, said to exist outside human time, is the complex presence of Borges' classics. For Borges, antiquity – and, in particular, its literary production – is a world that exists both in our own subjective time and in eternity. Thus, his interest is not only in the classical presences that we can account for in our cultural history, but also in the classical *absences* that we cannot explain but still somehow exist in our literary imagination. The category of 'classical presences' belongs to our time, and is what we call – not without much contestation and disagreement[12] – either 'classical' or 'world' literature, while 'classical absences' is a category of Graeco-Roman literature now lost to us; texts that have been temporally eclipsed from our memory, or even texts that could have been written but were not. This is what Borges would call 'Universal Literature' in its truest sense, and what would entail the impossible-to-grasp notion of 'Classics Whole'. Both classifications of literature, 'Classical/World' and 'Universal', can overlap at any time. They have their putative shelves in the Library of Babel, since, according to Borges' celebrated fiction, the eternal library includes all that can be uttered in the three tenses: past, present and future: 'its bookshelves contain all … that is able to be expressed, in every language. All' (*CF* 115). There, in the fictional world of Babel, we can locate the works of Homer, Virgil and Ovid, to name only three from the vast list of classical canonical authors that we still read and enjoy. We can also locate the lost books of Tacitus, Borges' example of lost classical literature *par excellence*, which we endlessly crave to inspect.[13] Babel furthermore houses Lucretius' *De rerum natura*, whose transmission has had a highly fluctuating history,[14] and whose pages have at times been placed close to the extant classical canon, and at others far away from it, somewhere closer to the lost pages of Tacitus. The history of this textual clustering is indeed inconstant and necessarily adopts the permanent form of a version. Rarely has the literature of ancient Greece and Rome taken such a spectacular journey in time in the modern

[12] For a discussion of 'world' as a category of 'literature', see Chapter 1, 20–1.
[13] For the complex history of their transmission of Tacitus, see Martin (2010: 241–52) and Murgia (2012: 15–22). For the fragmentary character of Tacitus' *Histories* and *Annals*, see Master (2012: 84–100) and Benario (2012: 101–22), respectively. I am also grateful to Ellen O'Gorman for sharing with me her knowledge of Tacitus' lost texts.
[14] See Reynolds and Wilson (1983: 218–22). Butterfield (2016: 22–53) and Deufert (2016: 68–87) also offer excellent case studies of the fluctuating history in the transmission of the *DRN*.

imagination as it does with Borges. And rarely has the modern reader been presented with such a formidable vision of the classical past.

Both infinity and eternity are therefore highly significant concepts in Borges' remapping of the temporality that punctuates the Graeco-Roman tradition, a tradition that in Borges' work operates between the poles of cultural history and speculative fiction. For Borges, the classical past can only be conceived fragmentarily, since its presence not only re-emerges through the generations as a version in flux, without beginning or end, but also constantly fluctuates between the realms of Classical/World and Universal Literature. At the core of this eccentric formulation of the classical tradition and its circulation in time and space is yet another temporal form that encompasses Borges' 'physics of reading' antiquity – that of cyclicality. Cyclicality marks the larger structural mechanism of Borgesian time, whether this refers to the texts that Borges imagines as circulating between eternity and our world *ad infinitum*, or just within our world alone.[15]

In 'Circular Time', published in 1941 (*SNF* 225–28), Borges traces three forms of cyclical renewal[16] that in philosophical terms we know as the notion of the 'eternal return' or 'eternal recurrence' and typically associate with Nietzsche, even though the idea has an extensive philosophical history.[17] The first and second forms discussed by Borges respectively concern the astrological formulations of Plato, Cicero, Lucilio Vanini and Thomas Browne and the 'algebraic principles' of Nietzsche, Blanqui, Hume and Russell (*SNF* 226). It is the third form of the eternal return that matters to Borges and his aesthetics of reading the past.[18] This refers to 'the concept of similar but not identical cycles' discussed by Marcus Aurelius in his *Meditations* 2.14, which Borges believes to be the most 'conceivable' way of interpreting the notion of temporal renewal. This concept, Borges tells the reader, can be traced in an 'infinite catalogue of authorities' on the subject, even though his focus is on a selected few:

> I now arrive at the final mode of interpreting eternal repetitions, the least melodramatic and terrifying of the three, but the only one that is concei-
> vable. I mean the concept of similar but not identical cycles. The infinite

---

[15] Bartoloni (2004: 317–33).

[16] In fact, the original title of this piece was 'Tres formas del eterno regreso'. The piece was published in the Argentine newspaper *La Nación* in 1941 and Borges later added it to his *History of Eternity*, published in 1953, which collects all his works concerning the question of time. Bernès (2010: 1531) in *ŒC*.

[17] On Nietzsche's eternal recurrence, as well as its impact in modern thought, see Loeb (2013: 646–71).

[18] On the three forms of the eternal return discussed by Borges, see Tcherepashenets (2008: 14–15).

catalogue of authorities would be impossible to complete: I think of the days and nights of Brahma; the epochs whose unmoving clock is a pyramid slowly worn down by a bird's wing that brushes against it every thousand and one years; I think of Hesiod's men, who degenerate from gold to iron; the world of Heraclitus, which is engendered by fire and cyclically devoured by fire; and the world of Seneca and Chrysippus, annihilated by fire and renewed by water; I think of Virgil's fourth *Eclogue* and Shelley's splendid echo; Ecclesiastes, the theosophists. Concordet's decimal history; I think of Francis Bacon ... Schopenhauer ... Poe's *Eureka* ... Out of this profusion of testimony I will cite only one passage, from Marcus Aurelius ... ('Circular Time' (1941: *SNF* 226–27))

In this passage, the form of Borges' method of citations is as important as the message these citations convey. Borges claims that the catalogue illustrating the third form of the eternal return is 'infinite' and 'impossible to complete'. This statement arguably makes sense if one recalls that in the Borgesian imagination literature belongs to two conceptual categories, World and Universal, and encompasses the entirety of the textuality of the past, present and future, as well as literature whose status remains potential. Thus, even though Borges recalls a particular group, his comment implies that, in theory, his catalogue of authorities could span both *ad infinitum* and *ad aeternum*. It is also worth noting the deliberate order that Borges' otherwise random method of citation of past literature exhibits. While our author chooses a range of examples that tends to move from antiquity to modernity and from East to West, he still preserves an aesthetic sense of randomness on his page. This is not only an important aspect of his art of citation, which reproduces Borges' own encyclopaedic habits[19] – it also allows the author to create a miniature cosmos illustrative of his thinking about the literary tradition in time, a tradition that he constantly globalizes from shifting and multiple perspectives, as has been demonstrated thus far.

Within this miniature cosmos of citations, Borges gravitates towards ancient Eastern thought and the philosophy and literature of the classical world. The thematic focus of this arrangement is that of renewal and its varied manifestations. This prompts Borges to begin with the units of time that mark the eternal cycle of rebirth in the days and nights of Brahma, the creator god of Hinduism. The examples then move to the Graeco-Roman world, and to a highly allusive reference to what must be Tacitus' *Annals* 6.28, which retells the strange appearance of the Phoenix in Egypt and the

---

[19] Carricaburo (2011: 461–73).

various local beliefs in the temporal frequency with which the mythical bird cyclically regenerates.[20] Then follow two explicit classical references with additional information: the shift from the Golden to Iron Age in Hesiod's *Works and Days* and the restorative yet equally destructive power of fire, as interpreted by Heraclitus, Seneca and Chrysippus. We next come to Virgil's *Eclogues* 4. The citation is only titular since, Borges must believe, his readers will know it refers to the sequence of the ages and the renewal of the age to come (*'talia saecla' suis dixerunt 'currite' fusis | concordes stabili fatorum numine Parcae* 46–7, 'Ages so blessed, glide on! cried the Fates to their spindles, voicing in unison the fixed will of destiny'). From Virgil onwards, the examples continue to emerge in a highly abbreviated manner, moving swiftly from antiquity to modernity until they reach Schopenhauer. The final citation, however, moves dramatically back to the second century AD, to one of Marcus Aurelius' meditations, which Borges cites verbatim:

> '[R]emember that all things turn and turn again in the same orbits, and for the spectator it is the same to watch for a century or for two or infinitely' (*Reflections* II, 14). ('Circular Time' (1941: *SNF* 227))

We may think that Borges is contradicting himself in this final illustration of the third form of eternal return. His previous examples clearly point to a form of renewal through the generations that exhibits 'similar but not identical cycles'. Marcus Aurelius, however, seems to be proposing that the history of man is no more than a series of observable repetitions whose salient characteristic is sameness. Yet Borges is eager to clarify his reader's possible misinterpretation of his citation of the Roman Stoic philosopher's words:

> If Edgar Allan Poe, the Vikings, Judas Iscariot, and my reader all secretly share the same destiny – the only possible destiny – the universal history is the history of a single man. Marcus Aurelius does not, strictly speaking, force this enigmatic simplification upon us ... *[he] affirms the analogous, but not identical, nature of multifarious human destinies.* He affirms that any time span – a century, a year, a single night, perhaps the ungraspable present – contains the entirety of history. (My emphasis) ('Circular Time' (1941: *SNF* 227–8))

---

[20] The phoenix is a favourite Borgesian figure and appears especially in Borges' late poetry. Borges is surely referring to Tacitus here. The connection becomes even more plausible when read in conjunction with discussion of the same passage with reference to death and repetition: in Barthes (1991: 111). 'La mort tacitéenne est un système ouvert, soumis à la fois à une structure et à un procès, à une répétition et à une direction ... tout se reproduit et pourtant rien ne se répète, tel est peut-être le sens de cet univers tacitéen, où la description brillante de l'oiseau-Phœnix (VI, 34) semble ordonner symboliquement la mort comme le plus pure moment de la vie.'

So does Borges affirm 'the analogous, but not identical, nature' of the equally 'multifarious destinies' of the classical tradition in world history and literature. This latter point will be the next focus of discussion, which involves antiquity's extraordinary cyclical journeys from the Bible to the Argentine Pampas, and from our collective memory to tacit oblivion, in Borges' fictional cosmos.

Heraclitean Receptions

While the classics permeate Borges' sophisticated thinking about time and the tradition of the classical past, the authors and texts that he cites tend to appear on his page in a markedly brief and often highly allusive manner. Heraclitus is perhaps the exception. Borges has his most far-reaching dialogue with the pre-Socratic Greek thinker, whose doctrine of change revealing time to be an ever-recurring phenomenon is at the very heart of Borges' classicism. Borges frequently refers to Heraclitus when invoking the inexorability of change, and he repeatedly cites the philosopher's comparison of time to a flowing river, into which no-one can step twice because the river is constantly changing.[21] Self-identity is an important and interrelated theme in this appeal to the Heraclitean metaphor, especially in poems and prose references articulating the idea that we, as human beings, are, like the notion we call time, in constant flux:

> [E]ach time I recall fragment 91 of Heraclitus, 'You cannot step into the same river twice,' I admire his dialectic skill, for the facility with which we accept the first meaning ('The river is another') covertly imposes upon us the second meaning ('I am another') and gives us the illusion of having invented it. ('A New Refutation of Time' (1947: *SNF* 322–3))

> We are the river you spoke of, Heraclitus.
> We are time.   'The Maker', *The Limit* (1981: *SP* 443)

> To look at the river of time and water
> And remember that time is another river,
> To know we are lost like the river
> And faces dissolve like water.
>   'Ars Poetica', *The Maker* (1960: *SP* 137)

---

[21] For fragment 91a, see Kahn (1979: 168–9) and Robinson (1987: 139–41).

Here, Borges is particularly interested in the power that the time-as-a-river metaphor has on our understanding of the self and self-identity. The Heraclitean 'river of time' is like a mirror that reflects images of our essence as human beings. We are like time, which in turn is like a river that flows infinitely. The metaphor seems to tell Borges that the moment we attempt to capture the essence of who we are – an ontological question – is the very moment we realize what we *are not*. For, in its reflection, the river that flows like time always shows us that we are 'another', i.e. that there is no single moment in the present tense that defines us wholly because we are constantly flowing, constantly changing.[22] Like the question of the identity of literature, our self-identity also seems to be fragmentary: we must be a version of someone who we cannot ever fully know. It is poetry and philosophy, Borges tells us, that on occasion give us glimpses of our whole selves, when our identity would putatively acquire a status that is fixed, or ideal, in the Platonic sense. Borges sublimely immortalizes this image at the closing of his 'Ars Poetica', as he continues to define the nature of art:

> They say that Ulysses, sated with marvels,
> Wept tears of love at the sight of his Ithaca,
> Green and humble. Art is that Ithaca,
> Of green eternity, not of marvels.
> It is also the river with no end
> That flows and remains and is the mirror of one same
> Inconstant Heraclitus, who is the same
> And is another, like the river with no end.
>
> 'Ars Poetica', *The Maker* (1960: *SP* 137)

While this poem begins with the question of the self, as I have shown above, it ends with the question of poetry, not without first mentioning Odysseus. Exhausted from his travels, the Homeric hero finally grasps a vision of eternity on earth in the image of his 'green and humble' Ithaca. Yet, when considered as an optical medium, Ithaca is not like the unimaginably daunting Aleph that offers a vision of eternity itself. Ithaca is, here, an ataraxic version of the idea of eternity that offers Odysseus the possibility of reflecting on his arduous past while simultaneously projecting his welcome future. Through the depiction of this instant, the maker of art (Homer and Borges, as we shall see in Chapter 3) has the ability to show us versions of what they conceive to be the status of the self in eternity. This,

---

[22] For Borges, the present tense is 'ungraspable'. See, for instance, *SNF* 228: 'He (Marcus Aurelius) affirms that any time span – a century, a year, a single night, perhaps the ungraspable present contains the entirety of history'.

for Borges, is the power of art. Meanwhile, Heraclitus is the profound thinker who, by means of his equally poetic time-as-a-river metaphor, places a mirror before us to reveal the inconstant nature of our selves in our time.

The flux of time that discloses the fragmentary nature of the self also crucially underpins the temporal and spatial framework through which Borges engages with the classical tradition. Borges remains convinced that this tradition responds to the same mechanisms one finds in the formation of, and in the same manner as responses to, all past and present literary, cultural and historical traditions of the Western world. This includes the question of how antiquity reveals itself in modernity. In spite of their contextual differences, antiquity and modernity are, for Borges, two sides of the same Heraclitean coin: they are manifestations of a series of cyclical repetitions that periodically re-emerge in multiple forms in our world to forge what we retrospectively know as its story, or history.

A clear illustration of this reading can be found in 'In Memoriam of J.F.K.'. In this highly condensed piece, Borges contextualizes the assassination of President Kennedy in 1963 in a myriad of historical and literary examples of assassinations of world leaders, including that of Julius Caesar by Brutus:

> This bullet is an old one.
>
> In 1897, it was fired at the president of Uruguay by a young man from Montevideo, Avelino Arredondo, who had spent long weeks without seeing anyone so that the world might know that he acted alone. Thirty years earlier, Lincoln had been murdered by that same ball, by the criminal or magical hand of an actor transformed by the words of Shakespeare into Marcus Brutus, Caesar's murderer. In the mid-seventeenth century, vengeance had employed it for the assassination of Sweden's Gustavus Adolphus in the midst of the public hecatomb of battle. In earlier times, the bullet had been other things, because Pythagorean metempsychosis is not reserved for humankind alone. It was the silken cord given to viziers in the East, the rifles and bayonets that cut down the defenders of the Alamo, the triangular blade that slit a queen's throat, the wood of the Cross and the dark nails that pierced the flesh of the Redeemer, the poison kept by the Carthaginian chief in an iron ring on his finger, the serene goblet that Socrates drank down one evening. In the dawn of time it was the stone that Cain hurled at Abel, and in the future it shall be many things that we cannot even imagine today, but that will be able to put an end to men and their wondrous, fragile life. ('In Memoriam J.F.K.' (1963: *CF* 326))

This piece, 217 words in Spanish, is arguably the most succinct example of the universalizing system and deliberately random temporality in which

Borges cites classical material. Pythagorean metempsychosis is the organizing principle of the artistic chaos that guides the reader from Cain to the unimagined future, from East to West, and from historical fact to fiction. Here, Caesar, Marie Antoinette, Socrates, Lincoln, Pythagoras, Christ, Gustavus Adolfus, Hannibal and many others coexist in a textual world that moves vertiginously between temporalities, histories and literatures. Within this eccentric whole, my focus is on Caesar. Borges cites Caesar via Shakespeare as a classical illustration of his main subject, the assassination of J.F.K. For Borges, the assassination of the American president in 1963 by Oswald is, in theory, no different from that of Julius Caesar by Brutus in 44 BCE: both involve a leader, a weapon and a killer, and both disclose the essential characteristics that mark the relief of the history (and story) of humanity and its affairs. Nor are these assassinations dissimilar to that of a local gaucho of the Pampas by a violent faction:

> To make his horror complete, Caesar, pressed to the foot of a statue by the impatient daggers of his friends, discovers among the blades and faces the face of Marcus Julius Brutus, his *protegé*, perhaps his son, and ceasing to defend himself he exclaims: 'You too, my son!' Shakespeare and Quevedo revive the pathetic cry.
>
> Fate enjoys repetitions, variations, symmetries. Nineteen centuries later, in the south of the province of Buenos Aires, a gaucho is attacked by other gauchos. As he falls, he recognizes the face of one of his godsons and says to him with mild reproach and slow surprise (these words must be heard, not read): '¡Pero che!' He dies, and he doesn't know that he's dying in order to repeat a scene. ('The Plot' (1981) (trans. A. Manguel))

'[H]e dies, and he doesn't know that he's dying in order to repeat a scene.' The scene that the gaucho repeats is the same as that implied in the citation of Caesar in Borges' 'In Memoriam J.F.K.'. In 'The Plot', however, the citation plays a central part and is subject to explicit variation. Here, Borges again incorporates Shakespeare's Caesar as an intermediary source, but this time in the context of literary, historical and staged drama. The focus is on the cyclical reiteration of Shakespeare's famous line 'Et tu, Brute?' in different contexts. This moves from Borges' translation (originally in Spanish) of the 'Et tu, Brute?' of Shakespeare's *Julius Caesar*, 'You too, my son!', through Francisco de Quevedo's '¿Y tú, Bruto?' in his *Vida de Bruto* (1964),[23] to Borges' unique reinterpretation in his Argentine Spanish '¡Pero che!'. '¡Pero che!' is truly untranslatable into English, as Alberto Manguel points out, but might be loosely rendered in this context as

---

[23] Costa Picazo (2010: 361 n. 83) in *OC* III.

'Come off it!' or 'Give me a break'. Its meaning also requires an understanding of the dramatic tone and the gestures with which it is typically
spoken in the Argentina of Borges' time.[24] This is why the narrator urges
the reader to hear rather than read the phrase, thus further relocating its
literary history to the Rioplatense stage.[25]

The gaucho who utters '¡Pero che!' is still a version of his predecessors.
Though historically, fictionally and linguistically disconnected, in these
two pieces, Caesar, J.F.K. and the gaucho from the Pampas are playing the
same part in a Shakespeare-inspired play that is our world history, even
though their interpretations and performances are different. The main
ingredients in this play respond to Borges' formula of tradition which
involves 'repetitions, variations, [and] symmetries' (and which reminds us
of Borges' reading of Marcus Aurelius' dictum in 'Circular Time'): an
assassination, a weapon, a killer and, in the case of Caesar and the gaucho,
the last words uttered by the victim. Furthermore, they all embody the
essential characteristics that punctuate, through cyclical repetition, an ever-
recurring aspect of human nature: the interplay of power, betrayal and
violence. Heraclitean time is at the centre of this dialogue between antiquity and modernity within the larger structure of what Borges understands as History, a history that, as we have seen, owes as much to fiction as
it does to fact.

One may find the commensurability of Caesar with Kennedy, or Caesar
with a local gaucho, as well as the blend of history with literature, an
uncommitted form of reading on our author's part. Yet, this seemingly
detached response to the interplay of antiquity and modernity is not
without complications in Borges' politico-historical thought.[26] Nor are
Borges' cyclical receptions simple, and passive, statements about how
modernity reiterates aspects of antiquity. Rather, what Borges sees in the

---

[24] I am grateful to Alberto Manguel for discussing this line with me. For a full discussion, see
Manguel's essay in *Translating Borges* (2012): "'¡Pero che!' is one of those local expressions whose
sense depends not only on the tone and the gestures with which it is spoken, but on a childhood
spent in a Buenos Aires neighbourhood, on conversations in dusky cafés and on obligatory
nostalgia. In the end, I came up with a lame "Come off it!", which doesn't even begin to do justice
to the irony and melancholy contained in the "*¡Pero che!*"'.

[25] 'Rioplatense': this refers to the region around the basin of the Río de la Plata, which includes
Uruguay and Borges' Buenos Aires, as well to the Spanish language spoken in the area.

[26] For which see Chapter 5. In his late poetry in particular, Borges often alludes to Heraclitean time to
refer to the renewal of dictatorial forces in twentieth-century Argentina and Europe, e.g. the seizing
of executive power by dictator Juan Domingo Perón in 1955, which had an impact on Borges' public
life and persona, or the establishment of the Argentine military junta during 1976–83, which he
notoriously first supported and then condemned. For this period of Borges' life, see Williamson
(2004: 326–41 and 428–67).

examples of Caesar, J.F.K. and the gaucho is how antiquity *renews* itself in modernity, while simultaneously pointing to the recurrent plots that put antiquity and modernity into dynamic interactions. In Chapter 7 ('Successors of Borges' Classicism'), we shall explore further implications of these ideas from the perspective of Derek Walcott's cultural criticism of Borges.

Receptions of the Unfinished Text

We have seen that Borges conceptualizes the classical tradition as a form of cyclical renewal. In this renewal of antiquity, we rediscover traces of Caesar in Marie Antoinette, J.F.K. and a gaucho, and of Brutus' dagger in the guillotine, in the rifle of Oswald, and in the violent attacks by Argentine gauchos. But this in turn suggests that the classical past is only partially renewed. J.F.K is not exactly Caesar, but is *like* Caesar. The gaucho of the Pampas utters something *similar* to Shakespeare's Caesar, but not quite the same. In Borges, the renewal of tradition is a process in which the histories we hear, read or recall are always transmitted in incomplete form. This theme is recurrent in his work, and it amounts to an important, and an influential, reconsideration of the identity of literature and its transmission in twentieth-century thinking. Ricardo Piglia, who, together with Alberto Manguel, is amongst the most perceptive readers of Borges, points to this notion in a recent public lecture on Borges:

> Borges most aptly conveys the sense of the unfinished text: the idea that there is always something left to read, even if this is lost or unknown, and that this very part which remains unread determines what and how we actually read.[27]

For Borges, literature, like history, is constantly renewed in the flow of time, and as such it never assumes a finished status and identity. From this perspective, Borges insists, the *Iliad* is not a definitive text that explains subsequent adaptations and translations (*SNF* 69–82). It is, rather, an unfinished text, or a version of an older oral version (of which we know so little), just as subsequent translations of Homer's epic in any language are versions of versions themselves. Like the river of Heraclitus, all literature is not only incomplete, but also crucially *in flux*.

This flux can also paradoxically reveal the concealment of texts, which sometimes occurs for generations. Borges' favourite example of this

---

[27] 'Borges, por Piglia', TV Pública, Buenos Aires, Lecture 1 (22/08/2013), my translation.

phenomenon is Lucretius' *De rerum natura*, a text which, he argues, becomes temporarily invisible to the flux of tradition, when early Christianity decides to favour the piety it finds in Virgil's *Aeneid* over the atheism it condemns in the writings of Lucretius ('On Lucretius').[28] Other texts, Borges tells us, are more permanently eclipsed, such as the epigrams of a minor poet of *The Greek Anthology*, whose full textuality now amounts to a word in an index:

> Where now is the memory
> Of the days that were yours on earth, and wove
> Joy with sorrow; and made a universe that was your own?
> The river of years has lost them
> From its numbered current; you are a word in an index.
> To others the gods gave glory that has no end:
> Inscriptions, names on coins, monuments, conscientious historians;
> All that we know of you, eclipsed friend,
> Is that you heard the nightingale one evening.
> Among the asphodels of the Shadow, your shade, in its vanity,
> Must consider the gods ungenerous.
> But the days are a web of small troubles,
> And is there a greater blessing
> Than to be the ash of which oblivion is made?
> Above other heads the gods kindled
> The inexorable light of glory, which peers
> Into the secret parts and discovers
>   each separate fault;
> Glory, that at last shrivels the rose it reveres;
> They were more considerate with you, brother.
> In the rapt evening that will never become night
> You listen without end to Theocritus' nightingale.
>
> 'To a Minor Poet of the Greek Anthology' (1964: *SP* 167)

The poem has several things to say about what Borges makes of the role of time and recollection in our knowledge of classical literature and its authors. It does so by a clever appeal to a cultural memory that rests solely on an indexed name in the anthology. The current of time, here expressed by a clear allusion to the Heraclitan metaphor of the ever-flowing river, has not only demoted an ancient Greek author of epigrams into a minor poet but, also pointedly, into a 'word in an index', whose name we, Borges' readers, don't even know. Unlike the memory of other glorified poets, which time has preserved partially through images carved in coins,

---

[28] *Conversations* II (2015: 264).

inscriptions of their lives and works, or the task of 'conscientious histor-
ians', we only know that this elusive poet has heard the nightingale. This is
the point at which the index of his unnamed name becomes a threshold of
interpretation, to use Genette's metaphor for paratexts.[29] For the nightingale, that bird which in Western tradition becomes a trope for sorrow
and lament,[30] directs our classical literary memory to the nightingales we
know a little more as, for instance, the *philomela* of Virgil *Georgics* 4, to cite
an intertext that resonates strongly in the context of Borges' text, who,
from the shadow of a poplar, laments Orpheus' loss of his wife Eurydice.[31]
And this more palpable memory of the Virgilian past stays with us as we
continue to read Borges' poem to its last line, when we are taken even
further back in time, to the singing of the *philomela* of Theocritus, to which
the minor poet now listens extra-temporally from his oblivion. And as we
retrace earlier lines of Borges' poem, this Theocritan setting is further
reconfigured into another well-known image, that of *Odyssey* 11 and 24,
in which the *asphodelos* is the symbolic flower of the shades. But Borges'
poem also seems to be working within a wider allusive network. In his note
on the minor poet, Pierre Bernès, the commentator of the Gallimard
edition of Borges' *Oeuvres Complètes*, tells us that Borges here is refereeing
to an '[i]llûstre poète de l'époque alexandrine (vers 315–vers 250 av. J.–C.)
qui cultiva l'idylle bucolique'. While this may be correct, Borges does not
give us any fixed clues. We may follow a contextualist approach and even
wonder if – especially because the poem alludes to Heraclitus via the river
metaphor (5), in composing this piece – Borges is also specifically thinking
about the Heraclitus of the *Greek Anthology* 7.465, the single epigram (and
thus the one and only index entry) that we possess by that author. That
epigram is also often read in conjunction with 7.80 by Callimachus, which
refers to Heraclitus' collected works as *Aëdones*, or *Nightingales*, and which
happens to associate spatial and temporal distance with loss, memory,
mourning and the favour of the gods:[32]

> Εἶπέ τις, Ἡράκλειτε, τεὸν μόρον ἐς δέ με δάκρυ
> ἤγαγεν· ἐμνήσθην δ', ὁσσάκις ἀμφότεροι

---

[29] Genette (1997) and discussed further in Jansen (2014).   [30] López-Baralt (2013: 73–4).
[31] I offer the example of the nightingale of *Georgics* 4 as a particularly resonant intertext in my own
reading of Borges' poem, and because Borges' poem calls for a strong Virgilian allusion via
Theocritus. The list of classical nightingales is long, however, and my readers may be thinking of
other instances when reading Borges' poem above, such Ovid's Philomela in *Metamorphoses* 6.519-
62, in itself a close intertext to Virgil's *philomela* and its tradition.
[32] I am thankful to Daniel Anderson for discussing this allusion with me. For a discussion of the
potential relationship between these *AP* 7.80 and 7.465, see Hunter (1992: 113–23).

ἥέλιον [ἐν] λέσχῃ κατεδύσαμεν. ἀλλὰ σὺ μέν που,
    ξεῖν᾽ Ἁλικαρνησεῦ, τετράπαλαι σποδιή,
αἱ δὲ τεαὶ ζώουσιν ἀηδόνες, ἧσιν ὁ πάντων
    ἁρπακτὴς Ἀίδης οὐκ ἐπὶ χεῖρα βαλεῖ.[33]

Someone told me of your death, Heraclitus, and it moved me to tears, when
I remembered how often the sun set on our talking. And you, my
Halicarnassian friend, lie somewhere, gone long long ago to dust; but they
live, your Nightingales, on which Hades who seizes all shall not lay his
hands. (Trans. W. R. Paton with minor alterations)

The Callimachean epigram contains the central themes explored by
Borges: nightingales, death, memory, time's passing and the capricious
favouring of the gods on some and not others. But whether Borges is
thinking specifically about Heraclitus' *Nightingales* (we simply don't have
enough internal or external evidence to know which author or poem this
may be)[34] is perhaps besides the point. His poem functions in such a way
that our memory of more allusive literary nightingales, such as those of
Heraclitus, or even those of Ovid and Keats, are equally possible within the
network of what Borges regards the Universe of Human Letters. He has
brought some memories of the history of the literary nightingale to the
textual surface of his poem, not all, and he will bring other memories
elsewhere in his late poetic oeuvre, such as in 'To the Nightingale' (*SP* 355).
His poem clearly thrives on a kaleidoscope of nightingale citations and
memories which may include even the Sufi tradition of the celebrated bird.

While the poem is open to a complex system of allusion and intertext, its
more direct content invites us to recreate a collective memory of what we
may regard as a most incomplete text: an index in an anthology, whose
actual text we don't know. But this index is no simple paratext: it is in this
case an entry point into recalling tangible yet distant memories of the
classical literary past. Thus, we are encouraged to remember not to forget
that the eclipsed poet of the anthology has heard the nightingale of
Theocritus' *Idylls*, which Virgil himself hears in his *Georgics* 4, as later
does Ovid in *Metamorphoses* 6, and that we may even hear in Heraclitus
and Keats. What is more, the eclipsed poet is now eternally surrounded by
asphodels, flowers we know best from our reading of Homer.
The narratology of this intertextual memory is, once more, based on the
temporality of the Heraclitan river metaphor, which, in its eternally running course, allows some texts to continue to be visible to us (Homer,
Theocritus, Virgil), while it eclipses others (such as our minor Greek poet

---

[33] Gow and Page (1965: xxxiv).   [34] Costa Picazo (2010: 526–27) in *OC* III.

who, we may wonder, could even be Heraclitus, whose *Nightingales* are now lost to us). Most provocatively though, because of Borges' unique form of reading the classics in time, we can now reconfigure our cultural memory of Homer, Heraclitus, Theocritus and Virgil, thinking of classical asphodels, rivers and nightingales also as indexes to our elusive poet of the anthology. It's all about the entry points and meaning in-between, and never about attempting to recuperate fully what we know, and accept, is lost or forgotten.

Borges and the Disclosure of Antiquity

Cyclical time gives a texture to the way we read the Universe of Human Letters, as Borges also likes to call the incompleteness of our literatures. It also canonizes parts of that universe, while obscuring other parts, such as the minor poet in Borges' poem whose memory was obscured for us. The texture of Borges' reading of classical literature as fragmentary phenomena thus rests on a series of zoomings-in and -out. In the case of the historical Caesar, he is part of a complex and dense intertextuality that fuses – and confuses – fact with fiction in the history of his character's tradition from Roman antiquity to Borges' Argentine modernity. The case of the minor poet, whom a fictional Borges has encountered while running his index finger through the last pages of the anthology, becomes a playful paratext with which he dramatizes the gaps in our memory of the minor poet's tradition and indirectly points to the way we read canonical authors, whose texts we know more fully. The knowledge of the lost and unrecoverable(?) books of Tacitus' *Annals* and *Histories* contained somewhere in the eternal Babel seems, therefore, to determine the way we read Tacitus. In a similar way, one could add that knowledge of an earlier version of Ovid's *Amores*, containing five books (whether in the literary imagination of Ovid or in some lost bookrolls), seems relentlessly to determine the way we approach our reading of the last of the Augustan elegists.[35] The list of examples of unfinished texts is vast, from Sappho onwards. Hence, Borges' physics of reading encourages us to plot literature as fragmentary phenomena that respond, not to our urge to know, but to the volatile eclipses and disclosures at stake in the flux of tradition.

Borges' disclosure of antiquity as a series of historical, intellectual and cultural events that flow fragmentarily in time in the scenarios of our histories and historical drama is an intrinsic aspect of his global classicism.

[35] Jansen (2012).

This form of classicism draws on the cross-cultural perspectives and post-colonial responses of New World literature, which Borges himself helps forge, as well as deeply influencing the successors of his classicism, as we shall see in the final chapter of this book. It not only sees the classics in a new globalized role with respect to formulations of modern identity, human history and world fiction, but it also makes for a fascinating chapter in the curious history of lost literatures. Furthermore, Borges' global classicism presents us with a therapeutic alternative to the search for the classical past – a persistent tradition in twentieth-century peripheral Western imagination – since the Argentine author believes that images of this past can never be recuperated to the full. All we can do, he tells us, is to accept the fragmentary character of ancient Greece and Rome as it reveals itself before us. As for the bizarre temporality of Borges' classicism, this arguably emerges in sharp contrast with the predominant manner of reading the Graeco-Roman past in the Western world, which, broadly speaking, seeks to recuperate in various ways, and as fully as possible, images of antiquity's intellectual, socio-political and material culture. Yet Borges is not exactly opposed to this kind of exegesis.[36] Rather, his stories subtly point to the methodological anxieties that this exegesis brings to bear in our endeavour to disclose past cultures almost as if we were glancing at them through the Aleph. For, as Borges would argue, it remains true that no matter how many lines we manage to restore or interpolate, how much material we find under the ground or scattered amongst ruins, or what new evidence we uncover, our knowledge of that past will always be transmitted to us in parts. Unless past and present were for the first time to unite in a single moment and place, responses to the lacunose Sappho will probably continue to be a matter of scholarly conjecture, the inscribed fragment of the *Res Gestae* of Augustus found in Ancyra will likely retain its beautifully fractured shape and the reasons for an Ovid in exile will remain a secret (or a ruse!) that the poet took to his grave. If, then, full pictures of past cultures, like those of the classical Greeks and Romans, can only be partially reconstructed, imagined or entertained, rather than fully known, Borges would ask why we insist in pursuing antiquity with such zeal. For Borges, our obsession with recuperating the classical world to the full is an enterprise of our modernity spectacularly doomed to fail. This is, in part, the moral of 'The Library of Babel', which retells the psychological highs

---

[36] For Borges' implicit influences on historicists, cultural and textual approaches to the study of literature, see Wood (2013) for an overview. For individual case studies in Borges as a new critical idiom, see Alazraki (ed. 1990).

and lows experienced by the librarians of the hexagons who, for endless generations, are obsessed with finding the 'Total Book' that will disclose all knowledge housed in the universal library (*CF* 115).

In his stories about unattainable universes, Borges implies that our own obsession with seeing 'classics whole' is no more than a hope and an illusion. This obsession with full cognition of the past entails something of a pathology that the French call *la douleur exquise*: a bittersweet pain of realizing, with certainty, that there are marked limits to our ability to obtain something whole, while simultaneously attempting to prevail over those very limits in the hope of succeeding anyway. The pursuit of antiquity as a *douleur exquise* also points to a realization that those of us involved in the study of the classical world may find hard to accept: we may not be after the end product, exactly, but rather after the *frisson* of the quest. The thrill of the quest is by no means a superficial aspect of our approach to knowledge acquisition. It powerfully suggests that what we are after can perhaps be found somewhere in-between: in-between the experience of not knowing and getting to know, and in-between the moments and spaces in which we position ourselves to contemplate the distant and often lost past. This is, in sum, Borges' therapeutic alternative to our obsessions with the recuperation of antiquity in the flow of Heraclitean time.

CHAPTER 3

The Idea of Homer

We do not know if Homer existed. The fact that seven cities vie for his name is enough to make us doubt his historicity. Perhaps there was no single Homer; perhaps there were many Greeks whom we conceal under the name of Homer.

J. L. Borges, 'Blindness' (1977: SNF 479)

The preceding chapters have shown that Borges constructs a new physics of reading antiquity, which privileges a vision of the classics as a part of a globalizing system, and transcends fixed ideas on the identity and circulation of the classical canon in the West.[1] Borges' Homer is the most experimental, if not perplexing, example of this vision. For the reader used to thinking of Homer as the father of Western literature, Borges' Homer is by no means easy to grasp, at least at first sight. As Borges resituates Homer's (pre)classical[2] past in the modernist scenarios of his oeuvre, his Homer becomes a nebulous figure, one that increasingly challenges received notions of his Western tradition.[3] Perhaps the best way to characterize the Greek poet in Borges' work would be that he is a figure capable of acquiring multiple versions of his former self. This portrayal of Homer emerges in implicit dialogue with the so-called 'Homeric Question', or questions, that have a considerable academic

---

[1] The title of this chapter owes to James Porter's work on Homer as the history of an idea, as well as to the title of his forthcoming monograph 'Homer: The Very Idea'. I am grateful to Porter for discussing this chapter with me and for his invaluable feedback.

[2] For Homer as a preclassical author, see Nagy (2010). For the importance of reading Homer as a preclassic in his cultural history, see Porter (2004). While I subscribe to Nagy's and Porter's arguments, for stylistic reasons I will use the term 'classic' rather than '(pre)classical' in the remainder of my discussion.

[3] As, for instance, Bloom does in his *Map of Misreading*, where he portrays the place of Homer in the Western tradition as a source of a subsequent 'anxiety of influence' (1975: 33): 'Everyone who now reads and writes in the West, of whatever racial background, sex or ideological camp is still a son or daughter of Homer'. For the problems and limitations of Bloom's vision of Homer in the twentieth century, see the excellent opening discussion by Graziozi and Greenwood (2007: 1–3).

history and had become well established by the time Borges was writing.[4] Namely, who was Homer? Did he ever exist? Was he one author or many? Did he enjoy a historical actuality and a concrete tradition,[5] or is he, after all, the product of an idea that has been occupying our scholarly pursuits and cultural imagination from antiquity onwards?[6] While Borges may have been aware of these issues in academic debates, his engagement with the question of Homer's identity appears to be in close dialogue with intermediary authors, such as Victor Hugo and Oscar Wilde, both of whom, Borges tells us, entertain the notion of many Homers existing in the postclassical imagination (*SNF*: 479). As Borges points out in the epigraph that prefaces this chapter, he seems inclined to believe in the 'cultural truth' of an imaginary Homer eclipsed by a plurality of Homers: 'Perhaps there was no single Homer; perhaps there were many Greeks whom we conceal under the name of Homer' (*SNF* 479).[7] Borges most innovatively explores this hypothesis and develops it as a narrative platform from which to launch his idea of the Greek poet, open to potentially infinite contexts and possibilities, like Borgesian literature itself. One of these, as will be discussed below, constitutes a poetics of reading Homer as a multiple, ever-expanding phenomenon, while another embodies Borges' interpretation of his own authorial identity and legacy after the image of his postclassical Homer.

This chapter will study these themes from two mutually complementary perspectives. First, it will explore the presence of Homer on the postclassical stage of Borges' 'The Immortal' (1949). In this story, Homer experiences multiple lives in the course of human history until he finally recalls his classical past via various clues, though not without losing sight of his new global place in Borges' narrative. A second section will consider a set of Homeric tropes that Borges traces in his work. These tropes speak of Borges' desire to associate his authorial identity to Homer's, a process that begins to define not just Borges' own cultural idea of his authorial persona in time, but ultimately Borges' profile as a global classicist. The chapter will close with a discussion of the contribution that Borges

---

[4] The 'Homeric Question', or questions, have a considerable academic history within Classics. It involves debates between 'oralists', who, building on Parry's seminal work on Homer and the oral tradition, have tended to argue that 'Homer' is more or less synonymous with 'the tradition', and those who believe that behind the *Iliad* and the *Odyssey* there was a single poet called 'Homer'. For a study of this debate and key bibliography, see Fowler (2004: 220–32).

[5] Haubold (2007) and Fowler (2004).   [6] For this cultural development, see Porter (2004).

[7] Of course, the notion of Homer's plural identity is by no means new to Borges. In fact, it is the very logic of Homer from the beginning, as well as from the early receptions of his persona For Homer as an 'invention' that begins in antiquity. For this latter issue, see Graziosi (2002).

makes to the question of Homer in the twentieth century, especially as part
of the 'history of an idea',[8] and as an authorial figure emerging between
world literature and the Western canon.[9]

Homer in Borges' Postclassical Landscapes

One of the most far-reaching effects of Borges' engagement with Homer is
the reconfiguration of the Homeric persona to a point that this persona
becomes almost synonymous with Borges' conception of literature. This
theme is central to the poetics of Borges' 'The Immortal' (1949), one of the
most complex treatments of Homer in twentieth-century writing.
Chapter 1 discussed how Borges reimagines Homer for his readers in
'The Maker', a short story published over a decade after 'The Immortal',
in which the figure of the Greek poet is made to forget his classical
canonicity then to remember it by the distant sound of a rumour.[10]
Despite its more intricate temporality and higher level of allusiveness,
'The Immortal' operates in a similar fashion for the reader.
Retrospectively speaking, the story develops on two main levels and directions. It presents us with a postclassical Homer barely recognizable to us, as
he moves through the centuries and his own immortality in fluctuating and
erratic ways, then to open new visions of Homer's distant classicism from
the wider perspective of Borges' literary landscapes.[11]

Only a few pages longer than 'The Maker', 'The Immortal' is a deeply
complex story.[12] In its original Spanish, it imitates a seventeenth-century
baroque form of the language and concentrates numerous Latinisms in its
vocabulary and syntax.[13] In terms of content, moreover, it features a high
level of erudition, especially in the encyclopaedic and geopolitical details
that dominate the narrative. Thematically, furthermore, the story requires
intensive reading and, as the history of its criticism attests, its idiosyncratic
structure is open to multiple readings and open-ended interpretations.[14]

---

[8] Porter (2004).   [9] Graziosi and Greenwood (2007).   [10] Chapter 1, 5.
[11] For a discussion of how Borges experiments with the notion of Homer's unrecognizability, see
Rabau (2012: 277).
[12] Though see Gallimard II (1617–18), which cites Borges' own critique of 'The Immortal', in which he
underlines certain excesses in its prose and style, as well as giving some details of how he would have
written the story years later. Citations come from Georges Charbonnier, *Entretiens avec J. L. Borges*
(1967: 120–212). In his interviews with Carrizo (1983: 232), Borges insists that 'The Immortal' was
over-written.
[13] Bernès (2010: 1618) in *ŒC*.
[14] It would take disproportionate space to cite the substantial list of bibliographical items on this topic,
all of which deal with specific angles of Borges' story. My reader may find a list of critical works on

The narrative follows a ramifying pattern that branches out potentially *ad infinitum*, though at times it forms labyrinthine and circular structures. Within this pattern, the classical Homer is concealed by a plurality of Homers who exist only postclassically. The tale of 'The Immortal' is told in five sections (I–V) that are embedded in the larger frame of Borges' fiction. It narrates the odyssey of Homer himself, who adopts the lives of several characters in social and cultural history, as well as those inhabiting the City of the Immortals. At the end of this odyssey, which coincides with the end of both his postclassical life and Borges' 'The Immortal', this Homer finally recalls that he once spoke Greek, and that he was the author of the *Iliad*, a text that he encounters in Pope's English translation of the epic.[15]

Homer's classical past is gradually revealed in sections III–V. Throughout sections I–V, the figure of Odysseus *polytropos* in *Odyssey* 1.1 and 10.330 ('much travelled' but also 'of many turns')[16] is apparent in the narrative, although Borges' Homer is subject to a much more elaborate temporality than that of Odysseus in the *Odyssey*: 'The Immortal' takes Homer through the centuries back and forth, as well as extra-temporally. His journey begins in 1929 London, and then continues in the third century AD by the Red Sea, where Homer drinks the waters of oblivion, until he mysteriously reaches the city of The Immortals (a version of the Underworld). After a timeless period in the City of The Immortals, Homer re-emerges in Tangier, here figured as one of the portals out of the immortal world, at an imprecise time. From that point onwards, his voyage on earth ramifies in various directions and times, as he wanders through 'new realms, new empires' (*CF* 192), from 1066 London back to seventh-century Cairo, where we find him transcribing 'the seventh voyages of Sinbad' (*CF* 193). As the centuries pass, he re-emerges in Bohemia as a teacher of astrology. In 1638, he moves to Rumania and later to Germany. We are not told what he did in these two locations, although he seemed to continue to carry out activities related to books and divination. In 1714, he suddenly appears in Aberdeen, Scotland, where he

---

'The Immortal' under the 'Criticism' section of the Borges Centre, Pittsburgh (www.borges.pitt.edu /criticism/articles-books-dissertations).

[15] In fact, this is how Borges summarizes the story in his interview with Carrizo (1983: 232).

[16] 'Much travelled' only captures one sense of this notoriously ambiguous epithet. The epithet also conveys other meanings in Homer which I evoke in Borges' Homer: 'of many turns' (i.e. 'wily') in the intellectual sense, as well as 'of many turns' in the sense of much travelled, for which see Heubeck, West and Hainsworth (1988) s.v. 1.1 and (1989) s.v. 10.330. There is also a debate about whether this adjective should be construed as active or passive; in the latter sense, it would mean something like 'turned round and round' – i.e. by Poseidon. For these interpretations, especially in the narratological sense, see de Jong (2001) s. v. 1.1 and n. 13.

subscribes to the six volumes of Pope's *Iliad*, which, as we are told at the beginning of Borges' story, contains the attached manuscript of 'The Immortal'. Finally, on his way to Bombay in 1921, Homer stops on the Eritrean coast, where he glances at the Red Sea and recalls his time as a Roman tribune in the third century, when the tale of 'The Immortal' begins. Throughout this narrative, the themes of memory and forgetfulness are predominant, as Homer moves from location to location and attempts to recall himself from the many identities that make up his postclassical existence.

Borges frames the tale of the immortal with a number of paratexts and authorial notes, most of which implicitly offer ways of understanding the character and scope of Homer's classicism in his allusive story. These appear in the following order:

1. An epigraph containing a verse by Francis Bacon's *Essays* LVIII. This concerns the fading character of memory as it moves in human history, as well as the power of forgetfulness in the formation of our cultural knowledge. The epigraph anticipates a notion central to the Homeric experience in 'The Immortal', i.e. that everything we come to know culturally is the result of a faint recollection of the things we once knew concretely but now have partially or fully forgotten.

2. An opening narrative taking place in 1929 London. This concerns the story of Joseph Cartaphilus of Smyrna (Smyrna being the first clue to Homer in the story), who gives a copy of Pope's 1715–20 translation of the *Iliad* (a second clue) to a character called the Princess de Lucinge. Cartaphilus dies in September of the same year.

3. An 'add-on' text, or epitext, containing the five sections that make up the story of 'The Immortal'. The Princess de Lucinge finds this manuscript attached to the last volume of Pope's translation. Retrospectively speaking, this is the first hint that Homer has had a postclassical biography composed by a mysterious author, which may be taken to be an extra-textual Borges.

4. A postscript by the Borgesian narrator written in 1950, and therefore postdating the publication of Borges' first edition of 'The Immortal' in 1949. The text lists some commentaries that have inspired the tale of 'The Immortal', i.e. sections I–V of Borges' story, as well as insisting on the authenticity of the manuscript found at the end of the copy of Pope's *Iliad*. We are told that the most noteworthy of these commentaries is titled *A Coat of Many Colours*, published in Manchester in 1948, a year before Borges' publication. Amongst this text's many

sources, Seneca and Pliny the Elder (*Historia Naturalis* VIII.8) are mentioned.

5. A dedication of 'The Immortal' by Borges to Cecilia Ingenieros, a past love. The dedication could be understood to work as a *mise en abyme* for Borges' readers: just as the Princess of Lucinge reads the tale of the immortal attached to the copy of Pope's *Iliad*, so will Cecilia Ingenieros read Borges' story of the same title, and so will the reader of Borges read about Cecilia Ingenieros' reading about the Princess of Lucinge's reading. And so on *ad infinitum*.

Throughout this multi-layered and potentially ever-expanding frame, which deliberately fuses and confuses the story's narrative organization with the material and editorial history of Borges' fiction, Homer emerges as possessing a series of bizarre, interconnected identities. Following the chronology of sections I–V, the most predominant of these are:

a. Joseph Cartaphilus from Smyrna, a book dealer from 1929 London, who gives the copy of Pope's *Iliad*, containing the attached manuscript of 'The Immortal', to the Princess of Lucinge.

b. Marcus Flaminius Rufus, a Roman tribune from the Diocletianic period. He is the first character of the tale of 'The Immortal'. Rufus is stationed in Northern Africa when the narrative of his journey to the City of The Immortals begins. Once he enters the City of the Immortals, he mysteriously takes the form of a troglodyte.

c. Rufus as a troglodyte lost in the City of The Immortals. The city is located somewhere in a virtual dimension beyond the Red Sea and the desert, where Rufus first loses consciousness and enters this alternative reality.

d. Argos, a dog accompanying the troglodyte in the City of the Immortals. He is as faithful to Homer as Argos was to Odysseus, before the hero's voyage begins. His identity eventually fuses with that of the troglodyte's. He is the first character to recall words from the catalogue of ships in *Iliad* II.294–759. Argos becomes the vehicle through which the troglodyte finally realizes that he is Homer and begins to recall his oeuvre.

e. A Borgesian narrator increasingly certain of having once been the author of the *Iliad* and the *Odyssey*. He is variously present in all the identities figured in the story, but becomes the most prominent voice towards the end of section V, after Argos, the troglodyte and Rufus fuse into a single Homeric identity.

f. A Homer who finally understands that he is Homer, as well as all the
    Homers in Borges' story (Rufus, the troglodyte, Argos and the
    Homeric narrator). At the end of section V, this Homer declares:

> As the end approaches, there are no longer any images from memory – there
> are only words. It is not strange that time may have confused those [words]
> that once portrayed *me* with those that were symbols of the fate of *the person
> that accompanied me for so many centuries.* (J. L. Borges, 'The Immortal',
> *The Aleph* (1949: *CF* 194))

This passage articulates most incisively Borges' unique understanding of
Homer and the Homeric tradition in the makings of cultural memory.
Chapter 2 explored Borges' conceptualization of antiquity in time, where
antiquity is only ever a version of itself that recurs through the generations in various forms, and operates within a temporal structure that
flows cyclically *ad infinitum*. In this passage, Borges implicitly refers to
this mechanism, as well as to the peculiar character of its formations in
the history of Homer as a cultural phenomenon. The passing of historical
time ('so many centuries') has operated in such a way that it has somehow
'confused' two evolving ideas of Homer into one. One of these threads
relates the story of a poet who has come to be known to us as 'Homer', the
author of the *Iliad* and the *Odyssey*, and whom the Homer of section
V represents as '*me*', after he finally recalls himself as a classical persona.
The other, which has somehow become interwoven with the first,
involves the linguistic symbols that have accompanied Homer as
a literary figure through the centuries, and in turn have made him the
subject of *a* tradition based on his historicized identity. While the Homer
at the end of 'The Immortal' does not appear to reject this tradition
(indeed, as we have seen, Borges' story includes several elements of this
tradition in the narrative), he nevertheless seems eager to *complement* it
with the fuller sense of self that he has acquired in the temporal and
locative depths of Borges' story (as outlined in 1–6 and a–f above). For,
with Borges' 'The Immortal', Homer has become an ever-expanding
phenomenon. He has outgrown the historical narratives that make up
the contours of his well-known tradition to inhabit the shifting forms and
scopes of Borgesian literature. This process has transformed him into
a deep reader of his persona in time and space,[17] including *before* and *after*
Borges:

---

[17] On deep reading, see Butler (ed. 2016), 1–19. On Borges as a deep reader of antiquity, see Jansen also
in Butler (ed. 2016).

I have been Homer; soon like Ulysses, I shall be Nobody; soon, I shall be all men – I shall be dead. ('The Immortal', *The Aleph* (1949: *CF* 194))

Here is a Homer who has gained a global vision of his cultural persona near the point of oblivion, and after his experience with immortality. He has left behind a specific understanding of his identity and place in evolving history, and is now able to see himself more wholly through the Aleph-like vision that Borges produces for him in 'The Immortal'. This Homer appears to capture *all*: his classical past, his postclassical proliferation, his immortality, the semiologies that have created certain stories of him, even the story of his future, as he is about to face the nothingness of death. In sum, and quite paradoxically, he is able to capture a panoramic vision of the ever-expanding, ever-multiplying character of his persona as it traverses the infinite paths and possibilities of Borges' narrative.[18]

The representation of Homer as a cultural identity that finally gains a quasi-totalizing grasp of the self from the privileged position of Borges' boundary-crossing literature has points of contact with the Shakespeare of 'Everything and Nothing' (*CF* 319–20), published in 1960. Like Homer, Shakespeare is depicted as a Protean figure who is keen to embrace the dimensions of nothing and all, many and none, as History grants him a final understanding of his identity and place somewhere on his way to death:

> History adds that before or after he dies, he discovered himself standing before God, and said to Him: *I, who have been so many men [. . .], wish to be one, to be myself.* God's voice answered him [. . .]: *I, too, am not I; I dreamed the world as you, Shakespeare, dreamed your work, and among the forms of my dream are you, who like me are many, yet no one.* ('Everything and Nothing', *The Maker* (1960: *CF* 320))

'History adds': Borges once more presents Historical Time as the author of a biographical 'fact' which, being fictional, we naturally don't know, but which has the effect of *supplementing* our idea of Shakespeare to the extent that makes it appear global in our cultural imagination.[19] This global self-reading even takes the playwright to the realms of divinity: it identifies him

---

[18] In this sense, Borges' Homer experiences the 'several [fictional] futures' of 'ramifying time' that the infinite labyrinth of the narrator-spy Ts'ui Pên constructs in 'The Garden of Forking Paths':

In all fictions, each time a man meets diverse alternatives, he chooses one and eliminates others; in the work of the virtually impossible-to-disentangle Ts'ui Pên, the character chooses – simultaneously – all of them. He creates, thereby, 'several futures', several *times*, which themselves proliferate and fork. 'The Garden of Forking Paths', *Fictions* (1944: *CF* 125)

[19] On Shakespeare's multiple historical destinies and the question of a creator's destiny, see Bernès (2010: 1150) in *ŒC*.

with God, here portrayed not only as the dreamer of his plays, but also as Shakespeare himself. The Homer of 'The Immortal' similarly enjoys a new global sense of his classical self, one that absorbs and moves beyond understandings of his tradition in Western literary history. However, unlike the Shakespeare of 'Everything and Nothing', this tradition does not place Homer next to (a Judeo-Christian?) God. Instead, it re-situates the author of the *Iliad* and the *Odyssey* in the vast dimensions of world literature, as conceived by Borges, the author of 'The Immortal' and other universal stories in *The Aleph* (1949), all of which continue to redefine the scope of Borgesian fictional narrative following *Fictions* and *Artifices* (1944). The potential of this bold reconfiguration of Homer in mid-twentieth-century writing seems boundless, even incalculable: what if our idea of Homer were made to transgress the confines of his Western canonicity to inhabit a literature that moves between World and Universe, cultural remembrance and forgetfulness, images and words, mortality and eternity, history and fiction, and finally, the ordering and chaotic nature of myth itself?

'The Immortal' develops from this complex hypothesis. It explores the immense capability of modernist fiction to accommodate, even thoroughly reconfigure, our understanding of long-established and authoritative classical traditions in the West, such as that of Homer as the father of the Western canon. Amongst its multiple meanings, 'The Immortal' comes to represent Borges' very first articulation of Homer as an ever-expanding notion in our modern imagination. Borges returns to this theme in a more synthesized fashion in 'The Maker' (1960). There, he takes into account the ideas that formed the Homeric persona in 'The Immortal' and applies them in order to raise another question: what if Homer once more forgot his classicism, as he does in 'The Immortal', but this time recalled it, not from the perspective of a postclassical odyssey, but from the deep and vast darkness of his blindness, as that past comes to him via a gentle rumour? Both 'The Immortal' and 'The Maker' invoke ways of 'seeing' the Homeric past through a reconfiguration of our traditional idea of Homer that is made to expand potentially *ad infinitum*. This is made possible by a literary platform designed to offer a limitless sense of space to multiple versions of a single idea. Yet this mode of representation goes further than recasting an ancient Greek poet of the distant preclassical past into a globalizing phenomenon of modernist literature. As we shall see, it also fundamentally helps Borges define his very own idea of Borges, as well as his own profile as a global classicist.

Homeric Identities and Identifications

In the course of his late life, between 1960 and the last years before his death in 1986, Borges incorporates details of his reconfiguration of Homer in the representation of his identity, and what he gathers has become the formation of a cultural idea of his authorial persona. The first example of this identification with Homer can be traced in 'Borges and I', published in 1960 in the same collection as 'The Maker' (*The Maker, CF* 289–324):

> I live, I allow myself to live, so that Borges can spin out his literature, and that literature is my justification. I willingly admit that he has written a number of good pages, but those pages will not save *me*, perhaps because the good in them no longer belongs to any individual, not even to that other man, but rather to language itself, or to tradition. Beyond that, I am doomed – utterly and inevitably – to oblivion, and fleeting moments will be all that survives [of me] in that other man. ('Borges and I', *The Maker* (1960: *CF* 324))

Before tracing a correspondence with Borges' configuration of Homer in this passage, it is worth considering in some detail how 'Borges and I' has been interpreted by those interested in the question of Borgesian identity, since this also contributes to the formation of a specific discourse about Borges' authorial persona. The piece has acquired the status of a *locus classicus* in biographies of Borges, and in studies of Borgesian autobiography, and commentators like Bernès are not wrong in pointing out that its criticism has rendered some 'pictoresque' and 'confused' readings and interpretations.[20] 'Borges and I' is the product of the beginning of the late period of Borges' career, when Borges was almost blind, and the practicalities of, as well as his approach to, his composition changed dramatically.[21] The piece deals with the question of the dual self, a topic that variously runs through his oeuvre. Critics and biographers tend to interpret this theme in terms of an inner conflict and sense of opposition that, they claim, exists at the core of the mid–late Borges, as he experiences not only an increasing loss of sight, but also the rise of his international fame. From the perspective of this reading, the private Borges claims to exist under the shadow of the public Borges, the man of letters, whose identity dominates the 'true' Borgesian self.[22] Other critics have analysed

---

[20] Bernès (2010: 1152) in *ŒC*.
[21] E.g. besides the assistance of his mother, and later on of his wife María Kodama, this is the period when Borges begins to work with note takers, Alberto Manguel being one of them. See Manguel (2006).
[22] Rodríguez Monegal (1983).

'Borges and I' in the context of the chronological development of Borges' early and mid–late literary career. For them, the author's sense of self-division emerges from two distinct phases in his writing, namely, the local (i.e. Rioplatense and Argentine) Borges, who creates a myth for a pre-European immigration nineteenth-century Buenos Aires in the first decade of his career, with works like *Fervor of Buenos Aires* (1923), *Moon Across the Way* (1925) and *San Martín's Copybook* (1929), and the 'speculative, cosmopolitan and universal' Borges[23] one finds in *Fictions* and *Artifices* (1944) and *The Aleph* (1949) onwards.[24]

If one considers this passage in conjunction with other later material, discussed below, it is not immediately apparent that 'Borges and I' betrays a sense of inner conflict within Borges. The piece instead articulates a notion of duality in terms of complementary contrasts, rather than oppositions. This view can be supported by reference to Borges' revisionary practices, many of which can be found in the author's later prefaces, or postfaces, added to earlier work. We know that, from the 1960s, Borges sets out to revise his earlier writing as it starts to be translated into several languages, removing in particular what he considers to be 'its baroque excesses' and 'sentimentalities' (*CP* 3). However, this desire for a revision of his early production does not necessarily mark a sense of inner conflict for the later Borges. On the contrary, it stresses the author's conception of his literary persona as an ever-evolving identity. Hence the editorial Borges of the prologue to *Fervor of Buenos Aires*, Borges' first publication, writes in 1969:[25]

> I have not rewritten this book (i.e. *Fervor of Buenos Aires*). I have moderated its baroque excesses, I have polished some rough spots [. . .], as I went through the work [. . .] I felt that the young man who wrote the book in 1923 was already essentially [. . .] the mature author [. . .]. We are the same person [. . .]. For me, *Fervor de Buenos Aires* foreshadows all that I would write afterwards. ('Prologue' to *Fervor of Buenos Aires* (1969: *SP* 3))

'We are the same person': i.e. the 'colourful' twenty-three-year-old Borges of *The Fervor of Buenos Aires*, and the literary experienced sixty-nine-year-

---

[23] Bernès (2010: 1153) in *ŒC*. See also Macadam (2013), who argues that Borges is 'playing with the opposition between the mortal man and the immortal but never-alive author, between living and writing', 144. Macadam furthermore makes associations between 'Borges and I' and the blind Homer (143). Wood (2013: 32–3) on the possibility of a Lacanian reading of 'Borges and I'.

[24] One can argue that this sense of division has been resolved in the work of Beatriz Sarlo (1993) who perceptively incorporates the traditions of the local and universal Borges into her study of Borges as an author on the edge of two cultures of the West, i.e. that of Europe and early- and mid-twentieth-century Argentina.

[25] Cajero (2006).

old Borges of works such as *The Self and the Other* (1964) and *In Praise of Darkness* (1969). When considered in terms of an authorial development in time, the two complement each other. The younger Borges writes literature, while the older Borges revises and polishes it from the standpoint of his prolific oeuvre, as well as his poetic training and wisdom. This sense of duality is articulated on another level in 'Borges and I'. It conveys a more dramatized version of this partnership between two Borgeses – the Borgesian '*me*', who writes pages of literature, and the other Borges, who now belongs to the sphere of tradition: 'but those pages will not save *me*, perhaps because the good in them no longer belongs to any individual, not even to that other man, but rather to language itself, or to tradition' (*CF* 324). There is no conflict of the self here, but rather a double vision of the authorial self in time. In 'Borges and I', Borges does not present himself in terms of 'one versus the other', but instead in terms of 'one *and* the other', two versions of Borges that have somehow become fused and confused. This understanding of his identity includes the mature author who, in 1969, experiences a duality of the self as his literary life evolves, and as he revises his first publication from 1923. Furthermore, it includes the author of 'Borges and I', who also traces a double persona on the page he writes: 'I am not sure which of us it is that is writing this page' (*CF* 324). The answer to this uncertainty is that two Borgeses do so – Borges the authorial actor, *and* Borges the author function who no longer belongs to the authorial actor alone, but to the sphere of 'language itself, or to tradition' (*CF* 324). From his first publication in 1923, through his editorial interventions in the 1960s, to an increasing awareness of the self as a discursive tradition, Borges presents himself as an evolving authorial figure with a clear double vision of the historical self.

It is against this background that the similarities between the Borges of 'Borges and I' and Borges' idea of Homer become increasingly palpable to the close reader. For, here, Borges begins to project a cultural image of his persona that looks towards a future reception, one that is built around aspects of his previous conceptualization of Homer in 'The Immortal' and 'The Maker'. We have seen that, in both 'The Maker' (1960) and 'The Immortal' (1949), Borges explores the theme of Homer's dual identity from the perspective of the Greek poet's loss and recollection of his classical memory. In 'The Maker', this dual identity is clearly outlined in the representation of two Homers, the classical and the postclassical. By contrast, in 'The Immortal', Homer's dual identity becomes blurred, as Borges conceals it behind a 'plurality of Homers', to use his own words (*SNF* 479), as the Homer of the classical past grows into multiple postclassical identities. In the passage from 'Borges and I' cited above, Borges draws on a sense of dual identity closer to that found in 'The Immortal'. Both 'Borges and I' and 'The Immortal' refer to a *'me'* (Borges' and Homer's, respectively) and to the Borgesian and Homeric persona and corpus that now belong to the sphere of language and symbols, i.e. to the formation of a tradition. It is worth comparing the close lexical and thematic correspondence between the two key passages in both pieces:

> [T]here are only words. It is not strange that time may have confused those [words] that once portrayed *me* with those that were symbols of the fate of *the person that accompanied me for so many centuries*. I have been Homer; soon like Ulysses, I shall be Nobody; soon, I shall be all men – I shall be dead. ('The Immortal', *The Aleph* (1949: *CF* 194))

> [B]ut those pages will not save *me*, perhaps because the good in them no longer belongs to any individual, not even to that other man, but rather to language itself, or to tradition. Beyond that, I am doomed – utterly and inevitably – to oblivion [. . .]. ('Borges and I', *The Maker* (1960: *CF* 324))

As we find in the Homer at the end of 'The Immortal', the Borges of 'Borges and I' has come to understand a specific development that has formed in the cultural imagination of his persona and oeuvre. This image is a result of a bifurcated vision – i.e. of the self, or *'me'*, that refers to Jorge Luis Borges the writer, and of the 'words' and 'symbols' that have shaped a tradition and encouraged a mode of reception of that *'me'*. As Borges foresees his inevitable death, he more fully begins to understand that Borges the man is doomed to oblivion, and that what will survive of him is an image, or *an idea*. As with the case of the Homer at the end of 'The Immortal', Borges projects a conception of the self in which Borges the man, who happens to be an author, becomes gradually absorbed by the historicity of his identity in time. The ultimate effect of this construction of the self in the history of his authorial life is of a Borges who coexists with *a specific vision* of himself and his work at a late point in time in his career. Borges amplifies this specific vision of the self by re-situating his authorial persona in the boundless and experimental scenarios entertained in his fiction, as he does with Homer and Shakespeare.

In his associations of Homer with Shakespeare, Borges gives History the role of supplementing our cultural knowledge and imagination of the afterlives of these authors ('History adds', 1960: *CF* 320). We find that Borges himself takes up History's supplementing role in a famous televised interview with the Argentine journalist and critic Antonio Carrizo in 1979, later published in book form in 1983. In this interview, Borges offers a casual, yet fundamental, rephrasing of the theme of double identity he presents in 'Borges and I'. In response to Carrizo's question about the title and central idea of this piece, Borges responds:

> I should have called it 'Borges and the Others', because two is too few. I was referring to the private and public man, but I would say that dichotomy is poor. As Stevenson also thought, I believe that we are many. I believe that this idea of man's plurality is an old, accepted idea . . . Some would tell Walt Whitman that he contradicted himself, and he would have said: 'I contradict myself. Yes, I contain multitudes in me'. That is to say, he knew that he was many. (*Borges el memorioso* (1983: 116–7) (trans. L. Jansen))

'I should have called it "Borges and the Others"': just as history 'edits' facets of Homer's and Shakespeare's afterlives, which has the effect of supplementing the tradition of these authors to the point that they become ever-evolving in our cultural memory and imagination, so here Borges offers a 'new edition' that complements our growing notion of his persona and tradition, as he approaches the last years of his life (Borges was turning 80 in his interview with Carrizo in 1979). This new edition, which he articulates in the shape of a titular revision, aims to correct our (miss) understanding of the Borgesian self as a duality in conflict to convey instead the notion of Borges as a multiplicity that conceals one author. This ontological presentation of his authorial persona, one that builds from Stevenson ('we are many') and from Whitman ('I contradict myself. Yes, I contain multitudes in me'), is similar to that in 'The Immortal': 'Perhaps there was no single Homer; perhaps there were many Greeks whom we conceal under the name of Homer' (1977: *SNF* 479). As is the case of Homer at the end of 'The Immortal', Borges does not reject the tradition of his double *'me'* that has emerged by the time he writes 'Borges and I', or even prevails by the time he speaks to Carrizo in 1979. Yet, as with his additions to the Homeric and Shakespearean afterlives, in the Carrizo interview he supplements the image of his persona just as his own career and life is about to end. This end will be the time when the Borgesian *'me'* concealed in a plurality of Borgeses will be no more, and his cultural memory will be in the hands of tradition (*CF* 324).

The supplementary image of the self as a multiple entity that Borges presents in his revision of 'Borges and I' in 1979 fuses with, and even transforms, our understanding of his cultural identity presented in that piece in 1960. As with Borges' classical revisions explored in Chapter 1, Borges' revisions of the self, and of Homer, have the effect of projecting authorial entities as ever-transforming phenomena, whose identities are always in flux, yet constantly striving towards wider, Aleph-like visions of the self in historical time. We have, nevertheless, seen in the examples of Homer and Shakespeare that these globalizing visions of the self, as authors at the moment of their death, do not gain closure in our time. Thus, Shakespeare reaches divinity and Homer coexists somewhere between life and eternity in the spaces and depths of Borgesian fiction. Borges also employs this trope for the construction of his own identity, as he sketches supplementary visions of the self outside human time that resonate powerfully in our imagination of his authorial persona. The *Odyssey*, the figure of Odysseus, and Ithaca are the very vehicles through which Borges builds this expanding image. As we shall see next, Borges creates this image by appealing to the Homeric text, and especially to this text's implicit open closures. Through these Homeric thresholds, the Argentine author represents himself as an Odyssean figure crossing boundaries between our mortal world and the post-historical realms of dreams and eternity.

Odyssean Voyages into the Post-Historical Self

> They say that Ulysses, sated with marvels,
> wept tears of love at the sight of his Ithaca,
> green and humble. Art is that Ithaca,
> of green eternity, not of marvels.
>
> 'Ars Poetica', *The Maker* (1960: *SP* 139)

Odysseus' *nostos* to Ithaca in Borges' 'Ars Poetica' (*SP* 137) deals with Borgesian notions of self-identity and self-knowledge both in our mortal world and in eternity. In Chapter 2, we saw that, in this part of the poem, Borges conveys a deeply poetic and philosophical idea of the self. Namely, that the self never manifests itself complete in historical time, and that a full grasp of its ontology would only be putatively attainable in a timeless, qua 'post-historical' reality that Borges calls eternity. For, according to Borges, eternity is a space where the three tenses that govern our human narratives, i.e. past, present and future, unite in a single whole, one where we would leave behind all versions of our fragmented self.[26] In 'Ars Poetica', Borges presents us with an Odysseus who leaves behind his past identity as a world wanderer, and presently comes closer to seeing a whole vision of the self, as he regards the verdant image of his 'eternal' Ithaca. Borges represents this vision not only as a paradigm of art, but also as an

---

[26] In this sense, Borges shows points of contact with Boethius and his view of eternity. I'm grateful to Charles Martindale for discussing this intertext with me.

ataraxic projection of the eternal self for the hero of the *Odyssey*. As he contemplates green Ithaca, Odysseus is able to synthesize, at least momentarily, his past, present and future, as he stands on a location that symbolically represents a threshold to a fuller self.

Borges variously incorporates elements of this image of Odysseus grasping the world beyond him in the representation of his own Borgesian fluctuating identity. One example of this reworking appears in 'The Dream', published in *The Unending Rose* (*SP* 341–67) in 1975.

> While the clocks of the midnight hours are squandering
> an abundance of time,
> I shall go, farther than the shipmates of Ulysses,
> to the territory of dream, beyond the reach
> of human memory.
> [. . .]
> I shall be all or no one. I shall be the other
> I am without knowing it, he who has looked on
> that other dream, my waking state.
>
> 'The Dream', *The Unending Rose* (1975: *SP* 349)

The themes of death and oblivion permeate *The Unending Rose*, and 'The Dream' is no exception to this pattern. The poem works on two main levels or structures. The world of human time, in which those enjoying life are not aware of time's passing day after day, and the territory of dreams, whose geopolitics involves no remembrance of the human past. While Odysseus' crew here move within the world of time, an Odyssean Borges, foreseeing the closeness of death, goes farther beyond the epic seas of the *Odyssey* to a reality alternative to the spheres of wakefulness and memory, i.e. to the oblivious landscape of dreams. There, Borges' identity will become blurred, and his death will paradoxically take him to a state of wakefulness. This eternal location will reveal whether he will become a Homeric multiplicity, of the kind we find in 'The Immortal', or an Odyssean οὖτις, as Odysseus calls himself before the Cyclops in *Odyssey* 9.366 ('I shall be all or no one | I am without knowledge', *SP* 349). This is a world beyond our world, where reality becomes a dream, and where he will finally gain a true and permanent understanding of self. Once more, the *Odyssey* becomes for Borges a symbolic vehicle taking identities towards self-knowledge. In 'Ars Poetica', Homer's text operates as a symbolic threshold for Odysseus' vision of the self in eternity. In 'The Immortal', it provides a platform for Homer to view his cultural identity as he approaches the realm of forgetfulness ('as the end approaches, there are no longer any images from memory', *CF* 194). In 'The Dream', it offers

Borges the possibility of exploring himself outside time, or post-historically , in the atemporal world of dreams, where, like Homer, Odysseus and Shakespeare, he may become 'everything and nothing'.

'The Exile' is another poem from *The Unending Rose* that reinforces the subterranean force of the *Odyssey* in Borges' construction of his identity in regions outside our world, such as Hades:

> Within the confines of the globe, myself, Ulysses,
> descended deep into the Hall of Hades
> [...]
> Someone today walks streets – Chile, Bolívar –
> Perhaps happy, perhaps not.
> I wish I could be he.   'The Exile', *The Unending Rose* (1975: *SP* 363)

The poem alludes to a series of interrelated themes, all of which are foreshadowed by the topic of death that dominates the collection. The first interrelated theme concerns the return of General Juan Domingo Perón (1895–1974) to executive power in 1973. For many like Borges, this event marks the beginning of a dark period in Argentine socio-political stability that will culminate in the coup d'état of March 1976.[27] The second theme relates to Borges' increasing desire to go into exile as a result of Perón's return. As Borges travels extensively around the world during this period, he considers exile in France or Geneva, or even in the city of Montevideo, Uruguay, where his nineteenth-century *criollo* relatives escaped during the dictatorial regime of another general, Juan Manuel de Rosas, in 1835–52. Another important allusive point in this piece is that, with the return of Perón in 1973, Borges loses his post as Director of the National Library Mariano Moreno in Buenos Aires, which he has held since 1955. This explains the reason for the reference to the streets Chile and Bolívar, located in the South of Buenos Aires, and looking towards México Street, where the Library was situated before it moved to the North of the city.[28] A further, parallel development, not mentioned in the poem, but which must have accompanied its interrelated themes, is the death of Borges' beloved mother, Leonor Acevedo Suárez, in 1975, which left a void in Borges' personal and literary life.[29]

---

[27] Perón dies in the summer of 1974 leaving his presidential chair to his wife Isabel Martínez de Perón, vice president of Perón's government between 1973 and 1974. Isabel Martínez de Perón's government comes to an end in the military coup of March 1976, which would last until 1983, when democracy is restored in Argentina. On the controversy around Borges' rather naïve initial support of the early period of the military junta, see Williamson (2004: 422–27).

[28] The Library was relocated to the North of the city in the Recoleta neighbourhood, where the author Alberto Manguel, Borges' notetaker during the 1960s and 70s, was recently made Director in 2016.

[29] Borges lived with his mother for most of his life. She was a poet, critic and translator, as well as managing several aspects of Borges' literary career and production.

These biographical details form the backbone of 'The Exile', as well as informing the two main spheres in which the poem operates. These are, the mortal world, specifically focused on the city of Buenos Aires and its local affairs, and the immortal world, represented by the Hall of Hades. Once more, Borges appeals to the *Odyssey*, but this time in the context of Odysseus' *katabasis* to Hades, where he portrays himself as seeing the shades of Tiresias, the blind seer of Apollo in Thebes and Hercules (*SP* 363), as Odysseus does in *Odyssey* 11.[30] Like 'The Dream', 'The Exile' plays with the crossing of narrative boundaries presented in the *Odyssey*. With Odysseus and the underworld as rhetorical vehicles, Borges discloses a version of his identity that exists beyond our mortal world of remembrance. There, in the immortal world, he is no longer a fragmented self, as Borges believes we all are in our time, but becomes technically *wholly oblivious*. He leaves behind the mortal world, and forgets his recent turbulent and sad past. Others, namely, the new directors who have followed his steps, now walk nearby the National Library, 'happy or not', while they continue to go through their historical time as ever-fragmentary, ever-changing identities burdened by human memory. Borges still wishes he could be that person he once was ('I wish I could be he'), but the circumstances around him prohibit it. Thus, while travelling around the world, he seeks refuge in the *Odyssey*, a text that allows him to envisage an alternative realm for his self, where memory and a tradition of him will remain in the mortal world of time, and he, the true Borgesian 'me', can be obliviously himself.

The Odyssean voyage into the beyond, whether this involves the alternative reality of dreams, or the sphere of oblivion offered by the immortal world, therefore acts as a symbolic threshold for Borges. In this threshold, he projects reconfigurations of his identity, which, like those of his Homer and Shakespeare, work towards gaining globalizing views of his persona and tradition, as it shifts from human time to visions of permanence and timelessness.[31] The Homeric texts continue to appear in other poems, whose central themes are the gods, myth, labyrinths and the nature of

---

[30] One wonders if the figures of blind Tiresias and Hercules may be faint allusions to Borges and Perón, respectively, since Perón was regarded by many in the Partido Justicialista, or 'Peronist' party, as a force defending society from social injustice.

[31] In the case of an author like Borges, who, for the most part avoided discussions about contemporary politics, one can only speculate as to how his 'Odyssean voyages into the post-historical self' relate to his stepping outside political reality, and possibly his own failures to take responsibility for/in such. Indeed, it is tempting to read between the lines and argue that, in 'The Exile', Borges does not simply couple History with the topic of time and notions of eternity but, also allusively, to contemporary politics.

the universe, amongst others. These will be explored in Chapter 5 ('Antiquity in the Poetic Cosmos'), where I will investigate the role of the classics in the makings of Borges' poetic world. For now, I would like to close where I began this section. Namely, with Odysseus' Ithaca in Borges' 'Ars Poetica', in which the hero's homeland offers an ataraxic vision of the self in eternity. For Borges, this is the city of Geneva:

> Of all the cities in the world, of all the private homelands that a man hopes to deserve in the course of his travels, Geneva seems to me the most propitious for happiness. Since 1914, I owe Geneva the revelation of French, Latin, German, expressionism, Schopenhauer, the teachings of the Buddha, Taoism ... and the nostalgia for Buenos Aires. And also love, friendship, humiliation, and the temptation of suicide ... Geneva, a little like Japan, has renewed itself without losing its past. The alpine alleyways of the Old City endure just as the clocks and fountains endure, but there is also the big city of bookstores and Western and Eastern shops.
>   I know that I will always return to Geneva, maybe even after the death of my body. ('Geneva', *Atlas* (1984) (my translation))

This short piece from *Atlas* (1984) is reproduced in part on a plaque placed outside Borges' home in the Vielle Ville of Geneva, on the Grand-Rue, where Rousseau also once lived. Borges lived in Geneva during the First World War (1914–18), when he studied at the Collège Calvin, now the Collège de Genève, and revisited the city throughout his life, until he finally returned to it to die after illness in 1985. On one level, Geneva is close to Borges' idea of ancient peripheral Greece, discussed in Chapter 1, which explored the significance that Borges places on Magna Graecia as both a fountain of knowledge and a cross-cultural model of East and West ('Geneva the revelation of French, Latin, German, expressionism, Schopenhauer, the teachings of the Buddha, Taoism ... Geneva, a little like Japan'). On another level, Geneva is an implicit version of Odysseus' Ithaca in the *Odyssey* and in Borges' 'Ars Poetica'. For it includes the themes of voyages ('in the course of his travels'), returning home ('I know that I will always return to Geneva'), as well as the ataraxic, quasi-platonic representation of the city as the optimal place in the world ('Geneva seems to me the most propitious for happiness').

This association is crucial to our discussion of how Borges explores the *Odyssey* as a threshold into alternative, post-historical realities for one's identity. For Geneva will become the place not only where the historical Borges will return to die in 1985, but also where he will *finally return* posthumously, i.e. after death ('maybe even after the death of my body'). In other words, Geneva is for Borges a vision of mortal and eternal bliss, as

Ithaca is for Borges' Odysseus. The Homeric and Odyssean undertones in this piece, which Borges composes near his death in Geneva, are allusive yet highly palpable to the close reader of Borges' Homer. The piece incorporates central themes from Borges' reconfiguration of Homer and the *Odyssey* in 'The Immortal' and 'Ars Poetica', respectively, and Geneva, here allusively portrayed as Borges' Ithaca, emerges as the locative threshold through which the author further amplifies his idea of Borges, as he moves closer to his end in historical time. Buenos Aires, another Ithaca for the young Borges living in Europe, offers further thresholds of interpretation. These will be detailed in the next chapter, especially in the context of the classicism of Borges' early poetry.

Borges' Homer in the Twentieth Century

This chapter explored how Borges presents a conceptualization of Homer and the Homeric tradition that becomes nearly synonymous with the cross-cultural and globalizing poetics of Borges' writing. Furthermore, it considered how this representation informs Borges' understanding of his own evolving authorial persona in time, one that he also substantially weaves into the text of the *Odyssey*, a narrative platform that allows him to launch his Homeric identity to the post-historical landscapes of dreams, immortality and eternity. This close correspondence between Homer and Borges in the Borgesian oeuvre has important implications for our study of Borges' classicism, especially in terms of how Borges' encounters with Homer further define Borges' mode of reading antiquity discussed thus far. This question can be fruitfully considered in the context of recent discussions of the place of Homer in the cultural shifts of the twentieth century, as well as in the history of Homer as a cultural idea. For Borges' Homer contributes significantly to the matter of what the Western canon and 'world literature' come to mean at the 'edge of the West', specifically in the peripheral culture of Borges' Argentina. Here, Borges' Homer fundamentally serves to frame Homer as a *universal* classic, and helps us position Borges as an author whose global classicism substantially redefines the horizons of twentieth-century 'world' literature.

Graziosi and Greenwood have examined the complex place that Homer comes to have between world literature and the Western canon in the twentieth century.[32] From the perspectives of Comparative Literature, Cultural History, and Post-Colonial Studies, their volume investigates

---

[32] Graziosi and Greenwood (2007).

a tension in scholarly and artistic treatments of Homer that is part of a paradigmatic shift in the larger cultural landscape of our recent modernity. Both the editors and their contributors trace receptions of Homer in culturally and geographically diverse national literatures, such as Albania, Ireland, Southern-East Europe, the Caribbean and the Unites States, all of which mark in various ways a distancing from the genealogical model that presents Homer as the father of the Western canon. While these readings do not deny Homer a vital place in the Western tradition, their engagement with the Greek poet and his epics nevertheless points to a cultural turn in conceptions of the character of the Western canon and the evolving notion of world literature.[33] This important study does not include twentieth-century receptions of Homer in Latin America, and this is where Borges can help broaden the scope in two specific ways.[34] First, Borges is considered a precursor in postcolonial thinking about the relationship between national literatures and the Western tradition.[35] In 'The Argentine Writer and Tradition' (1951), which I introduced in Chapter 1 ('Borges' Classical Revisions'), Borges considers the case of Jewish and Irish writers as examples of how their literature operates simultaneously yet autonomously within their own cultures and the European and British tradition, respectively: 'they act within that culture and at the same time do not feel bound to it by any special devotion' (*SNF* 426). Borges contends that something similar could be argued about Argentine and South American literature in relation to the Western canon, the latter of which Borges identifies as 'European subjects':

> I believe that our tradition is the whole of Western culture, and I also believe that we have a right to this tradition . . . I believe that Argentines, and South Americans in general . . . can take on all the European subjects, take them on without superstition and with an irreverence that can have, and already has had, fortunate consequences. ('The Argentine Writer and Tradition' (1951: *SNF* 425–26))

Here, Borges can be seen to form part of the cultural shift traced by Graziosi and Greenwood, especially in terms of how a twentieth-century

---

[33] Graziosi and Greenwood (2007: 3–4).
[34] The absence of twentieth-century Latin American treatments of Homer may have its own logic in the volume's focus. As Güthenke points out in her detailed review of the volume, the volume focuses on 'areas where the challenge and the discourses of nationalism and national identity, often in relation to a Western, central, or other "canon", have been of great importance in the twentieth century, which is, after all, also a century of national conflicts (i.e. in the centre of the West)'. See Güthenke BMCR (2008: February 10).
[35] Aizenberg (ed. 1990).

writer reformulates the relationship between his national literature and the Western canon. Yet, in the case of Borges, this cultural shift and reformulation are informed considerably by his rhetoric of geographical distance and literary appropriation, one that stresses the peripheral position and identity of Argentine writers working with European themes, which, as we know from Borges, include classical antiquity. Borges implicitly turns the technical geographical distance between the Western 'centre' and its 'periphery', here represented by Western Europe and South America and Argentina, respectively, into a rhetorical advantage from which he advances his cross-cultural and globalizing literary ideals.[36] From this strategic viewpoint, he contends that Argentine literature can take on 'any European subject [. . .] with irreverence' to produce a literature with 'fortunate consequences'. When it comes to Borges' chosen subject, i.e. Homer, the felicitous outcome of his 'irreverent treatment' is the projection of a whole new vision of *the* classic of all classics of the Western canon, one that acquires a *universal* place and identity, as we have seen. In turn, this takes us to a second consideration of Graziosi's and Greenwood's thesis. Namely, how twentieth-century national cultures collectively serve to redefine conceptions world literature. We have examined in detail how Borges' reconceptualization of Homer, from a distant classical identity to a proliferating postclassical multiplicity, raises central questions about the scope and depth of Borgesian literature. For Borges' Homer not only transgresses the confines of his established Western canonicity, but also dramatically *transcends* his status as a world classic in a literature that, as I have contended, moves between World and Universe, cultural remembrance and forgetfulness, images and words, and mortality and eternity. In recasting Homer as a boundary-crossing, ever-evolving figure, Borges manages to re-situate the figure of the Greek poet in a version of world literature rarely experienced before, as well as expanding the horizons of this literature to a category that we may call 'universal', and whose exegesis would involve a whole new intellectual vision and set of tools. From a cross-cultural standpoint, carefully cultivated from the 'edge of the West', Borges thus presents us with a Homer who ultimately helps to draw new coordinates for a literary space that moves not only between Europe and the globe, but, also vertiginously, between the globe and beyond.

This extraordinary, indeed exorbitant, redefinition of world literature and its relation to the Western canon leads us to a final point of discussion, namely, that of Homer as a cultural idea in the modern imagination. In his

---

[36] For which see de Toro (1995: 11–43) and Aizenberg (1997).

study of 'Homer: The History of an Idea', James Porter considers Homer
and the Homeric texts as 'cultural icons, as signifiers of value, and as
landmarks in the evolving relationship between literature and culture'.[37]
In addition, he argues that to approach Homer in this way 'is to consider
his place – the very idea of Homer – in the culture wars of antiquity and
modernity [...] and [in] the intellectual and cultural history of value'.[38]
With a focus on Western receptions of Homer, beginning with classical
antiquity and nineteenth-century England and Germany, Porter traces
a set of issues, one of which concerns 'the construction and sustaining of
Homer's ever-imaginary identity'.[39] Once more, this is where Borges
makes an important contribution. We saw at the beginning of this chapter
that Borges believes in the 'cultural truth', already cultivated in antiquity,
of a historical Homer eclipsed by a plurality of Homers: 'Perhaps there was
no single Homer; perhaps there were many Greeks whom we conceal
under the name of Homer' (*SNF* 479). Furthermore, we have traced the
ways in which Borges most innovatively explores his hypothesis on Homer
as an ever-evolving identity in and out of historical time, one that is open to
potentially infinite contexts and possibilities, like literature itself. In what
has become the history of Homer as a cultural idea rooted at the heart of
our imagination, Borges contributes a truly outstanding chapter. It begins
with the narrative of Homer's socio-cultural and literary afterlives around
the globe and beyond, a journey that moves between memory and forgetfulness, and culminates in the thresholds that lead the Greek poet to his
'post-history', where his 'ever-imaginary identity', to use Porter's words, is
re-situated in the immortal, eternal world, outside human time. As we have
seen, Borges himself retraces the steps of his postclassical Homer in order to
associate his own Borgesian authorial persona increasingly with the cultural monumentality and obliviousness of this Homer. The result of this
bold and rare experiment, based on the logic of Homer as a plural identity
from his classical beginnings, indeed challenges the modern imagination,
so much that my discussion in this chapter is no more than a starting point
and a suggested map for future reading. For, through his reading of Homer
and his classicism more broadly, Borges asks us to grasp a literary universe
that moves in and out of our historical sphere, where the classics proliferate
in landscapes that are truly unknown to us. Ultimately, Borges' Homer can
be plotted as the cultural history and the story of a constantly evolving
phenomenon that has no beginning or end, and spans the spaces of
nothing and all, to such an extent that we would need an Aleph to conceive

[37] Porter (2004: 324).   [38] Porter (2004: 324).   [39] Porter (2004: 325).

it in its ungraspable totality. In sum, Borges' experiment amounts to a formidable reconfiguration of the Homeric identity in the modern imagination in which there is no 'authentic', nor 'original' Homer, but instead an idea of Homer that travels in deliberately erratic ways through history and beyond. This idea takes yet another eccentric form in Borges' physics of reading the classics, as we encounter Borges' recasting of Virgil as a classic belonging as much to ancient China as it does to the urban landscape of modernist Buenos Aires.

CHAPTER 4

Virgil's Touch

It is very strange . . . [his is the work of] a *précieux* poet, a poet who felt
each line, the special quality of each line, [he] used that meticulous art
(*in tenui labor*) for a vast poem.
    'Virgil', *Conversations* II (2015: 236) (trans. T. Boll with minor alterations)

Borges' Virgil gives us an equally extraordinary vision of a classical canonical author, one that coheres with, and indeed supplements, Borges'
globalizing readings of Homer and the classical past more broadly. Yet
there is a specific difference between Borges' Homer and Borges' Virgil.
Borges' Homeric thought-matrix is centred on the figure of a *self* and
a voice (as we saw in the 'The Maker' and in 'The Immortal'), whereas
Borges' thinking about Virgil is, as we shall see, more oriented toward the
point of contact between hand and page and the materiality of text. Borges
reimagines Virgil as a classic with an intensely transcultural – and sensory –
impact on our world, which we may characterize as the poet's 'global
touch'. For Borges, the figure of Virgil's touch takes many forms, all of
which challenge conceptions of Western cultural history, the makings of
a classical presence worldwide and our profile as readers of antiquity. At the
core of this version of Virgil, Borges finds a deeply aesthetic impulse.
As Borges tells Ferrari in the epigraph prefacing this chapter, Virgil is for
him 'a poet who felt each line' he wrote, 'the special quality of each line',
and who employed this haptic approach to compose 'a vast poem'.[1] For
Borges, this poem is the *Aeneid*, and, also, as it will be in this chapter, the
entirety of the Virgilian corpus, a body of literature that takes part in an
immense network in Borges' cultural thought. In recalling Virgil and his

---

[1] Cultural studies in the topic of the sense of touch in antiquity are also numerous. My understanding
of the nature of touch in Borges' encounter with Virgil and Graeco-Roman antiquity has benefited
greatly from Purves (2017). This excellent collection rethinks the question of the haptics of Graeco-
Roman culture from the point of both conceptions of touch in classical antiquity and recent
theoretical rethinking on the topic. I am very grateful to Alex Purves for allowing me to consult
her volume and bibliography prior to publication.

tradition, Borges' memory moves dynamically between East and West, North and South, as well as between antiquity and Borges' modernity. Indeed, centrelessness and non-linearity are key factors in the directions of Borges' cultural reading of Virgil. It is characteristic of Borges' outlook that he resists situating Virgil in any particular tradition, or according to the established orders of Virgilian literary history.[2] Instead, his focus is on the ubiquity of Virgil's presence, as well as the impact of his poetry, worldwide. Ultimately, for Borges, Virgil's globalizing quality and appeal lie in his capacity to 'touch' us all and make us *feel* the haptically troped effects of his writing, whether we envisage ourselves in ancient China, in the Anglo-Saxon regions of last two centuries of the first millennium, in thirteenth-century Venice or in modernist Buenos Aires.

This chapter explores Borges' encounters with Virgil from two main interrelated points of discussion. The first of these concerns the geo-cultural spaces that Virgil occupies in Borges' memory, a memory that maps out a constellation of Virgilian presences across various locations and temporalities. My main focus is on Borges' conversations with Ferrari in 1984–85, since these dialogues, conducted in the last two years of Borges' life, not only offer a retrospective panorama to Borges' classicism, but also crucially disclose the discursive forms of Borges' approach to Virgil and the transmission of the Virgilian oeuvre. Here, Borges' physics of reading antiquity comes into play once more, as the Argentine author considers the reiterated presence and gravitational pull of Virgil in space and time in the context of various levels of Homeric and Lucretian absence. Section two will take stock of this discussion to explore in detail Borges' Virgil in a series of Borgesian poems, fictional essays and lecture material, many of which are not available in English. It will examine the manner in which Borges retraces selected lines from the Virgilian corpus and transforms them into poetic ideas whose sensory quality have the effect of 'touching' readers through time. The chapter closes with a theoretical discussion of Borges' cultural memory of Virgil as a new paradigm for reading the Roman poet in the twentieth century, and will highlight the part that geopoetics and the senses play in Borges' globalizing presentation of Virgil and his tradition. Furthermore, it will assess the contribution that Borges' Virgil makes to Borges' conception of world literature, especially in view of his understanding of world and universal literature that we have found in his encounters with Homer and the classics thus far.

---

[2] Cf. Eliot, who, in his address to the Virgil Society (1944), celebrates the *Aeneid* as the 'classic of all Europe'.

The Cultural Geography of Borges' Virgil

Borges' dialogue on Virgil with Osvaldo Ferrari, reproduced in about seven pages in Tom Boll's English translation, does not follow specific chronologies, nor does it function systematically as a cultural commentary on Virgil. Prompted by Ferrari's profound knowledge of Borges' oeuvre, literary thought and encyclopaedic mind, the dialogue instead moves dynamically and open-endedly between geographies, temporalities and texts, all of which recreate a geo-cultural landscape of Virgilian presences. Within this flexible frame, Homer and Lucretius emerge as the primary classical background to Borges' recollections of Virgil, as do Dante and Victor Hugo, two crucial intermediary authors whom Borges plots as offering contrasting visions of Virgil's canonicity. As with much of Borges' classicism, it is not the Virgilian topics that Borges deals with that are necessarily new. Rather, it is the stance and strategy that he adopts to review such topics that ultimately gives rise to his thoroughly new perceptions of Virgil and Virgil's oeuvre. As we shall see, it is through various degrees of literary absences and interventions that Borges' Virgil gains his geographical presence and an increasingly global impact at crucial points in our cultural history.

One primary way to consider Borges' mode of plotting Virgil's presence in space and time is to examine Borges' remarks on the *Aeneid*:

> And we must bear in mind that in the Middle Ages, and perhaps until the Romantic movement, the great poem was the *Aeneid*, since they respected Homer but that was no more than an act of faith. ('Virgil', *Conversations* II (2015: 236) (trans. T. Boll))

With these few words, Borges captures a specific historical moment in which Virgil's 'vast poem', the *Aeneid*, gains – and preserves – the weightiest of literary presences in European culture. This turns out to be a long period spanning the Middle Ages and the Renaissance, until roughly the beginning of Romanticism, the earliest of our modern, Western artistic movements which, as Borges claims a year after the *Conversations* in his prologue to 'Virgil, *The Aeneid*' (*SNF* 519), 'denied and almost erased [Virgil]'. This is an *Aeneid* whose presence dominates the European literary scene considerably at the expense of Homer, until its impact declines with the advent of an early-nineteenth-century aestheticism that seeks to reinvigorate an interest in ancient Greece.[3] It is worth pointing out at this

---

[3] This is a vast field. For the texture and dimensions of the renewal of this interest, see Billings (2016: 49–65). On Romanticism and Hellenism, see Webb (1982), on classical standards in the Romantic

juncture that, in a mind like Borges', the measure of time by periods and artistic movements is deliberately imprecise.[4] We know from previous discussion in Chapter 2 that Borges regards temporal labels of this kind as no more than convenient generalizations of otherwise complex temporalities at play that often escape the linear aspects of historical time.[5] Within the volatility of this temporal framework, Borges explicitly contrasts Virgil's long-lasting cultural impact in Europe with the destinies of Homer: 'they respected Homer but that was no more than an act of faith'. Here, Borges draws significantly from his own classicism. He combines two ideas that predominate in his reading of the classical past: his plotting of classical presences through the phenomenon of classical absences and his idea of Homer, which, we recall, develops from the hypothesis that the Greek poet acquires the status of a 'cultural truth' in our imagination, a truth that we come to believe given the lack of tangible evidence concerning his historical life.[6] With Borges, this Homer becomes one of the most extraordinary classical presences in mid-twentieth-century fiction. Yet, looking back in time, the period between the Middle Ages and the outset of Romanticism projects a more eclipsed image of the author of the *Iliad* and the *Odyssey*: according to Borges, Homer becomes the object of quasi-religious faith, as he remains a distant, respected precursor to Virgil's epic. It is in the context of this partial eclipse of the Homeric figure and its tradition that Borges frames the *Aeneid* as once 'the great poem' of Europe.

For a highly discerning and subtle mind like Borges', this reads as an atypically grand statement on his part. Yet we should be careful not to confuse his presentation of the *Aeneid* with that of T. S. Eliot, who in 1944 links Virgil's epic with the Roman Empire, as he proclaims Virgil 'the classic of all Europe'.[7] By contrast, Borges is not passing a final, authoritative judgment on the status of Virgil' epic just before the mid-twentieth century. Instead, he is offering a panoramic vision of the far-reaching

---

period, see Fry (2000: 7–28), and for the most recent discussion of the relationship between Romanticism and Roman antiquity, see Saunders, Martindale, Pite and Skoie (eds. 2012). For the decline of Virgilian authority in England, see Caldwell (2008).

[4] Borges, here, uses the word 'perhaps'. This is not a mere adverbial addition on his part. Elsewhere in the *Conversations*, Borges is reluctant to mark the outset of Romanticism with a particular date, even often to call it a 'movement'. Instead, he prefers to identify certain works from France, Germany and England as the first manifestations of some shared characteristics that we nowadays identify as 'Romantic' (e.g. Victor Hugo's *Hernani*; Bishop Percy's English and Scottish ballads; Coleridge and Wordsworth's *Lyric Ballads*; and Macpherson's *Ossian*). See *Conversations* II, 230–31.

[5] On this issue, see *Conversations* II, 227–28. See also Levine (2013: 47).

[6] Borges, 'Blindness' (1977: *SNF* 479), discussed in Chapter 3, 53   [7] See note 4 in this chapter.

influence of the *Aeneid* on 'sixteen hundred years' of cultural history, as he
claims in his prologue to Virgil's epic (*SNF* 519), a history that, in Borges'
literary thought, nevertheless remains subject to ontological and temporal
fluctuation. Borges projects this vision of the *Aeneid* by zooming to
a moment when the poem appears to have gained a geopoetical gravitas
across certain cultural centres in Europe. From this perspective, as Borges
makes various observations in his dialogue with Ferrari, he subtly begins to
deconstruct the spatial landscape in which Virgil and his oeuvre operate,
sketching their cultural destinies principally through the lens of Homer,
and then through the conspicuous absence of Lucretius.

Ferrari opens the conversation by reinstating what readers of Borges
already know well: that Borges has always preferred the *Aeneid* over the
Iliad, 'perhaps', as Ferrari suggests, 'because of the subtlety with which
the *Aeneid* is written'. Indeed, the subtle texture of Virgil's writing and the
materiality of the Virgilian text are reasons for Borges' preference, as will be
argued in the next section. The other reason is his profound admiration for
the *Odyssey* and, broadly speaking, for epic with a flavour of adventure and
voyages, rather than battles, as is the case with other modernists such as
Joyce.[8] Borges agrees with Ferrari, and immediately turns to consider the
Aeneid in the context of English and German translations of Homer:

> Clearly [I prefer Virgil's *Aeneid*]. Besides, I know the *Odyssey* through
> various versions ... in English. I think that in English there are thirty-
> something versions of the *Odyssey*. There are fewer of the *Iliad*, since well,
> England and the sea are a single identity. On the other hand, more versions
> of the *Iliad* have been made in German, because Germany and the land, like
> England and the sea, go together, no? ('Virgil', *Conversations* II (2015: 236)
> (trans. T. Boll with minor alterations))

From a scholarly viewpoint, we may charge Borges with too generalized
a view of epic, a view that he builds on the basis of how cultural identities
may be shaped by geography.[9] His concern, rather, seems to be with the
quasi-psychological aspect of the reception of epic in the region, which he

---

[8] 'Epic Flavour', *Conversations* II 103–11.
[9] One could also add that the complex history of the translations of Homer in English and in German
may not necessarily accord with Borges' statement. His claim that there are more translations of the
Odyssey in English and the *Iliad* in German may well respond to knowledge genuinely available to
him (Borges may be thinking of Voss?), or to bibliographical access, rather than from actual fact.
Furthermore, Borges knows well that *the* great translation of Homer in English was Pope's *Iliad* (cf.
'the Homeric Versions', 1932: *SNF* 72). An even more apologetic view would be that he, as ever, is
not exactly preoccupied with scholarly precision, since his encyclopaedic and globalizing mind
would always regard this kind of fact to be subject to the flow of time, as well as constant revision
(Chapter 2, 'The Flow of Heraclitus').

sketches from a transcultural outlook.[10] Indeed, there is an implicit geo-poetical strategy to Borges' thinking. This is to plot the cultural impact of Virgil's work through a double lens, at least when considering the transmission of the *Aeneid* in the North: in a move familiar to scholars of Virgil, Borges splits Virgil's epic poem into an 'Iliadic' and an 'Odyssean' *Aeneid* (underwritten by the 'second prologue' of *Aeneid* 7), two classifications which, in his view, appear to respond to translation demands, as well as to the taste for classical epic intrinsic to 'land' and 'sea'.[11] By separating Europe into land and sea, Borges therefore first opens the *Aeneid* to two routes of reception in the North, especially in England, Germany and Scandinavia.

Still with a focus on the North, but already turning their attention eastwards, Borges and Ferrari proceed to comment on what may be called 'Troy-oriented' receptions of the *Aeneid*, once more, through the lens of Homeric epic. Here, Borges concentrates on one of his favourite passages from the *Aeneid*: book 2.324–7, in which Aeneas relates his sufferings to Queen Dido in terms of what his nation had been and what it will never be again:[12]

> uenit summa dies et ineluctabile tempus
> Dardaniae. fuimus Troes, fuit Ilium et ingens
> gloria Teucrorum; ferus omnia Iupiter Argos
> transtulit [. . .]
> 　　　　　　　　　　　　　　　　　　*Aeneid* 2.324–7

One way to plot these lines is around the structure of time and the transfer of divine power that this structure conveys. In his description of the fall of his homeland, Aeneas tells Dido that Troy could no longer fight its present time (*ineluctabile tempus*, 324) and that, as a result, its land, peoples and immense glory ceased to be what they once were (*fuimus Troes, fuit Ilium et ingens | gloria Teucrorum*, 325–26), since the fortunes of time were such that Jupiter carried all (things/power) to Argos (*ferus omnia Iupiter Argos | transtulit*, 326–27). In other words, time was once with Troy, until it was given to Argos. This is the kind of close reading that appeals to Borges. Indeed, one phrase in this passage that fascinates him is *fuit Ilium*. A year or so after the *Conversations* take place, we find Borges commenting on the phrase in his *Prologues to a Personal Library*:

[10] Retrospectively speaking, this is an outlook that has points of contact with the dynamic brand of transcultural literary history proposed by Pettersson (2008: 463–79).
[11] For a now seminal argument about the Odyssean and Iliadic *Aeneid*, see Anderson (2005: 1–26).
[12] For an excellent analysis of how this line operates in a 'subterranean' fashion in Borges' aesthetics of translation, see García Jurado and Salazar Morales (2014: 111–2).

[Virgil] does not write that Troy was destroyed, but rather, 'Troy was'.
(J. L. Borges, 'Virgil's *Aeneid*' (1986: *SNF* 520))

This statement encapsulates succinctly Borges' discussion of *fuit Ilium* in
the *Conversations*, where he argues that a good translation of the phrase in
Spanish should capture the pathos of it:[13]

> He produced that wonderful expression *Troya*[14] *fuit*, which is generally
> translated very badly into Spanish 'Aquí fue Troya', which loses all of the
> expression's power. On the other hand, 'Troya fue' is tinged with
> sadness ... 'Troya fue' is like saying: Once one could have said 'Troy is'
> but now we can only say 'Troy was'. That 'was' is wonderful. ('Virgil',
> *Conversations* II (2015: 236) (trans. T. Boll))

In the *fuit* of Virgil's *Ilium fuit*, Borges hears a trace of a presence behind the
form of an absence: for it is not that 'Troy was once here' ('Aquí fue Troya')
and is no more, but that the city that existed in the present tense now exists
in the past tense. In this sense, Troy becomes an absent-presence, since its
ontology is made up by a presence and absence that are intrinsically co-
involved, not isolated phenomena. For Borges, this is one of the wonders of
Virgil's lines, as well as the pathos, that his vast poem conveys to its
audiences. In the case of Troy, the pathos experienced by the semantic
possibilities of the verb to be is such that the ancient city, now technically
'absent' after its obliteration, gains an enduring – and worldwide – presence
in our cultural imagination of the classical past worldwide:

> Of course, [*Troya fuit*] is a literary device, but all literature is made up of
> devices. I remember now that Chesterton notes that the whole world, every
> country, has wanted to be a descendant of the Trojans rather than the
> Achaeans. ('Virgil', *Conversations* II (2015: 236) (trans. T. Boll))

'[T]he whole world, every country, has wanted to be a descendent of the
Trojans rather than the Achaeans': it is at this juncture of the *Conversations*,
and always through the lens of Homer, that Borges first opens the reception of the *Aeneid* to a global level.

We may not perceive this move on a first read of the dialogue. Yet, on
a second reading, we begin to notice that the directions of Borges' transcultural thinking have already been guiding us towards this amplified
vision of the *Aeneid* and its reception. Prompted by Ferrari, Borges first

---

[13] The complexity behind the translation of *fuit Ilium* to which Borges refers revolves around the verb
'to be' which in Spanish can split into the verbs 'ser' and 'estar'. Borges here combines a locative sense
of in his use of 'ser' with the idea of a frustrated ontology: 'Aquí fue Troya' only gives us the image of
where Troy 'was'. 'Troya fue' gives us the pathos that 'Troy was'.
[14] 'Troya': as it appears in the Spanish original.

directs our attention northwards to the 'split' impact of the Homeric *Aeneid* on land and sea readerships. Once he reaches this cardinal point, he leads us eastwards to the pathos of Virgil's Troy, and now, with a firm stand on Troy, he opens his vision far and wide to the world at large, beginning with its reception in the literary cultures of the Saxons and Scandinavians. Here, it is not exactly Achilles and the Greeks, but Hector and Troy and, by implication, Aeneas and Troy, who become the key protagonists of a global story of fate:

> BORGES: And that brings us to the suspicion that the real hero of the *Iliad* – for us, and perhaps for Homer too – is Hector [. . .] the Trojan [. . .] and the title is proof, *The Iliad* [. . .] Ilion [here Ferrari adds, 'to Ilion, that is to Troy'] because [the poem] could have been called the *Achillea*, like the *Odyssey*, but no, it's called the *Iliad* . . . Hector knows that he is defending a city that is condemned to fire and extermination. Hector [a tragic figure] struggling for a lost cause.
>
> FERRARI: One appreciates the Greek sense of fate there.
>
> 'Virgil', *Conversations* II (2015: 238) (trans. T. Boll)

The sense of Greek fate that Borges plots in the story of Ilium directs his attention to the North once more. Here, he draws interesting thematic parallels between English and Scandinavian mythological literature and Troy. He reminds us of the fascination that the North and the Saxons have for the *Aeneid*, one that some scholars have traced in the epic *Beowulf* (*Conv.* 239), produced some time between the eighth and eleventh centuries by an anonymous author known as the 'Beowulf poet'.[15] Furthermore, Borges here recalls linguistic connections between Troy and the North. For instance, he points out that the Old English term for fate is 'wyrd', which we find in the 'weird' or 'fatal sisters' at the beginning of Shakespeare's *Macbeth*, and can be considered an echo of the Greek notion of fate, just as 'Thor' is a distant echo of Hector, or Hector's brother, in the Scandinavian god Thorn (*Conv.* 239). The dialogue continues to make observations about Scandinavia, before beginning to steer southwards following the exposure of the *Aeneid* and its treatment of Greek fate to a transcultural reading, whose focus had so far been Medieval and Elizabethan receptions.

The dialogue then becomes truly Borgesian. It begins to shift more vertiginously to other geographies and temporalities, as Ferrari reminds Borges of the way the European North has always wanted to establish cultural connections with the classical South. At this point, Borges takes us

---

[15] A view that now has become unfashionable. See Klaeber (2008: xxv–xxxv and clxii–clxxxvii).

rather unexpectedly to Hitler in the early twentieth century, and to the
Mongols of the thirteenth century onwards, after their invasion of China:

BORGES: . . . the Scandinavians, stranded up there in the North, wanted – well,
    contradicting Hitler the future ethnologist – to be Trojans . . .
FERRARI: It's an example of the North's need to feel connected to the South . . .
BORGES: Yes [and] the prestige of Rome, always the prestige of Rome.
FERRARI: Of the ancient culture.
BORGES: Yes. A classic case would be the Tartars. The Tartars or the Mongolians
    conquered China, and then, within two or three generations, they became
    Chinese gentlemen studying the *Book of Changes* and the *Analects* of
    Confucius.
            'Virgil', *Conversations* II (2015: 239–40) (trans. T. Boll with minor
                                                                adaptations)

This section of the dialogue is most insightful when it comes to the
interplay between periphery and centre that informs Borges' classicism.
Borges comments on the magnetic pull that the classical world, here
represented by 'the prestige of Rome', has had on the northern 'edge' of
Europe. In this sense, Borges' globalizing views of the *Aeneid* recognize that
ancient Rome, the new site of Troy in the West, acts as a cultural base, or
centre, from which the culture of the Western world develops and spreads
outwards to form a reception category that we may identify as 'peripheral'.
Yet we recall from previous discussion in Chapters 1 and 3 that, for Borges,
Western peripheral cultures are also 'centres' in their own right, which do
not blindly absorb the paradigms of the hegemonic centre. For Borges,
peripheral nations, as different as, for instance, Ireland or Argentina,
capitalizing on a sense of geographical distance and otherness, cultivate
cultural strategies of their own, from which they develop their own profiles
and agendas. This ought to be taken into account when Borges comments
on the 'North's need to be connected to' the prestige of the Classical South
(Troy and Rome), especially when one follows closely Borges' deep engagement with Anglo-Saxon and Scandinavian culture and literature elsewhere
in his oeuvre.[16] Furthermore, in his observations about how the North
connects to the prestige of the South, Borges brings other forces into play
that reinforce what may initially appear to be simplistic readings on his
part. One of these is Hitler, ironically presented by Borges as the 'future
ethnologist'. At this juncture, Borges begins to blur the temporal structure
in which he frames his cultural comments on Virgil's *Aeneid*. For not only
has the dialogue moved dynamically between cardinal points, but now it

---

[16] See especially, 'Mythologie scandinave et épopée anglo-saxonne', *Dialogues* I (2012: 256–63).

also begins to shift temporalities to reach the Nazi era in the twentieth century. In the context of this part of the dialogue, it is interesting to note that Hitler implicitly comes to represent the anti-globalist *par excellence*, at least in the sense that the global operates in Borges' cultural vision. Here, Hitler stands obstructively between the European North and the classical South, threatening to obliterate their long-standing cultural dialogue in his ambitious aim to consolidate the power of a single ethnic group that seeks to dominate European culture. When conceived from the viewpoint of Borgesian temporality, the peripheral Scandinavians 'stranded up there in the North' centuries before Hitler were *already* somehow 'contradicting' the future ethnological voice of the Nazi Germany that will pose a threat to their cross-cultural outlook. This is why, in Borges' view, the North then wished to enter into a dynamic dialogue with the literary jewels of presti-gious Rome, and, in doing so, contribute to, for example, the increasingly global transmission of the Homeric and Virgilian epics.

While Borges' comments on the relationship between the Northern periphery and the classical South take him to the twentieth century, his mind simultaneously takes him back to the thirteenth century and to the Far East. In this case, he appeals to a syncretist view, one that we have already come across in previous discussion. As with most of his syncretist moves, Borges appeals to the Far East as a mode of comparing cultures that have had little or no contact with one another. Here, the Scandinavians resemble 'the Tartans or the Mongolians' of the thirteenth century who conquer the Song Dynasty that rules China. Located peripherally with respect to a vast centre of a cultural power, like the Scandinavians, these conquerors look towards the rich heritage of the Chinese empire, then the very heart of the Eastern world, by engaging with their canonical literature and philosophy. Indeed, one could take this syncretist perspective further by turning back to the classical world. For imperial Rome's engagement with the prestige of ancient Greece, most famously captured by Horace in *Epistles* II (*Graecia capta ferum uictorem cepit et artes | intulit agrestic Latium*, 1.156–57, 'Greece, the captive, made her savage victor captive, and brought the arts into rustic Latium'), can also become a fruitful syncretist parallel to the phenomenon of the Mongols' reception of China mentioned by Borges. This part of the dialogue between Borges and Ferrari truly opens Virgil's presence and the impact of his epic to a transcultural vision, one than moves radically between cardinal points, periphery and the centre, historical times and blurred temporalities, as well between phenomena that trace parallels connecting different modes of reception of the cultural past.

As the dialogue with Ferrari comes to an end, the conversation moves towards the South and Lucretius:

FERRARI: Coming back to the South, it surprises me that Virgil acknowledged
that he was a follower of Lucretius, given that he was such an idealist ... in
contrast to the materialism of Lucretius, who followed on ... Epicurus
BORGES: Yes, one doesn't seem to sense any similarity between them, but
Lucretius must have had an influence on Virgil.
'Virgil', *Conversations* II (2015: 240) (trans. T. Boll with minor adaptations)

It should not escape us that, behind these casual observations on Virgil and Lucretius, there lies Borges' profound understanding of the interconnections one can plot between the two poets. When Borges claims that 'Lucretius must have had an influence on Virgil', it is probable that he is thinking about the ubiquitous allusive presence of Lucretian language and figures in the *Eclogues* and *Georgics*,[17] which Borges knew well.[18] It is also worth noticing that the two poets are not presented as opposites but, rather, as contrasting figures in allusive dialogue with one another, as if one were to put Marx's materialism, which builds on Epicurus and Lucretius, in poetic dialogue with the idealism of the Romantics, or even with Plato's ideas. In fact, the potential of these imaginary dialogues is palpable in the dual character of Borges' own authorial persona:

FERRARI: And who do you feel closer to, Borges, Lucretius or Virgil?
BORGES: ... It's difficult to answer that, I think that, let's say, intellectually
Lucretius, but in literary or poetic terms – Virgil.
'Virgil', *Conversations* II (2015: 241) (trans. T. Boll with minor adaptations)

Just as Homer is a constant referent in Borges' plotting of the geo-cultural impact of Virgil's *Aeneid*, we can appreciate here the extent to which Lucretius is also a constant presence in Borges' Virgil. Following Borges' sense of temporality, one could even argue for the reverse, i.e. that it would be inconceivable to think of Borges' Homer and Lucretius without reference to his Virgil. Such is the intrinsic nature of Borges' own classical self, one in which a myriad of Graeco-Roman presences and absences are co-involved and inform his global outlook on the world: he can be an idealist as much as a materialist, a Heraclitean visionary or an ahistorical Homer. Borges' transcultural outlook provides further glimpses of Virgil's foretold

---

[17] For a study of presence of Lucretius in Virgil's cultural and historical narratives, see Hardie (2009: 11–41).
[18] Aside from his citations of Virgil's early poetry *passim*, we know that Borges held a Loeb copy of Virgil volume I, which contain the *Eclogues*, the *Georgics, Aeneid* 1–6, and whose pages offer several marginal annotations. See Rosato and Álvares (2010: 339–40).

canonicity, one that is aided by the full erasure of Lucretius in Christian European literature, specifically in Dante:

> Now, naturally, Dante doesn't mention Lucretius ... five poets welcome him ... as an equal [in] *The Divine Comedy* ... Virgil, Homer, Horace, Ovid and Lucan. But Lucretius is excluded. Well, naturally, Lucretius was an atheist so he has to be excluded, no?[19] ('Virgil', *Conversations* II (2015: 240) (trans. T. Boll with minor adaptations))

Our recollection of Virgil's postclassical canonicity often stops with Dante. Yet we owe it to Borges' global classicism for his reminder that Lucretius is not excluded in Victor Hugo's *Shakespeare*, but that Virgil was:

> That's why Hugo, who clearly wasn't a Christian, in his book on Shakespeare, makes a list of great poets ... and he begins with Homer and continues with Lucretius, and ... excluded Virgil and Dante. ('Virgil', *Conversations* II (2015: 241) (trans. T. Boll with minor adaptations))

In his dialogue 'On Lucretius', Borges reaffirms this reading by reminding us once more of the canonical destiny that Virgil could have had if Victor Hugo's atheist text possessed more impact than Dante on his Christian audiences:

> Lucretius has been deliberately forgotten, because ... he has sung the praises of atheism and wanted to free men from the terror of the afterlife, well, that can't earn the approval of believers. However, a notable exception would be Victor Hugo ... who ... makes a catalogue of poets ... and Virgil is excluded ... ('Lucretius', *Conversations* II (2015: 264) (trans. T. Boll with minor adaptations))

We have come to understand Virgil the way we do because literature behaves in a volatile manner in the flux of Heraclitean time, which allows for some texts to become more visible than others, thus shaping the texture of our cultural memory. In his reading of Virgil, Borges emerges as a crucial exponent of this idea and process. He first amplifies our classical vision to show us how classical texts like the *Aeneid* are plotted and transmitted through the cultural pacts and wars that historical time reveals. Then he reminds us that cultural history can also be read in different ways if we pursue alternative texts from our literature, whether this is Victor Hugo's *Shakespeare*, or indeed Borges' oeuvre. Borges' unique paradigm even

---

[19] Borges here possibly ignores that Dante will have not read Lucretius, an author 'rediscovered' in the early Renaissance. For the discovery of Lucretius by Poggio, see Greenblatt (2011). For studies in the reception of Lucretius in the Renaissance, see Reeve (2010: 205–213), Prosperi (2010: 214–26) and Palmer (2014).

encourages us to consider momentarily what some of the authors discussed thus far might have to say about the way literary history and tastes develop, especially if they had had the chance to become successors rather than precursors:[20]

> How strange that a poet should work towards future poets, who he can't predict, and who perhaps wouldn't understand or wouldn't like. Because one would have to know if Homer, or the Greeks we call Homer, would have approved of the *Aeneid* – possibly not. And what would Virgil have thought of *The Divine Comedy*? ('Virgil', *Conversations* II (2015: 236) (trans. T. Boll))

We can do no more than speculate on these Borgesian questions. Yet, we can still follow their lead and sense of inverted temporality to formulate similar speculations, prompted by Borges' unique reading of Virgil and the eclipses of antiquity that give Virgil his vast presence in cultural history. What if Lucretius' *De rerum natura* had been 'the great poem of all Europe'? How would we have plotted our cultural memory of Virgil? What fragmentary echoes would we have heard instead? What if the *Aeneid* had been a more eclipsed text, and other texts had been more predominantly present? What vision of Virgil would we have today in our modern imagination? And, if this were the case, what author would Dante have been? Would Victor Hugo have welcomed Virgil and Dante in his list after all? The chain of possibilities in the Borgesian history of literature that 'was not but could have been' is endless. It reveals the story of hidden and/or potential texts, of how history shapes our thinking and of how central our reception in the flux of time is to the destiny of our cultural memory. In the next section, we shall see that Borges gives us a glimpse of how this alternative history could have been in his extraordinary revision of Virgil's touch from ancient China to modern Buenos Aires.

The Slow Hand and the Tears of Things

Until now, we have 'sensed' Virgil's touch through the weight of his transcultural classical presences. In what follows, this rhetorical figure becomes associated with bodily and emotional sensation, as well as with the materiality of the page and the power of writing,[21] which, in Borges' classicism, has no geographical nor cultural boundary. It is in this context

---

[20] Cf. 'Kafka and his Precursors', *SNF* 363–65, discussed in Chapter 1, 8–9.
[21] For an outstanding exploration of this theme, see Butler (2011).

that I would like to pursue two of Borges' favourite Virgilian motifs: that of the poet's *lenta manus* (lit. 'the slow hand'), found in several of Borges' writings, and the *lacrimae rerum* (lit. 'the tears of things'), uttered by Aeneas as he observes the tragic tale of his Troy carved on the Temple of Juno's door at Carthage.

There is an excellent sourcebook, published in 2010 by two curators from the Biblioteca Nacional Mariano Moreno, Buenos Aires' national library where Borges was director from 1955 to 1973, three years before the Argentine military junta came to power.[22] The curators' monumental task has been to compile a comprehensive catalogue of hundreds of books donated to the library by Borges in 1973 from his private collection, and which remained forgotten in the library's basement until 2005. The publication of the catalogue is a treasure house for anyone attempting to detect some of the thinking behind Borges' citation of classical material. The catalogue registers marginalia and paratextual material, as well as heavily annotated bookmarks, receipts, dozens of tickets from the local bus that took Borges from home to work daily; even scattered pieces of paper that draft the formative stages of some of his famous fictions and poems. When it comes to the entry for Virgil, the catalogue lists a copy of Fairclough and Goold's Loeb edition of the *Eclogues, Georgics* and *Aeneid* 1–6, volume I (there is no record of a copy of volume II). While the catalogue reproduces a wealth of images of books and pages annotated by Borges, it unfortunately does not reproduce an image of the pages of the Loeb edition owned and annotated by the author, as it does, for instance, with the entry for Juvenal, which offers illustrations of Borges' OCT copy. The curators nevertheless offer a full description of Borges' notes that contribute greatly to our exploration of Borges' Virgil.

The catalogue first comments on Borges' highlighting of line 7 of *Eclogues* 4 (*iam noua progenies*), along with words in the closing lines of the same *Eclogue*, where the Virgilian narrator playfully suggests that he would emerge victorious for his song about the Golden Age if he were to have a *certamen* (a 'contest') with the poets Orpheus and Linus. The lines are not fully elaborated in Borges' writings, though they are often cited in lectures and interviews, where he speaks about the belief in the oracular quality of poetry, as well as about the desire of all major poets to become the Orpheus of their own generation.[23] Most interestingly, in the same

---

[22] Borges was director of the National Library during 1955–73 when the library was situated on México Street, as I showed in Chapter 3, 68–9.

[23] Discussed in Borges' Norton Lectures (1967–68), Lecture 1, 'The Riddle of Poetry', 1–20.

Loeb copy, Borges also highlights and writes marginal notes next to *Georgics* 2.118–21 on the origin of silk, which goes as follows:

> quid tibi odorato referam sudantia ligno
> balsamaque et bacas semper frondentis acanthi?
> quid nemora Aethiopum molli canentia lana,   120
> uelleraque ut foliis depectant tenuia Seres?

In the margins of the Latin text, Borges enters a brief note clarifying Virgil's mistaken belief in the origins of silk (line 121), i.e. that silk was not, as Virgil seemed to have believed, directly taken from tree leaves in Asia, but instead the result of a process in which silkworms produce the textile material we know as silk.[24] However, Borges' interest in Virgil's silk has little to do with correcting a small factual error. In fact, his interest in Virgil's silk turns out to be one of the most far-reaching and stimulating readings of the poetics of composition in early Virgil. Next to his marginal note, Borges adds the phrase *lenta manus*, which, as we shall see, Borges is keen to translate with a sense of 'prolongation' in mind as the 'slow' and/or 'lingering hand', rather than the 'malleable' or 'pliant hand' of, for instance, a Camilla thrusting her sword in battle in *Aeneid* 11 (*pharetrata Camilla | et nunc lenta manu spargens hastilia denset*, 649–50). The *lenta manus* motif is familiar to the reader of Borges, but for the reader of Borges' Virgil it becomes highly evocative. Borges will use it on several occasions to recreate the figure of the Virgilian author through a body part – the hand. It is this hand that Borges tells us 'caresses and writes (on) Oriental silk in the *Georgics*'. This motif is first adopted in 'El oriente', or 'The Far East', a poem from Borges' 1975 collection, *The Unending Rose*:

> The hand of Virgil lingers
> over a cloth with the freshness of water
> and interwoven shapes and colours
> which the remote caravans of time and sand
> have brought to his Rome.
> It will survive in a verse of the *Georgics*.
> He had never seen it. Today it is silk.
>
>   J. L. Borges, 'El Oriente', *La rosa profunda* (1989: *OC* III: 114)
>   (trans. L. Jansen and A. Laird)

It is worth considering the temporal aspect of the *lenta manus* figure that Borges annotates in his Loeb copy, and which we find in this poem. Virgil's hand lingers over silk to feel its liquid freshness, colourful patterns, even its

---

[24] García Jurado and Salazar Morales (2014: 102–3).

long and tiring journey to Rome. At the end of the passage, however, we learn that the poet has not seen this material, nor has his hand touched its smooth texture. What the poet has done is first to recreate the tactile feeling of his hand on the silk and then write a dactylic based on that sensorial image as if he were doing so *slowly*: word by word, foot after foot. We can take this writing event even further into the world of material poetics. Borges prompts us to think of the Virgilian line, a product of a creative process, as also the material product of a cultural and economic exchange between the peripheral East, with its exotic commodities, as viewed by the centre of the West, and the West, represented by the power of Rome, with its endless desire to consume them. As we imagine the haptic quality of the *lenta manus* that has produced the line on silk in the *Georgics*, Borges also teases us with an alternative vision of how the Roman world of Octavian[25] demands, and consumes, Eastern materials. Furthermore, the reader of Borges' Virgil might begin to detect an allusive interplay between the two authors: in his poem, Borges cites Virgil's *Georgics* as a reference to how the Roman poet 'feels and writes silk', but when we return to that actual line in Virgil's didactic poem (*Georg.* 2.121), we strangely seem to miss Borges' reference, one that provides a background story about how Virgil came to compose the line in the first place. In other words, we don't have Borges to explain his Virgil. Regardless of the traditionally accepted orders of literary and historical time, Borges' method of citation encourages us to think that Virgil can be an allusive reference to Borges' text, just as Borges is an actual reference to Virgil's.

We have already encountered this kind of speculative experiment in a passage discussed in the previous section, in which Borges imagines a Homer reading Virgil and Virgil reading Dante ('On Virgil', *Conversations* II, 2015: 241). Borges applies the same speculative practice in 'The Far East' by which he conjures up the idea of a Borges as a necessary precursor to Virgil's *Georgics* 2.121. Without this image, our vision of Virgil's *lenta manus* would otherwise remain eclipsed.

In his 'Mil y una noches' conference in 1980, Borges continues to expand on these ideas in connection with Chinese civilization:

> Let us look at another example of this long and frequently tragic dialogue. Let us think of the young Virgil feeling a printed piece of silk from a remote country. The country of the Chinese, which he alone knows is nearby and

[25] 'Octavian': Augustus' name before he becomes first emperor of Rome. Virgil's *Georgics* were composed immediately before the Principate, which was established ca. 30 BC, though the poems were published in ca. 29 BC.

peaceful, very large, and which encompasses the furthest confines of the Orient. Virgil will remember that silk in the *Georgics*, that unstitched silk, with images of temples, emperors, rivers, bridges, lakes different from those he knew. (J. L. Borges, 'Mil y una noches' (1989, *OC* III: 233) (trans. L. Jansen and A. Laird))

The motif of Virgil's hand is further developed in this passage. The poet's *manus* is here not simply imagined to caress the material, but also the land of the Chinese in all its expansion. Borges envisages this hand's touch reaching the confines of the eastern side of the world and then returning all the way to the Virgilian page, and to Virgil's Rome, where the poet's geopolitical and cultural feast of the imagination will endure in a line of the *Georgics*. Thinking again in terms of citations, we may argue that the passage above implicitly becomes an essential reference to read an implicit poetics of empire in early Virgil, for, without Borges, the line in Virgil remains a description of the mistaken origins of silk. Of course, the linear orders of history compel us to admit that, without Virgil, the Borgesian reference would have never existed. If we follow this logic, the system of citations by which Borges rereads Virgil then operates only as a cross-reference for the reader of Borges as well as for Borges' Virgil. Yet, if we follow Borges' understanding of time and temporality, then the idea that Borges remains an essential reference to his copy of Virgil is equally possible. In 'The Hymn', Borges finally adds the epithet *lenta* to the hand of Virgil:

> The slow hand of Virgil caresses
> the silk brought
> from the kingdom of the Yellow Emperor
> by caravans and ships
>
> J. L. Borges, 'The Hymn' (1989, *OC* III: 307)
> (trans. L. Jansen and A. Laird)

These lines powerfully condense Borges' sustained engagement with Virgil's *Georgics* 2.121, which thus far in my discussion has emerged in the form of more scattered references to Virgil's slow hand caressing and writing silk in Borges' corpus. Elsewhere, the poetic motif of the slow hand of Virgil tracing the path of silk from East to West becomes a geographical reference. This is the case of a critical essay entitled 'Marco Polo: the description of the world', which inspires Italo Calvino to write his famous *Invisible Cities*. We may term this form of reference the 'Silk Road' that the Venetian merchant would follow to reach the land of the Chinese:

Through the silk-road, through the arduous path which wore out ancient caravans so that a cloth with figures would reach Virgil's hands and prompt his hexameter, Marco Polo, crossing the mountain ranges and sands, arrived in China. (J. L. Borges, 'Marco Polo: A Description of the World' *Miscellanea* (1996, *OC* IV: 485) (trans. L. Jansen and A. Laird))

Borges' imagined journey of Virgil's hand touching silk from East to West, and then inscribing it in the *Georgics* hexameter, now becomes a literary road in the material world of Marco Polo. Strangely, we are invited to imagine a version of Marco Polo who can only make sense of the role that Virgil's hand has in the poetic history of the Silk Road by reference to Borges' Virgil. The method of citation is, here, no longer cross-referential but, more tangibly, a *necessary reference*, even in the form of an atemporal road map, without which Marco Polo's road to the Far East, as envisaged by Borges, cannot exist.

The dialogue between East and West and the role of perception through imagined physical contact are also at the heart of Borges' reading of the poetics of the *Aeneid*. In his brilliant discussion of how Virgil emerges in Borges' translation practices, García Jurado has identified six lines from the *Aeneid* 1–6 that appear throughout Borges' oeuvre.[26] Borges touches on these lines in his 'Prologue to a personal library' (*SNF* 520), which I discuss at the end of this chapter. We can also locate the lines in Borges' paratextual annotations and underlining in his copy of the Loeb edition listed in the catalogue discussed above. The lines are very famous for readers of Virgil.[27] These are:[28]

1. sunt lacrimae rerum, et mentem mortalia tangunt (*Aen.* 1.462)
2. fuimus Troes, fuit Ilium (*Aen.* 2.325)
3. dis aliter uisum (*Aen.* 2.428)
4. tacitae per amica silentia lunae (*Aen.* 2.255)
5. nudus in ignota, Palinure, iacebis harena (*Aen.* 5.871)
6. ibant obscuri sola sub nocte per umbram (*Aen.* 6.268)

---

[26] García Jurado and Salazar Morales (2014: 99–143). I am grateful to Francisco García Jurado for discussing his excellent work with me, as well as my translations of Borges into English.

[27] As Charles Martindale has suggested to me, in one way the Virgilian lines reflect a personal selection for Borges, but from another perspective they reflect a communal preference in the history of the reception of the *Aeneid*.

[28] (1) 'There are tears for events and mortal things touch the heart'; (2) 'We Trojans are no more, Illium is no more'; (3) 'But the gods' will was otherwise'; (4) 'Amid the friendly silence of the tacit moon'; (5) 'Naked you will lie, Palinurus, on the unknown sand'; (6) 'On they went, hidden in the lonely night, amid the gloom' (trans. by Fairclough, whose edition Borges worked with, with adaptations of mine to address aspects of Borges' interpretation and Spanish).

Several observations can be made on the modes and aspects of Borges'
translation techniques in items 2–6, and my reader can explore these in
García Jurado's in-depth analysis.[29] My focus is specifically on Borges'
elaboration of *Aeneid* 1.462 (item 1). The line is uttered by Aeneas as he
observes the tragic tale of his Troy carved on the Temple of Juno's doors at
Carthage: *sunt lacrimae rerum et mentem mortalia tangunt* ('There are tears
for things and mortal things touch the mind'). We find that Borges paraphrases the line at several points throughout his oeuvre. For instance, in his
'Prologue to the *Unending Rose*', he elaborates on the role that the senses have
for readers of poetry, with the specific example of the *Aeneid* line:

> All verse should have two obligations: to communicate a precise instance
> and to touch us physically, as the presence of the sea does. I have an example
> of Virgil:
>> sunt lacrymae rerum et mentem mortalia tangent (J. L. Borges, 'Prologue
>> to the *Unending Rose*' (1975: *SP* 342))

As we have seen in his reading of Virgil's slow hand, for Borges, poets
like Virgil write through the senses and then communicate their imagined
experiences in writing for the reader, who in turn is *touched*, not simply
emotionally, but also – metaphorically – physically. In his prose piece
'Abramowicz', Borges recasts the *Aeneid* line again, this time concentrating
on its key words: *lacrimae*/tears – *rerum*/(of) things – *mortalia*/mortal,
living things – *tangunt*/touch:

> Tonight I can cry as a man, I can feel the tears roll down my cheekbones,
> because I know that there is nothing on earth which is mortal and which
> does not project its own shade. ('Abramowicz', *Los conjurados* (1989, *OC* III:
> 467) (trans. L. Jansen and A. Laird))

Readers of Borges do not necessarily need to interpret this passage as
a paraphrase of the *Aeneid* line, but readers of Borges' Virgil may have
already done so, especially if they are familiar with it in Borges' magnificent
'Elegy', written in the last years of his life:

> Without anyone knowing, not even the mirror,
> he has cried some human tears.
> He cannot imagine that they commemorate
> all the things that deserve tears:
> the beauty of Helen he has not seen,
> the indivisible river of the years,

---

[29] For example, paraphrasis, expression, ellipsis, 'conscious error', order, hypallage, or transferred
epithet, and word use. See García Jurado and Salazar Morales (2014: 99–143).

the hand of Jesus on the timber
of Rome, the ashes of Carthage,
the nightingale of the Hungarian and the Persian,
the brief good fortune and the anxiety awaiting Virgil,
Virgil, made of marble and music, he
who sang the toils of the sword,
the configurations of the clouds
of each new and unique sunset,
and of the morning that will become evening.
From the other side of the door a man
made of solitude, of love, of time,
has just wept in Buenos Aires
for all those things.
Borges, 'Elegy', *La cifra* (1986, *OC* III: 309) (trans. L. Jansen and A. Laird)

The poem paraphrases the Virgilian line while preserving its three central ideas: tears, things and living things that touch or move us to the point of tears. The same Virgilian hand that Borges imagines had touched silk – and then wrote about it in the *Georgics* – has now written a line in the *Aeneid* that has touched the Borgesian narrator physically, to the extent that his own hand now writes a poem about that sensorial experience. In this poem, Borges teaches us how to read his own Virgil while training us to read Borges himself. Here is the slow hand of Borges rewriting the slow hand of Virgil, the exemplary writer of 'the tears of things'. These 'things', the *res* of poetry, are in Borges' poem a catalogue of the classical and non-classical past: the mythical Helen; the philosophy of Heraclitus; the death of Jesus; the burning of Carthage; the alternative literary history of the nightingale; *and* the Virgilian production as a whole: all the 'tears of things' implied in one line of the *Aeneid* have touched the Borgesian author as reader and writer. This sense of touch is also multi-spatial. For it expands on the topographies that Borges presents us in his 'slow hand' and 'Silk Road' motifs in early Virgil. The trajectory here is no longer from the Far East to the Roman West, but becomes a reading path that takes us all the way from Greece to Argentina, while casually detouring in Rome, Carthage, Hungary and Persia. The tears of things that move us is then a motif that makes the *Aeneid* a text whose impact goes beyond its tradition in Europe, following an errant journey all the way to twentieth-century Buenos Aires.

Borges' Virgil in Cultural History and Aesthetics

Borges' Virgil is an author who, ultimately, touches us physically as he writes a text that, for Borges, truly operates as a universal classic. In his inaugural lecture to the Virgil Society, T. S. Eliot also identifies a universal quality to Virgil. Like Borges, Eliot was an author on the edge of two different cultures of the West, where early- and mid-twentieth-century America, specifically the America of his origins – i.e. the Missouri located along the Western Bank of the Mississippi River – meets that of the Ivy League and Oxbridge academy. For Eliot, the universality of Virgil rests in his 'relatedness to other literatures and cultures', specifically those intimately influenced by the Roman Empire and that ultimately crystalize his tradition as '*the* classic of Europe'.[30] Eliot's Virgil thus retains a demarcated kind of universality, one to which the educated scholar of English and North American culture can more fully relate. Likewise, as an author who writes at the crossroads of two different cultures of the West, twentieth-century Europe and Argentina, Borges, also in erudite fashion, detects a universal texture in Virgil. But he extends Eliot's reading. Borges' Virgil responds to a turning point in our reading of the Roman poet from the edge of the West: when South American modernism gradually became postmodern, and when readings of the classics in the early postcolonial imagination became highly experimental in their endeavour to offer visions of the Graeco-Roman past that contrasted with those of their respective cultural centres in Europe.[31] This is a Virgil whom a late Eliot would have been partial to.[32] And this is surely a Virgil whom a Kafka or Joyce would have loved to read, and that we know Italo Calvino and Derek Walcott celebrate: as a multi-dimensional and far-reaching citation, as a writer who maps out the arduous, global journey of the senses, an author who tells us that poetry recreates the tears of things, things that touch men as they regard the world through literature, whether this occurs in Hungary, in Persia, in China or in a distant room in Buenos Aires. In fact, we could say that Borges' Virgil is in many ways Borges' response to the image of the monumental presence that Western cultural history once gave the Roman poet from the Middle Ages to the end of the Renaissance. In turn, this leads to another important question in Borges' vision of Virgil: that of the cultural war between History and Aesthetics:

> Virgil's preeminence lasted for sixteen hundred years in Europe; the Romantic movement denied and almost erased him. Today he is threatened by our custom of reading books as a function of history, not of aesthetics. (J. L. Borges, 'Virgil, *The Aeneid*', *Prologue to a Personal Library* (1986: *SNF* 519))

---

[30] For the complexity and dimensions of this claim in Eliot, see Martindale (1997: 1–4).
[31] Hardwick (2007: 1–14).   [32] For a change of vision in the late Eliot, see Pollard (2004: 14–6).

Borges' complex conceptions of time, of memory and forgetfulness, and of the literary absences that make 'our' literature present, play a crucial part in this passage. History, not aesthetics, has for a long time explained Virgil's 'preeminence'. Our tendency to read the Roman poet as a 'function of history', by which Borges means 'cultural history', has meant that a single dominant paradigm has given us one version of Virgil only: despite contrasting treatments and philosophies, this is, in part, the Virgil of Christian readers, of Dante, and, to a certain extent, of T. S. Eliot. Borges gives us an alternative version of Virgilian presence. This begins, paradoxically, with a Romantic perspective, which is somewhat strange when we consider that, historically, the 'Romantic movement denied and almost erased [Virgil]', and reaches a climax in the landscapes and temporalities of Borges' classicism. As an advocate of reading Virgil 'as a function of aesthetics', by which Borges means his own physics of reading, he gives us a unique vision of Virgil's presence in space and time, while simultaneously drawing our attention to the absences that silently support this vision. Virgil himself would have approved of this Borgesian story of his ontology in the time that followed his historical life. For, in his unique, Kafkaesque manner, Borges ultimately gives us, in 1986, the year of his death, a Virgil who might have been a keen reader of Borges:

> Virgil does not tell us that the Achaeans waited for darkness to enter Troy; he speaks of the friendly silence of the moon. He does not write that Troy was destroyed, but rather, 'Troy was'. He does not write that a life was unfortunate, but rather 'The gods understood him in another way' ... He does not condemn the aggressive madness of men; he calls it 'the love of iron'. He does not tell us that Aeneas and the Sybil wandered alone amongst the shadows in the dark night; he writes: *'Ibant obscuri sola sub nocte per umbram'*. This is not a mere rhetorical figure, a hyperbaton 'alone' and 'dark' have not changed places in the phrase; both forms, the usual and the Virgilian, correspond with equal precision to the scene they represent. (J. L. Borges, 'Virgil, *The Aeneid*', *Prologue to a Personal Library* (1986: *SNF* 519))

Here is a Virgil who chooses to read Troy, Aeneas, the gods and the Sybil in characteristically Borgesian fashion. The palpable aesthetic communion between the Roman poet and Borges, as presented in this passage and throughout this chapter, makes us think that, for every time we consider Borges' Virgil, we also feel the absent-presence of Virgil's Borges. In the next chapter, this aesthetic experience becomes intensified for readers of Borges' global classicism as our magnificent reader of the classical past takes us on a vertiginous journey through the Möbius effects of his vast poetic cosmos.

CHAPTER 5

Antiquity in the Poetic Cosmos

A man sets himself the task of portraying the world. Over the years he
fills a given surface with images of provinces and kingdoms, moun-
tains, bays, shifts, islands, fish, rooms, instruments, heavenly bodies,
horses, and people. Shortly before he dies he discovers that this
patient labyrinth of lines is a drawing of his own face.

J. L. Borges, 'Epilogue', The Maker (1960: SP 142)

The main focus of discussion up to this point has been on Borges' narrative
prose, essays, lectures, interviews and marginal notes, with the occasional
appeal to poems in which antiquity receives a considerable treatment. This
chapter concentrates fully on Borges' poetry, especially his late poetry,
composed between 1960 and 1985, where the presence of Borges' classicism
emerges more frequently, albeit idiosyncratically.[1] Here, the classics figure
in their most abbreviated and encyclopaedic manner. As one moves from
one poetic collection to another, even the briefest of glances detects
a number of scattered, yet fairly frequent, classical citations, references
and allusions, ranging from the names of canonical authors and the titles of
their works, through historical and mythological figures and events, to
empires, cities, libraries and geographical locations. The overall effect of
this treatment can be intensely kaleidoscopic, and therefore perplexing to
grasp, as when, for instance, one attempts to make visual and conceptual
sense of the fascinating yet impossible constructions of Escher's lithographical work.[2] The Graeco-Roman past in Borges' poetry forms part of
a dense constellation of multiple references to Eastern and Western literatures and cultures, as well as a complex system that is metaphorically
structured around reflections, labyrinths, asymmetries and circularities.
Indeed, classical and non-classical citations visually come together to

---

[1] For a general discussion of Borges' early and late poetry, see Wilson (2013: 186–200).
[2] E.g. Escher's 'Relativity' (1953). For two important studies of Borges and Escher, see Lapidot (1991:
607–15) and Martínez Pérsico (2010: 112–18).

'make up' the texture of Borges' otherwise abysmal and giddy poetic page. The challenge for the reader of Borges' classicism could not be more daunting, therefore. Yet one can detect the delicate force of two organizing principles at play in this design. One of these is the interplay of depth and surface, two conceptual categories that guide us into the global dimensions of Borges' poetics. The epigraph that prefaces this chapter encapsulates this interplay perfectly. Here, the portrayal of the world represented by a creator ultimately turns out to be no more and no less than the wrinkled appearance of his own face before death. This is no mere description of a correspondence between man and his world. The image invites us to consider the labyrinthine depths that exist underneath the surface of the creator's face. For his face is made up of lines that commemorate his lifetime, his way of experiencing the world around him, his stance vis-à-vis that world and thus his vision of that world, just before he discovers himself about to enter his post-historical oblivion, as was the case with Borges' Homer and Shakespeare (Chapter 3, 'The Idea of Homer'). What the creator ultimately turns out to discover is that his wrinkled skin charts the latent processes that have given rise to his whole life's experience and production. In the previous chapter, we followed Virgil's (and Borges') hand as this body part disclosed palpable connections between distant geographies and the materiality of the Virgilian and Borgesian page. In the example of the maker, the materiality of the page is represented by his face, which offers a road map to the depths of his identity and creative vision. As we shall see in this chapter, the metaphor becomes paradigmatic of the system that informs Borges' own poetics, as well as his disclosure of antiquity in his poetry.

The second principle that offers a template to plot the conceptual aspects organizing Borges' poetic design is the interplay of order and chaos. As Borges himself explains in an early interview of the *Conversations* regarding his art of poetic composition:

> I begin by being disordered, that's chaos. How amazing that the word 'cosmetic' has its origin in cosmos. The cosmos is the great order of the world and cosmetic the lesser order that a person imposes on his face. It's the same root – cosmos, order. ('The Eternal Traveller', *Conversations* I (13))

Here, our author bases his explanation on the etymology of the Greek word 'cosmos' (*kosmos*), i.e. 'order' or 'arrangement' that relates to the adjective 'cosmetic' (*kosmētikos*) and the verb 'to arrange' or 'to adorn' (*kosmein*).[3]

---

[3] s.v. κοσμος and DER. 6. *EDG* (2010).

He appeals once more to macro and micro orders of 'world' and 'face',
this time emphasizing a connection with his poetic thought, one that is
primordially informed by chaos, but which results in the 'cosmetic order'
of a poem, a poem that ultimately reflects his vision of the world. One
could argue that Borges' poetic cosmos resembles the cosmos of Borges'
Babel. For the eternal library, like the face of the creator and Borges'
poetic page, also exhibits a 'cosmetic appearance' in the form of a series of
equal hexagonal libraries cataloguing the knowledge 'visible' to us in our
time, i.e. our fragmentary literatures (Chapter 2, 'The Flow of
Heraclitus'). Yet, underneath this organized façade, Babel conceals the
chaos that holds and contains the eternal knowledge of *all* – the absences
and eclipses, the 'post-histories', the knowledge well beyond our reach.
Borges' late poetry, like his fiction and non-fiction, operates with this
blueprint in mind. For every classical citation or brief treatment that we
encounter on the surface of Borges' poetry, we are invited to recall the
Babelian system of cultural knowledge that lies beneath it, in the chaotic
dimensions of Borgesian thought. Such is the texture of Borges' poetic
classicism.

   The aim of this chapter is to explore this texture, and to demonstrate
that classical antiquity is in itself a globalizing agency in Borges' poetic
thought, to such an extent that it would be unthinkable to consider
Borges' poetry without a consideration of his classicism. In what follows,
I will build my case from two specific, interrelated points. The first
section will trace the presence of the classics chronologically, from
Borges' early to late poetry, paying close attention to Borges' presentation
of his poetic collections as 'miscellanies' or 'casual assembles'. It will
contend that it is precisely this 'aesthetics of randomness' in Borges'
poetic collections that gives the classics their specific presence and effects.
The second section will consider Zeus and Hades, Oedipus, Janus and
Proteus, 'threshold' figures who are granted a unique role in sketching the
coordinates of Borges' complex global vision in his poetry. It argues that
the presence of classical myth in Borges' poetry becomes fundamental to
Borges' exploration of the horizons of his own brand of poetry (and
literature more broadly). Once more, Heraclitean time is the measure of
this poetic vision, as well as the code for our own reception of Borges.
The closing of the chapter will trace this programmatic idea in a poem
called 'Cosmogonía', first translated in English for the present book,
which readers of Borges' poetry can interpret as a neat sum of his 'deep'
classicism.

Classical Fragments in Borges' Poetic *Siluae*

One way to begin thinking about antiquity on the surface of Borges' poetry is to consider the presence of the classics chronologically throughout Borges' verse collections, from 1923 to 1985. Borges' poetic activity falls into two main periods. These usually are referred to as his early and late poetry, which respectively come before and after prose works such as *Fictions* (1944) and *Artifices* (1949).[4] While these periods do have some points of contact, they are, thematically speaking, in fact markedly different. The early poetry (*Fervor of Buenos Aires*, 1923; *Moon Across the Way*, 1925; *San Martín's Copybook*, 1929) has a distinctively local tone. Its thematic focus is on nineteenth-century national heroes and battles, as well as the affairs of local characters, such the *criollo* and the *compadrito*,[5] who occupy the urban scene prior to the arrival of Southern Europeans during the immigrations of 1920–30. In these early collections, Borges creates an avant-garde mythology for his native city and country that combines national and modernistic traditions.[6] There are almost no citations of classical themes in these works and, when they do appear, their presence is mostly allusive, as well as elusive. Some readers have detected a Homeric allusion in *Fervor of Buenos Aires* (1923). They argue that in this first collection Borges represents his return to his native city around the figure of Odysseus' *nostos* to Ithaca, a theme that Borges later weaves into the last verse of 'The Maker', as discussed in Chapters 2 ('The Flow of Heraclitus') and 3 ('The Idea of Homer').[7] While the allusion in *Fervor of Buenos Aires* is telling – and tempting to elaborate on – in my opinion there is no tangible detail for the development of a classicizing argument; not in the way one finds in 'The Maker' or in Borges' 'Geneva' (Chapter 3).

The second period (*The Maker*, 1960; *The Self and the Other*, 1964; *In Praise of Darkness*, 1969; *The Unending Rose*, 1975; *The Iron Coin*, 1976; *The History of the Night*, 1977; *The Limit*, 1981; *Atlas*, 1984; and *Los*

---

[4] For two excellent general discussions of these periods in English, see Olea Franco (2013: 172–85) and Wilson (2013: 186–200).

[5] In Argentine Spanish, and especially in the nineteenth century, a 'criollo' was someone of 'pure' Spanish descent. A 'compadrito' originally was a local character whose ancestors fought in the War of Independence from Spain. The semantic application of 'compadrito' keeps changing in the early twentieth century. Borges tends to use the word to mean a young man of a lower social class, dwelling on the coast of the Rioplatense area that covers Argentina and Uruguay. The compadrito enjoys nightlife and tango, and shows his virility in knife fights. Compadritos are recurrent characters in tango and Rioplatense literature. With time, the term acquires the connotation of a 'show-off' or 'cocky' character.

[6] The bibliography on this topic is vast. I have found Olea Franco (1993), Cédola (1994: 169–89) and Balderston (2008: 19–36) particularly revealing for my work.

[7] See Cédola (1994), esp. 169–74.

Conjurados, 1985) marks a shift in Borges' poetry.[8] The collections are punctuated by questions of time, identity, history, Western and Eastern thought, the library, the encyclopaedia, infinity and other themes also found in Borges' *Fictions* (1944) and *Artifices* (1949). A survey of this second period shows that references to the classics increase, becoming somewhat condensed and intensified. For instance, in *The Maker, The Self and the Other* and *The Limit*, Greek themes and genres predominate, drawn especially from myth, pre-Socratic thinking and tragedy, while Roman topics are limited to a specific few, becoming instead the subject of intensive repetition throughout (Rome and Carthage; the Virgilian persona and corpus; and Julius Caesar – themes we have already studied in preceding chapters). This development coincides with aspects of Borges' own historical life. One of the most crucial is blindness, which becomes more pronounced in the 1950s, when Borges becomes Director of the National Library in Buenos Aires ('Poem of the Gifts', *SP* 95). With the loss of sight, we trace a move towards thematic abstraction and inward reflection, and the classics, as well as the literature of the past, form part of, and inform, the author's renewed poetic voice. Also significant are the last twenty years of Borges' life when he travelled extensively around the world, with several stops in Sicily, Greece and Asia Minor, and when he revised his overall perceptions of antiquity from an increased globalizing perspective ('The Eternal Traveller', *Conversations* I).

On the whole, classical citations in Borges' late poetry operate intra- and intertextually, and in tandem with a mosaic of memories from Borges' vast, encyclopaedic knowledge of world literature and thought.[9] One significant effect of this appeal to antiquity is a further reinforcement of the cross-cultural classicism that we already find in Borges' prose during the 1940–50s. Yet one also notes a new development in the conceptual role that Borges grants antiquity in the construction of his biographical profile as 'hacedor', or 'maker'.[10] In fact, *El hacedor* is the title in Spanish of

---

[8] The chronological sequence follows Coleman's edition of Borges' poetry, *Selected Poems* (1999, Penguin). The proposed study works simultaneously with editions of Borges' poetry in Spanish (*Obras Completas I–IV*, Emece) and in French (*Oeuvres completes I–II*, Gallimard).

[9] For intertextually in Borges, see O'Sullivan (1990: 109–21) and Wood (2013: 35–6).

[10] See Williamson (2013: 216–23). Williamson plots the evolution of Borges writing into three autobiographical dimensions: the 'Author as Hero' (1914–30); the 'Author as Reader' (1930–64) and the 'Author as a Weaver of Dreams' (1965–85). These categories roughly coincide with the division of Borges' work into prose and poetry. While these are convenient categories for our analysis, it is doubtful that Borges would have enjoyed them. On this issue, see Alberto Manguel's lecture on 'Borges Lector', delivered in Casa América, Buenos Aires, 2011 in www.youtube.com/watch?v=8QXvUWq7nYU.

The Maker, published in 1960. The noun 'hacedor', related to the verb 'hacer', 'to make' or 'to do', depending on English usage, has become one of those *intraduisibles* ultimately going back to the Greek noun *poiētēs* ('maker').[11] The Penguin edition of Borges' *Selected Poems*, which includes 'The Maker', translates 'hacedor' as 'maker', yet the Gallimard edition in French has opted for 'auteur'. In their decision, the translators first consider a variety of possibilities in French that give a full range of what Borges means by 'hacedor' in Spanish, e.g. 'fabricateur', 'artisan', 'ouvrier'.[12] 'Auteur' may not sound quite like 'hacedor' and 'maker', yet it conveys an important idea that the Spanish and English versions do not: the notion of an author as someone who *augments*, as one finds in the Latin noun *auctor*, and the verb *augeo*, whose literal meaning is 'to augment', 'to increase'.[13] As they emerge in Borges' late poetry, the classics are instrumental in Borges' self-representation as an *auctor* in this sense. Namely, as a poet who augments the dimensions of his poetic cosmos, from its early beginnings in the local myths of nineteenth-century Buenos Aires to the realm of the universe at large. As I will show in the rest of this chapter, this process ultimately becomes for Borges a foundational question about the space of literature, as well as its shifting horizons.

The interplay of augmentation and the classics in Borges' poetic cosmos is furthermore complemented by what I call Borges' 'aesthetics of randomness', to which I allude in my use of *'siluae'* in this section's subtitle. First of all, it is important to bear in mind that the collections in the late period assemble both poetry and prose. The prose comes in the form of prefaces and postfaces, as well as dedications and other short pieces, such as voyages and descriptions of cities and dreams, as we find in *The Limit* (1981) and *Atlas* (1984). In this chapter, I take these prose pieces into account as part of my study of Borges' poetry because this is how our author conceived of the collections and its many revisions: as an assembly of material in which all literature is understood to be poetic.[14] Borges' aesthetics of randomness also exhibits a nuanced structural design. He first introduces the concept of randomness in the 'Epilogue' to *The Maker* (I enter the relevant Spanish in brackets):

---

[11] I use *'intraduisibles'* in the sense developed by Barbara Cassin (ed. 2004) in her *Vocabulaire européen des philosophies* and Apter (2013) in her uses of 'untranslatability' in the semantics of 'world literature'.

[12] Bernès (2010: 1127) in *ŒC*.

[13] S.v. *augeo* 1 and 2 in *OLD* and s.v. *augeo* in *EDL*. For discussion of *augeo* and *auctor* in this sense in Latin authors, see Barchiesi (1988), 103 and Jansen (2012: 12).

[14] Bernès (2010: 1244) in *ŒC*.

> God willing, the underlying sameness (*la monotonía esencial*) of this
> collection (*miscelánea*) will be less apparent than the geographical and
> historical diversity of its themes. Time has brought these pieces together,
> not I . . . of all the books I have delivered to the printer, none I think, is as
> personal as this unruly jumble, this florilegium (*colecticia y desordenada
> silva de varia lección*), for the simple reason that it is rich in reflections and
> interpolations. (J. L. Borges, 'Epilogue' (1960: *SP* 143))

This note is crucial to Borges' socio-literary dialogue with his readers.
We know that Borges thought of the postface as a delayed variation of
the preface, an idea that becomes highly influential to later twentieth-
century thinkers, such as Genette in his study of paratexts, and Derrida in
his deconstruction of the preface.[15] This conceptualization of the postface
also encourages a revisiting practice on the reader's part. Thus, in the
epilogue to *The Maker*, Borges offers an implicit code for re reading the
collection at the structural level based on the 'authorial instructions' that he
offers at the point of closure. The code is to (re)consider the collection as
a 'miscellany of sameness' compiled in *and* by time, by which Borges means
Heraclitean time, a temporal form of reading that discloses literature's
renewal in a fragmentary manner, as we have seen in detail in Chapter 2
('The Flow of Heraclitus').

Those involved in the study of classical and neo-Latin literature may
already have perceived another meaning, however. For Borges' use of
'miscellanies' has a strong resonance in the Latin concept of *siluae*, literally
meaning 'forests', but used by classical and postclassical authors to describe
the (supposedly) disorderly and eclectic character of their poetic collections, as we find, for instance, in Statius, Martial and Poliziano,
respectively.[16] While Borges was surely acquainted with these works,[17] it
is most likely that in this instance he is thinking of the Spanish writer Pedro
Mexía (1497–1555), who in 1540 publishes *Silva de varia lección*, exactly the
same words Borges uses in the epilogue above.[18] As Bernès points out in his
entry to Borges' *The Maker*, Mexía's collection featured '[une] vaste
collection d'anecdotes, de narrations, de miracles, de faits divers'.[19]

---

[15] For a discussion of Borges' poetics of the prologue, see Cajero 2006, 102–8. For prefaces as postfaces,
see Genette (1997: 237–62), Derrida (1981: 6).

[16] For a recent discussion of *siluae* as a form of re-embedding collected material in Statius and Martial,
as well as of the reception of this procedure in Poliziano, see Roman (2015: 451–54). On 'variety' as
a Roman concept, see Fitzgerald (2016), esp. 149–95 on miscellany and the Roman book.

[17] While I have not found explicit citations of these canonical authors in Borges literary oeuvre and
other materials, such as interviews and dialogues, I find it hard to believe that, at the very least, he did
not know their names and works.

[18] Bernès (2010: 1129) in *ŒC*.   [19] Bernès (2010: 1129) in *ŒC*.

While Borges might have had Latin *siluae* in mind, Mexía's own *siluae* appears to be a principal model for Borges, or at least the most immediate one. After *The Maker*, this understanding of *siluae* continues to be the structural notion guiding Borges' aesthetic of randomness, as we find in later collections, where the author explains that his 'compilations' respond to the 'instance of time', 'moods' and 'predictable monotony' (*SP* 147). However, as we reach *Atlas* (1984), a 'poetic geography' made out of prose texts and photography, Borges' aesthetics of randomness acquires a truly global dimension, one sustained by the collection's multi-mediatic and transcultural character:

> During the pleasant course of our stay on earth, María Kodama and I travelled across and took delight in a good many countries, which gave rise to a good many photographs and texts. Pezzoni saw these photographs, and Girri observed that they could be interwoven with the texts, in a book that is sagely chaotic. Here is this book. It is not made up of a series of photographs explained by epigraphs. Each title encompasses a whole, made of images and words. (J. L. Borges, Preface to *Atlas* (1984) (my translation))

Here, Borges' *siluae* become identified with Borges' globalizing vision. The passage presents us with three interpretations of *Atlas* as a collection, the first two by the Argentine poet-critics Pezzoni and Girri, from the Argentine Journal *Sur*, and the third by Borges.[20] Enrique Pezzoni (1926–89) reads *Atlas* as an *intertexture* of image and word ('interwoven with the texts'), while Alberto Girri (1919–91) plots it in terms of its 'wise' or 'intelligent' chaos ('sagely chaotic'), a reading that recalls Borges' appeal to 'cosmetics' in the description of the disorder that informs his poetic world ('I begin by being disordered, that's chaos. How amazing that the word 'cosmetic' has its origin in cosmos.' *Conversations* I: 28). Borges' response then supplements these views from a further perspective, which is to contend that each title, each piece, *englobes a totality*, or *whole*. In other words, each piece in the collection represents a cosmos in itself, one that those more trained in Borges' classicism, as we now are, can easily associate with other global visions in Borges, such as those of Magna Graecia, Geneva or the Homer of 'The Immortal'. In turn, this helps us further refine our own conception of how the global operates in Borges' classicism. For our author gives us specific visions and perspectives of the world around us that ultimately form the cosmos of his poetics of reading the cultural past: his global outlook consists of a series of focuses and shifts, which are both everywhere and nowhere at once, as is the case of the

---

[20] Borges' writings for *Sur* have been collected in *OC* I–IV and are published by Emecé (1999).

interplay of heterotopia and atopia that one finds in Pascal's sphere, discussed in Chapter 1. As we have seen in our discussions throughout this book, Borges' cultural approach to the past can be simultaneously 'pan-Mediterranean', 'pan-Anglo-Saxon', 'pan-Eastern', 'pan-Latin American', to mention a few instances in which his global approach exhibits momentary focal points. Each sphere 'encompasses a whole' that is 'intertexted', as Pezzoni suggests, and also produces a 'wisely chaotic' form, as Girri maintains.

In the context of Borges' twentieth-century poetic *siluae*, and following the significance of Heraclitean time as a mode of plotting literature, the presence of the classics is fragmentary at best. In this sense, each classical citation emerging on the surface of Borges' poetry trains us to become not just deep readers of his global classicism, but also of his poetics of recollecting of the cultural past. As a way of illustration, one can explore two instances of this procedure, one in prose and one in verse, as we encounter Virgil in fragmentary form in a collection titled *The Limit* (1981):

> I now say your name, María Kodama. How many seas, how many gardens of the East and West, how much Virgil. ('Inscription', *The Limit* (1981: *SP* 419))

> The silent friendship of the moon
> (I misquote Virgil) has kept you company
> 'The Limit', *The Limit* (1981: *SP* 459)

'The silent friendship of the moon | (I misquote Virgil)': as with all of Borges' classical presences, there lies, even behind a minimal citation (such as a deliberately misquoted line), a world of absences, eclipses, vague memories, variations, told and untold stories. Arguably, our most tangible memory of this citation, especially if our field is Classical Studies, is Virgil's own *tacitae per amica silentia lunae* (*Aeneid* 2.255), which in 'The Limit', as well as other texts, Borges cites as a 'deliberate error'.[21] Yet our memory of Borges' classics may equally lead us to recall other, less immediate, instances of Borges' Virgil. One of these could be the Virgil whose hand touches Chinese silk in Borges' imaginary *Georgics*, or the Virgil who charts the Silk Road from fourteenth-century Venice to the Far East in Borges' literary cartographies. Likewise, we cannot forget that this same Virgil made our Argentine author feel the 'tears of things' in his modernist

---

[21] García Jurado and Salazar Jurado (2014: 107 and 115–16). Also compare Virgil's own deliberate paraphrasing according to Borges: 'Virgil does not tell us that the Achaeans waited for darkness to enter Troy; he speaks of the friendly silence of the moon', we recall Borges saying in his 'Prologue' to the *Aeneid* (1986: *SNF* 519) (Chapter 4, 'Virgil's Touch').

Buenos Aires in 1986, when 'Elegy' was published; and, further, that the Roman poet still continued to invigorate our cultural memory in 1981, as we follow his transcultural impact, this time in the form of the Virgilian corpus' global journey 'East and West' with Borges and Kodama. 'How much Virgil', says Borges in his prefatory dedication to his wife entitled 'Inscription'. This Virgil surely refers to the Virgilian oeuvre that María Kodama reads to an almost blind Borges during one of his last world tours, as well as to Borges' increasingly partial preference for recalling Virgil in his late life ('49. Happy are those who hold in memory words of Virgil [. . .], for these will brighten their days', as he declares in 'Fragments from an Apocryphal Gospel', *SP* 293). Yet, 'Virgil' also silently operates as a multi-directional, minimal classical reference that – perhaps paradoxically – can disclose a chain of bifurcating memories that illustrate the temporal and locative breadth of Borges' global encounters with the past.

A similar mnemonic process is at play with other minimal citations of antiquity in Borges' late poetry, especially in contexts that aim at projecting an encyclopaedic scope of human endeavours, events and histories, as well as our author's increasing awareness of his own mortality. Amongst these frequent insertions of the classics, far too many to mention here, one could cite the intense repetition of proper nouns, such as 'Carthage', 'Ganges', 'Rome', 'Caesar', 'Alexandria', as well as of the Latin language and the Latin hexameter, most of which have already been discussed.[22]

Myth, Poetry and the Möbius Effect of Literature

We have seen that Borges' classicism promotes a literary space that challenges received ideas on the status and scope of literature, and especially of the literature we call 'world', as Borges constantly connects this space with the realms of dreams and oblivion. Some of the most powerful examples of this Borgesian phenomenon and approach are the 'eclipsed' poet of *The Greek Anthology*, whose memory has been almost forgotten in our cultural history; Tacitus' lost texts, shelved somewhere in the eternal Babel; and Homer's postclassical ontology, one that transgresses historical time. In other instances, Borges' classicism charts the space of literature transculturally, disclosing the convoluted temporalities and topographies that make up Borges' geopoetical memory, and hence his own unique mode of plotting cultural history. Borges'

---

[22] These citations are ubiquitous in the late poetry. Some examples can be found in *SP* 85, 91, 95, 117, 129, 163, 177, 181–3, 201, 225, 337, 351, 365, 411, 423, 433 and 411.

Virgil is the perfect example of this transcultural impulse, as Borges reimagines the haptic impact of the Virgilian oeuvre around the globe and through the centuries. Borges' classicism furthermore deliberately fuses and confuses the space that literature typically occupies in history and vice versa. This was the case of Borges' treatment of Julius Caesar, the figure that renews itself in both local, socio-political histories, such as those of a nineteenth-century gaucho from the Pampas, and the realm of fictional drama and political essays in Shakespeare and Quevedo, respectively. There is one more dimension in which Borges' classicism invites us to consider the spatial status of literature at a global level. This can be traced in the interplay of classical myth and liminality, which is familiar to students of classical mythology, but acquires innovative meanings and forms in Borges' late poetry.

While the presence of antiquity in Borges' late poetry tends to be highly fragmentary, as has been shown, in some instances, these classical fragments are marginally more complete. This is the case with poems in which Borges appeals to Graeco-Roman myth to deal with fundamental questions about human identity, condition and self-knowledge vis-à-vis the nature of reality, both in our world and beyond. In this type of narrative, myth occupies a liminal zone, one that constantly reconfigures the horizons of the Borgesian poetic page through a structure that appears to be circular but, in fact, operates as a Möbius strip. The Möbius strip is a band that at a given point features a twist causing the band to have a single surface. Thus, if we were to draw a line along the band on one side, we will see that it joins up with the point at which we began, without turning the band over. This unique design is implicit in Borges' 'Parable of Cervantes and the *Quixote*', a short text concerned with the ways in which an author's fiction can become imperceptibly – even inexplicably – intertwined with their historical life and literary production:

> For in the beginning of literature there is myth, as there is also in the end of it. (J. L. Borges, 'Parable of Cervantes and the *Quixote*' (1955: *CF* 315))

Broadly conceived, parables are allegories that reaffirm an important truth. For Borges, the truth that can be drawn from his Quixote parable is that literature, a phenomenon that for him encompasses all branches of knowledge and modes of expression, including poetry, has 'origins' and 'ends' in myth. By 'myth', Borges here implies a mixture of two notions: one is the most general meaning of 'story' or 'legend', while the other has the more specific connotation of *mythos* as 'plot', as Aristotle develops it in his study of Greek tragedy in *Poetics* 13 and 14.

It is this interpretation of myth that ultimately informs the blurring contours of, what Borges understands to be, the literature produced in our historical time:

> Defeated by reality, by Spain, Don Quixote died in his native village around 1614. He was survived only briefly by Miguel de Cervantes. For both of them, for the dreamer and the dreamed, the *tissue of that whole plot* consisted in the contraposition of two worlds: the unreal world of the books of chivalry and the common everyday world of the seventeenth century. Little did they suspect that the years would end by wearing away the disharmony. Little did they suspect that La Mancha and Montiel and the knight's frail figure would be, for the future, no less poetic that Sinbad's haunts or Ariostos' vast geographies. For myth is at the beginning of literature, and also at its end. (J. L. Borges, 'Parable of Cervantes and the *Quixote*' (1955: *CF* 315))

'[T]he *tissue of that whole plot*': in this parable, Borges plays with the idea that Don Quixote and Miguel de Cervantes are ultimately woven into a text whose global plot '[wears] away' the distinction between historical and fictional reality. This ambitious 'myth' somehow harmonizes the two realities to such an extent that Cervantes' life and his fiction become a single whole. It begins with the death of Don Quixote in the fictional year of 1614, and ends with the now legendary fame of La Mancha and its municipal town of Montiel, as well as the frail figure of Don Quixote, after Cervantes produced them. Yet, in claiming that the literatures of our time begin and end in myth, Borges is not making a circular or, more precisely, a teleological argument. For his point is not that myth is the grand structure that explains the historical reality of literature. Rather, it is that in our literature one can locate a moment in which the historical reality of, for instance, a Cervantes and his novel curiously folds – as happens in a Möbius strip – and fuses with the mythical realities of his Don Quixote de La Mancha. Thus, when we visit or think about La Mancha, we arguably cannot help connecting it to the legend of Quixote, just as when we consider the legend of the Quixote, we cannot help thinking of the historical Cervantes who dreamed that novel.[23] Similarly, we could say that, when we visit Virgil' tomb in the *cripta napoletana* in Naples, this part of the complex biographical history of Virgil is also inextricably a part of the fictional story of Virgil's afterlife,

---

[23] There have been several studies on Borges and Cervantes, especially on the question of Cervantes' influence on Borges' conception of authorship and the aesthetics of fiction. On these topics, I have found Madrid (1987), Williamson (1994), Wood (1994), Fine (2003), Giskin (2005), Sagastume and Martínez-Sáenz (2005) and Laín Corona (2009) particularly enlightening.

infused as it is with a wealth of local legends, as well as the legendary visits of Dante and Petrarch.[24] The Möbius-strip effect that imperceptibly develops a globalizing plot that bizarrely harmonizes literary history and literary fiction into a 'tissue', or text, as Borges articulates it in his parable, is characteristically 'non-orientable'. That is to say, it is a *turning point* in which, at least momentarily, we become disoriented and feel unable to distinguish where literature begins and ends. For Borges, this theme takes several variations, ones that he explores with particular interest in his classicism. As with much of Borges' late poetry, mirrors and reflections, labyrinths, multiple realities and metamorphosis form the shifting structures of Borges' experiment with the borders of his literature.

This mystifying point, or zone, that is said to exist somewhere at the silent borders of our human reality and artistic accounts becomes the playground of Zeus and Hades, Oedipus and the Sphinx, Janus and Proteus in Borges' late poetry. Borges situates these mythological figures at various points of this liminal space. Furthermore, he represents them as having various levels of ability to decode complex global plots, ones that ultimately align historical and, what I have termed in Homer, 'post-historical' spheres.[25] We have seen that Cervantes appeals to Quixano's dream about Don Quixote as a rhetorical strategy for his readers that ultimately blurs – and expands – the horizons of the seventeenth-century Spanish novel. So does Borges, in his role of *auctor,* as we have discussed above, appeal to classical myth as a vehicle for exploring, amongst other things, the uncharted spaces of his poetic experiments in the twentieth century. Let us begin with Zeus and Hades in a poem concerning labyrinths, the blind, literary self and the possibility of otherness:

> Zeus himself could not undo the web
> of stone closing around me. I have forgotten
> the men I was before; I follow the hated
> path of monotonous walls
> that is my destiny. Severe galleries   5
> which curve in secrets circles
> the end of the years. Parapets
> cracked by the days' usury.
> In the pale dust I have discerned
> signs that frighten me. In the concave   10
> Evenings the air has carried a roar

---

[24] Ziolkowski and Putnam (eds. 2008: xxxiv–xxxv, 130–32 and 411–13).
[25] A notion that already can be plotted in, for instance, Lucretius *De rerum natura*, for which see Kennedy (2002) and (2007: 276–96).

towards me, or the echo of a desolate howl.
I know there is an Other in the shadows,
Whose fate is to wear out the long solitudes
which weave and unweave this Hades.   15
And to long for my blood and devour my death.
Each of us seeks the other.

J. L. Borges, 'The Labyrinth', *In Praise of Darkness* (1969: *SP* 275)

This piece belongs to Borges' *In Praise of Darkness* (1969), a collection of poems whose most prominent theme is Borges' experience as a man, author and reader who has lost his sight.[26] In terms of its classicizing themes, the Borgesian narrator exhibits several points of contact with Borges' Homer in 'The Immortal' and 'The Maker'. This is the case when the narrator mentions his past: multiple ontologies (2–3); his hearing of echoes and other sounds from the distance that reveal faint aspects of his identity (9–12); and the experience of that moment prior to the end of his own mortality (16–7). Structurally speaking, furthermore, the labyrinth becomes the conceptual topography of Borges' daunting experience of blindness. Borges fully identifies this labyrinth with a version of Hades (15), a maze whose plot the author tells us can be woven and unwoven (15).[27] Here, the use of the language of textuality to refer to Hades should not escape us. For Borges implicitly presents this mythical space as a *textum* encompassing not just the spatiality of his experience, but also the conceptual space of his poem. The poem opens with a line that strongly recalls the opening words in Greek of the Hymn to Zeus in Aeschylus' *Agamemnon* 168 (οὐδ' ὅστις πάροιθεν ἦν μέγας, '<u>not even</u> he who before was mighty'). As far as I can tell, this close lexical intertext has not been noticed before, and while there is no certainty that Borges was thinking about the Aeschylus' line, or perhaps working through intermediary texts that had cited or recast it, the classicizing connection is highly plausible. If the intertext with Greek tragedy is allowed to stand, then one could contend that Borges begins his poem by problematizing Zeus' profile as the enforcer of world-order in the first play of the *Oresteia*. In Aeschylus, Zeus

---

[26] Bernès and Ibarra (2010: 1242) in *ŒC*.

[27] Like time, the labyrinth extends across Borges' work. As Borges puts it in 'The Garden of Forking Paths', the labyrinth is the 'fabric of times' that 'contains all the possibilities' (*CF* 127). Yet men can only attempt to decipher the labyrinths that obey 'human laws', since 'divine labyrinths' remain beyond their intellectual capabilities and understanding. At the heart of this formulation is the 'Greek labyrinth', which Borges recurrently cites as a metaphor for the intricacies of human paths and choice, the piecing together of clues, or the ways meaning circulates in one's mind. Bibliography on Borges and the labyrinth is vast. A now established discussion can be found in Barrenechea (1965). For a recent treatment of this topic, see Mualem (2012: 209–34) and González Echevarría (2013: 127–36).

is mentioned third (173) as the grandchild of Uranos (168) and son of Chronos (170).[28] Uranos and Chronos no longer have power over human affairs, while the mighty Zeus does. Then Borges begins 'The Labyrinth' by claiming that 'not even' mighty Zeus, the most powerful of the Olympian gods, can 'undo' the web that is the Hades in which he finds himself. From this perspective, our author presents us with a Zeus who, while still considered divine, turns out to be a limited reader of complex structures, especially those that demand a high level of perception ('I have discerned' 9) and, were we to decode them, they would lead us to enlightenment and certainty ('I know' 13). But who can 'undo' this version of Hades, one that not only represents a form of death, or 'darkness', in life, but also strongly emerges as a Babelian structure of time ('galleries | which curve in secret circles | to the end of the years' 5–7) enclosing the author ('the web | of stone' 1–2; 'path of monotonous walls' 4? As it turns out, Borges' Hades is a labyrinth whose 'signs' and deep, hollow sounds only Borges can just about decipher and hear, respectively ('In the pale dust I have discerned | signs that frighten me', 9–10; 'In the concave | Evenings the air has carried a roar | towards me, or the echo of a desolate howl' 10–12).

In 'The Labyrinth', Borges considers two types of liminal readers. One is Zeus, who, despite his divinity and mightiness, fails to make sense of the complex space described in the poem. The other is the Borgesian narrator, an adept reader, able to discern a way out of his own Hades, as well as the moment in which his mortality will inexplicably blend into his ahistorical oblivion ('I have forgotten | the men I was before 2–3; I know there is an Other in the shadows 13). In representing his Borgesian narrator as a competent decoder of his Hades, Borges offers an important example of a reader who potentially can transcend his own narrative space and locate the turning point from which he is able to weave 'the tissue of the whole plot', as Borges tells us in his 'Parable to Cervantes'.

While Zeus turns out to be a limited reader of Borges' globalizing textualities, Oedipus emerges as *the* liminal reader *par excellence* in a poem concerning the tragic hero's encounter with the Sphinx on his way to Thebes, before becoming king:

> Four-footed at dawn, in the daytime tall,
> And wandering three-legged down the hollow
> Reaches of evening: thus did the sphinx
> The eternal one, regard his restless fellow

---

[28] For οὐδ' ὅστις, see Fraenkel (1950) s.v. 168 and Bollack (1981) s.v. 168. For a discussion of Zeus in the context of liminal space and time in the *Oresteia*, see Widzisz (2012: 34–5).

Mankind; and at evening came a man   5
Who, in terror-struck, discovered as in a mirror
His own decline set forth in the monstrous image,
His destiny, and felt a chill of terror.
We are Oedipus and everlastingly
We are the long tripartite beast; we are   10
All that we were and will be, nothing less.
It would destroy us to look steadily
At our full being. Merciful God grants us
The ticking of the clock, forgetfulness.

J. L. Borges, 'Oedipus and the Enigma',
The Self and the Other (1964: *SP* 227)

The poem incorporates several Borgesian themes already familiar to us, above all, those relating to images, contemplation, eternity and the interplay of memory and forgetfulness. Borges' recasting of the myth does not concentrate on Oedipus' destruction of the Sphinx after decoding her enigma, or on the origins of the Sphinx, as we find them in classical sources.[29] His focus is rather on the moment in which Oedipus faces the Sphinx, here described as eternal (4), and becomes aware of the dreadful condition of mankind, his decline and destiny. In one sense, the Sphinx operates for Oedipus as Ithaca does for Odysseus in 'The Maker' (Chapter 2). Both heroes are returning home, i.e. Thebes and Ithaca, respectively, and both of them are presented with a daunting vision of eternity, in the Sphinx (4) and Odysseus' island. Yet, we recall that Ithaca acts as an ataraxic image of eternity for the hero of the *Odyssey*, while in 'Oedipus and the Enigma' the Sphinx projects the terrifying image of man's everlasting, tragic condition ('We are Oedipus and everlastingly | We are the long tripartite beast' 9–10), as well as the daunting prospect of seeing our pitiful selves *whole* (11). Were we to capture it, this latter image would be enough to destroy us. This is why, as he closes the poem, the narrator is thankful that we are able to forget the terrifying notion of who we really are: three-legged beasts (13–5). Meanwhile, Oedipus the mindful has captured a total vision of this reality, since he possesses the unique ability to decode Sphinx's enigma.

Through the lens of myth, tragedy and liminality, 'Oedipus and the Enigma' presents us with an optimum reader of the complex and daunting plot of humankind. In fact, the Oedipus of this poem would be a highly competent reader of, for instance, the totality of Borges' Homer, his

---

[29] E.g. Hesiod *Theog.* 326ff.; Aeschylus *Septem* 776f.; Sophocles *Oedipus Tyrannus* 391ff.; Apollodorus *The Library* 3.5.8. See Hutchinson (1985) s.v. 776 for an overview.

cultural memory and oblivion. For not only is he capable of decoding the truth of our human condition, but he also possesses the ability to capture 'the whole plot', i.e. the whole text of one's life and afterlife, something we, like Borges, can only *imagine*. Standing right before the borders of his own reality, Borges' Oedipus therefore is the quintessential reader of the reflections that reveal the actuality of who we *really* are, when forgetfulness no longer serves – and preserves – us, and when we find ourselves roaming the daunting space of 'all that we were and will be, nothing less' (11).

Borges' Janus is another sublime reader of Borges' global plots in his late poetry. Yet, unlike Zeus and Oedipus, Janus' liminal status and power is the direct result of his privileged position as presider of the gates that come between place and time:

> No one is to open or close a single door
> without homage to me, who see two ways,
> door's tutelary. Horizons lines
> of stable land, unstable seas, yield to my gaze.
> my two faces penetrate the past,   5
> discern the future. Common to both I see,
> drawn swords, evil, discord;
> one who could have removed them let them be
> and does so still. Missing are my two hands.
> I am of stone fixed in place. I cannot say   10
> for sure whether the things that I behold
> are future disputes or quarrels of yesterday.
> I look about my ruins: truncated column,
> faces powerless to glance each other's way.
>
> J. L. Borges, 'A Bust of Janus Speaks',
> *The Gold of the Tigers* (1972: *SP* 321)

Amongst various important Borgesian themes, the poem deals with the question of double identity, time and temporality, as well as the bizarre ability to grasp an Aleph-like vision of the self, themes that we have discussed in detail in previous chapters. Furthermore, the poem is possibly informed by – and blends – two classical sources. One of these could be Propertius 4.2, in which a statue of Vertumnus, the god of change, speaks to a passer-by on his way to the forum.[30] The other source must be Ovid's *Fasti* 1.89ff, in which the Ovidian narrator asks Janus about his etiology in the month of January, while describing the attributes of the two-faced god. Janus' liminal vision is enhanced by Borges' choice of language and

---

[30] For the complex origins and etymology of Vertumnus, one that surely must have fascinated Borges, see Hutchinson (2006: 86–9).

imagery. For instance, Janus' vision captures vast, unidentified geographies: 'horizon lines | of stable land, unstable seas, yield to my gaze' (3–4). In these lines, it is worth noticing that the Penguin translator, A. S. Trueblood, chooses the more idiomatic 'yield to my sight' when rendering the verb 'abarcar' in Borges' original Spanish ('Abarco el horizonte | de inciertos mares y de tierra cierta' 2–3). However, a principal meaning of 'abarco' in English is 'I encompass', a translation that admittedly would lack the poetic tone of 'yield to my sight', but that nevertheless would fit technically well with the 360-degree vision Borges aims to recreate. Janus' vision furthermore encompasses time: past and future (5–6), though these tenses are subsumed in that vision and become an inseparable form of eternity ('I cannot say | for sure whether the things that I behold | are future disputes or quarrels of yesterday', 10–2). Once more, it is worth bearing in mind the original Spanish when it comes to the language of global perception. In line 5, the same translator uses 'penetrate' in connection with Janus' ability to 'see through' the past, while Borges uses the 'divisar' ('divisan' 5), which conveys the visually panoramic, rather than piercing, power of the god to capture the scope of time. Finally, Janus possesses an Aleph-like type of vision, of the kind that allows viewers to observe not only the entire universe, but also themselves in it. Through his deep, vast vision, the god can even see himself in time in the poem ('I look about my ruins' 13). This process presents us with a potential *mise-en-abîme* structure, in which characters 'step out' of their narrative as they gain an external vision of themselves, and seemingly enter the realm of the reader. In turn, this becomes a Möbius point in Borges' poem, when the narrative momentarily disorients us as to the territory of our reading, one that keeps blurring the boundaries between characters and readers, texts and life.

One last liminal figure worth exploring at this point is Proteus. Borges writes two poems about Proteus, cited in full below, that appear in sequence in *The Gold of the Tigers* as 'Proteus' and 'Another Version of Proteus'.[31] Borges' choice of titles, as well as his placement of the two poems one after the other, surely aims at conveying the god's ability to shift form:

> Before the oarsmen of Odysseus
> would leave their mark upon the wine-dark sea,
> I can divine the indefinable forms

---

[31] Proteus also appears as a 'minimal citation' throughout Borges' prose and lectures, especially in connection with questions of identity. For a discussion of Borges as a 'literary Proteus' with a focus Platonic philosophy, see Mualem (2012: 175–208).

of that old god whose name was Proteus.
Shepherd of the wave-flocks of the waters   5
and wielder of the gift of prophecy,
he liked to make a secret of his knowledge
and weave a pattern of ambiguous signs.
At the demand of people, he took on
the substance of a lion or a bonfire   10
or a tree, spreading shade on the river bank
or water which would disappear in water.
Proteus the Egyptian should not surprise you,
you, who are one, but also many others.

    J. L. Borges, 'Proteus', *The Gold of the Tigers* (1972) (trans. A. Reid)

Inhabitant of suspicious-looking sand,
half-deity, half animal of the deep,
he lacked memory, which bends to keep
watch over yesterday and things that end.
But he was tortured by another engine   5
at least as cruel, and that was prophecy:
to know the door that shuts eternally,
the fate of the Achaean and the Trojan.
Held captive, he looks on unstable matter
in shifting forms, a tempest or a bonfire,   10
a golden tiger or a shadowy panther
or water that cannot be seen in water.
You too are made of wavering, unsure
Yesterdays and tomorrows. During, before . . .

    J. L. Borges, 'Another Version of Proteus', *The Gold of the Tigers* (1972) (trans. R. Mezey)

These poems (for convenience, henceforth abbreviated as 'P' and 'AVoP') feature a series of themes that are not only central to Borges' oeuvre, but also to his classicism. Amongst them, the most prominent are the acquisition of unreachable knowledge (P 5); the presence of signs (P 8); pre-Socratic thinking, especially in the references to water and fire as blending elements in Proteus' transformations (P 10 and 12); the interplay of no memory (AVoP 3) and prophecy (P 6); eternity as a form of reality (AVoP 7); the *Odyssey* as an ancient text that emerges between pre- and postclassical realities (P 1–2; AVoP 8); the presence of wild felines, such as panthers, tigers (AVoP 11) and lions (P 10) (an obsession throughout Borges' works); the sea, the river and water as metaphors for change (P 11–2; AVoP 12); and, finally, of course, time (AVoP 4; 15). Out of the poems encountered in the last few pages, the Proteus pieces betray Borges' closest, most direct engagement with the classics, in this case, Homer's *Odyssey* 4.351–569 and

Virgil's *Georgics* 4.387–529 and, in turn, with Virgil's own engagement with Homer.[32] Both the narrative elements and vocabulary are Homeric (and Virgilian via Homer) throughout, and it is worth noting that Borges describes Proteus as 'old' ('that old god whose name was Proteus' P 4), both in the sense of 'aged' and 'primordial', as we find Homer's calling of the god γέρων (γέρων ἅλιος νημερτὴς 4.384). As for Proteus' attributes, Borges concentrates on three: his ability to change forms; his (burdening) power to propheticize; and the fact that he lacks a memory of the past.

We have seen that, while Janus represents for Borges a metaphor for liminality itself, the two-headed god remains a fixed liminal point from which he captures 360-degree panoramic views of place and time. By contrast, Borges' Proteus represents the kind of liminality that is constantly shifting, and that can unexpectedly renew itself anywhere and nowhere at once. In that sense, Proteus has a strong point of contact with Borges' conception of Pascal's Sphere as a metaphor for centrelessness, or, more precisely, placelessness, or 'atopia'.[33] Namely, there are no territorial borders that the old god of change observes, as he recycles himself in 'indefinable' (P 3), 'suspicious' (AVoP 1), 'unstable' (AVoP 9) and 'wavering' (AVoP 13) ways from place to place, and from present to future. Proteus can also be associated with Borges' Heraclitus, as the two Protean poems substantially allude to the thinker of Ephesus, especially in terms of the reference to water ('he looks on unstable matter | in shifting forms ... [in] water that cannot be seen in water' AVoP 9–10 and 12). The constant sense of uncertainty, secrecy and blurriness in Proteus' renewable flow in both pieces gives them their mystic Heraclitean atmosphere. Furthermore, the language of weaving used in the two poems points, once more, to the textuality that has been the playground of Borges' interplay of classical myths, and which sustains the image of a crossing between realities (P 8). Like Pascal's Sphere and Heraclitus, Borges' Proteus weaves and unweaves a globalizing pattern that, in theory, endlessly charts the ever-shifting dimensions of literature, a literature that secretly exhibits Möbius effects, and potentially trains readers to decode the moments in which '(classical) myth is the beginning and end'.

---

[32] For Virgil's intertextual engagement with *Odyssey* 4. 351–569 in *Georgics* 4.387–529, see Farrell (1991: 265–6) and Morgan (1999: 201 and 219–21).

[33] One can also read this phenomenon as a 'heterotopia' in the sense that Foucault develops it, i.e. the realm where tropes, such as the library or indeed Proteus, undermine centrisms. For a study of Borges' through the lens of Foucault's heterotopia, see O'Sullivan (1990: 109–21).

Heraclitus between Chaos and Universal History

It is worth finishing this chapter with Heraclitus in Borges' late poetry. Heraclitus has been a constant presence in our study of Borges' classicism, disclosing Borges' complex conception of time and its role in our global encounters with antiquity. Through Heraclitus, Borges discloses a form of interpreting the Graeco-Roman past in one's present arguably without precedent: his Heraclitus shows us that it is not texts but *time itself* that is the measure of our receptions. Borges' Heraclitus teaches us to read time, a lesson that is initially daunting and hard to grasp, as we confront Borges' labyrinthine engagement with classical texts, but which potentially, albeit after much training, opens a wealth of interpretative possibilities. One of these possibilities is 'deep reading', in itself a metaphor for 'deep time', a phenomenon that 'places us [...] face-to-face with almost unthinkable timespans, [while confronting] us with the no less awe-inspiring *presence* of the distant past'.[34] This is one of the 'deep' themes of a sublime poem in Borges' *The Unending Rose* (1975), titled *Cosmogony*:

> No darkness or chaos. Darkness
> depends on eyes that see, just as sound
> and silence depend on hearing,
> and the mirror on the shape that settles in it.
> No space or time.   5
> Not even a divinity premeditating
> the silence prior to the first
> night of time which will be infinite.
> The great river of Heraclitus the Obscure
> has not taken its irrevocable course   10
> which flows from the past towards the future,
> which flows from oblivion to oblivion.
> There is something it already suffers. Something it implores.
> Then comes universal history. Now.
>
> J. L. Borges, 'Cosmogony', *The Unending Rose* (1975)
> (trans. L. Jansen and A. Laird)

The poem can be considered as a key expression of Borges' deep classicism. It charts no less than the temporal movement from invisible chaos to the concrete 'now' of the history of our world (14). It does so by zooming to the very moment before our cosmogony begins, a cosmogony whose temporal motor will be Heraclitus' river of time. The poem moreover evokes three contrasting ideas of time. The first is the atemporality of Chaos, where all is

---

[34] Butler (ed. 2016: 4).

eternal in the Borgesian sense, i.e. where the three tenses (past, present and future) exist simultaneously. The second is a sense of time between the atemporality of Chaos and our 'universal history', which the Borgesian narrator beautifully describes as 'the silence prior to the first | night of time' (7–8). The third idea of time is our time, which turns out to be 'irrevocable' as the course of a river (10) that will flow 'from the past towards the future' and 'from oblivion to oblivion' (11–12). Finally, a (pre)classical thinker, Heraclitus, becomes the close focus of Borges' deep reading. For, in the eyes of the Borgesian narrator, there exists in the entire universe, in the textuality of all, a Möbius-like, disorienting moment in which Chaos and the order of our world meet inexplicably to explain the depth of all, the whole plot. Borges' Heraclitus is the outstanding reader of this incalculable plot, and thus deserves a focal point in the cosmogonical narrative of Borges' poem. Once we have grasped that Heraclitean point, our reading can be constantly readjusted to other focuses in space and time, while we contemplate the fragmentation of the past in our present, remember the absences of our cultural past, while momentarily forgetting the presences that dominate our historical narratives, and imagine the afterlife of that past, one that includes the eternal realm of blissful oblivion. For Borges, this is one fruitful way of reading 'world literature', which includes our beloved classics. Most fittingly, 'Cosmogony' ends in 'universal history' (11), that 'moment' in our deep time that the Borges of the prologue to the *Conversations* with Ferrari says the peripheral Greeks of Magna Graecia organically set in motion. Their *dialogos* becomes an ever-flowing, open-ended phenomenon that still reverberates in our time:

> The best event recorded in universal history happened in Ancient Greece some 500 years before the Christian era, namely, the discovery of dialogue . . . Remote in space and time, this volume (the *Conversations with Ferrari*) is a muffled echo of those ancient conversations. (J. L. Borges, 'Prologue', *Conversations* I: ix)

This universal history, one that owes so much to the cross-cultural Greeks, then becomes the 'patient labyrinth of lines' that draws our face ('Epilogue', *The Maker*), our fuller identity, as we move to our oblivion, where we shall be somewhere closer to the whole story of our fragmentary classics. We owe this deep reading to Heraclitus and his sublime time-as-a-river metaphor, but also to Borges, whose encounter with Heraclitus transforms our own encounters with the cultural past, as well as with the mysterious atemporalities that may occur outside our Heraclitean time.

CHAPTER 6

Interlude
Borges and Global Classics

The preceding chapters have considered Borges' global classicism in tandem with Borges' larger preoccupation with the status and spaces of literature, which the author plots as a constellation landscape that spans world and universal spheres. Borges' global remapping of the territory of antiquity and its legacy in the twentieth-century imagination offers an opportunity to rethink the cultural identity of the classical canon, especially as it emerges in, and moves away from, Anglophone models of classical reception. The model of classicism found in Borges' oeuvre furthermore suggests the possibility of a more far-reaching dialogue between Classical Reception Studies and the complex question of 'world' literature that preoccupies recent work in Comparative Literature.[1] Indeed, global Classics, a research area still in need of clearer criteria and agenda,[2] emerges predominantly at the crossroads of these two fields. The discussion that follows will explore this interdisciplinary engagement with a view to raising some future research questions for the study of global Classics, as it unfolds in Borges' encounters with the Graeco-Roman past. My focus will be on the metaphors and idioms that guide Borges' global thought and the circulation of classical antiquity in his work. The discussion also aims to prepare readers for Chapter 7 on the successors of Borges' classics, who further illuminate and expand on Borges' global project and global classicism more broadly.

Global Classics and the Centreless Perspective

'That intellectual sphere, whose centre is everywhere and whose circumference is nowhere' (*SNF* 352): Pascal's sphere has offered an overarching

---

[1] Chapter 1, 20–1.

[2] Now discussed online in 'Encounters with Classical Antiquity in Latin America' (http://campuspress .yale.edu/classicalantiquityinlatinamerica/), the proceedings of a workshop organized by the Departments of Classics and Comparative Literature at Yale University under the umbrella programme, 'Humanities/Humanity' (October 27–8, 2017). One of the two central focuses of discussion of this workshop is on 'Globalizing Classical Antiquity: Future Questions'.

metaphor for exploring the centreless, non-gravitational character of Borges' global classicism, as well as for the boundlessness of the space in which classical antiquity operates in his oeuvre.[3] One of the most powerful examples of this trait in Borges' writings is Homer's multi-topographical movement from his (pre)classical identity, through his postclassical life, to his 'post-history'. Heraclitus' emergence at the crossroads of chaos and the 'world history' that his river metaphor sets in motion offers an equally powerful illustration, as do the liminal zones between self-knowledge and ignorance that Oedipus inhabits as he faces the disorienting Möbius effects of literature. These and other examples explored throughout this book confront ideas about the identity of the classics received by the cultural history of the West, especially when this identity is open to a cross-cultural reading, such as we have Borges develop at the intersection of the Western canon and twentieth-century literature of the peripheral West. It is from this cross-cultural point that Borges' classics are globalized and become subject to radical revision.

Over the last decade, Classical Reception Studies with a focus on the twentieth century have significantly expanded their areas of investigation beyond Europe and North America to include regions such as Africa and the Caribbean. These readings have been instrumental in shaping the agenda and scope of the field, as well as offering tremendous insights into the classical discourse of postcolonial and decolonial modernity.[4] By contrast, the study of classical receptions in Portuguese and Spanish Latin America has been slower to develop, and it is only recently that we are witnessing a more tangible and increasingly cohesive advancement in this area of research.[5] Awareness of Borges' classicism contributes to the overall effort to expand the study of reception to regions in Latin America and, especially, Argentina and Rioplatense literature.[6] Yet equally important is the contribution that the classicism found in Borges' work makes to the

---

[3] Chapter 1, 23–6.

[4] E.g. Hardwick and Gillespie (2007); Goff and Simpson (2007); Greenwood (2010); McConnell (2013).

[5] In this sense, my study of Borges' Classics aims to contribute to the efforts of classical scholars who seek to open up new avenues of research in the classical traditions of Latin America and their reception (e.g. Andrew Laird's major research project on Latin writing and ethnohistory in Central and Latin America; Rosa Andújar's study of Greek drama in Cuba and Puerto Rico; Moira Fradinger's forthcoming monograph for Oxford University Press's *Classical Presences* series on the Latin American tradition of adapting Antigone; and Rodrigo Gonçalves' research on anthropophagy in Brazilian classical receptions).

[6] As previously discussed, this refers to the literature produced in the region around the basin of the Río de la Plata, which includes Uruguay and Borges' Buenos Aires, as well to the Spanish language spoken in the area.

emerging field of global Classics. Here, *perspective* or, to be more precise, a stance that plots the reception of the classical past as a transcultural phenomenon that does not identify with a specific cultural centre, plays a key role. As it unfolds in his oeuvre, Borges' transcultural, non-gravitational vision opens up at least two issues for consideration in future research in global Classics. These are a need for (1) a refinement of under-standings of the interplay of centre and periphery in the formative stages of reception work on non-Anglophone cultures beyond the Western tradition and (2) a multi-perspective approach from which the periphery is con-ceived not only as a centre in its own right, but also as a centre with its own local, multi-local[7] and global preoccupations and goals.[8] These issues can be pursued even further. Borges' centreless perspective invites a rethinking of the criteria and agenda of classical reception studies that prevail in the Anglophone academic world: such a rethinking would include greater focus on multi-cultural Europe and North America, while extending the scope of the field to a truly global level. The study of global Classics should aim precisely at undertaking this kind of rethinking.

Antiquity as a Fragment

The notion of fragmentation is not unique to Borges' poetics of the classical past and its legacy, but is part of the aesthetics characteristic of modernist movements from the late nineteenth and twentieth centuries.[9] What is distinctive to Borges' poetics is his conceptualization of classical antiquity as a fragmentary phenomenon punctuated by the flow of Heraclitan time, as explored in Chapter 2. In his treatment of Heraclitus, Borges reveals a rare – even unparalleled – understanding of antiquity and its legacy: when we read the classics, we must also read time, for time is what determines how the classics renew themselves as fragmentary phe-nomena through generations, cultures and geographies. This philosophy of

---

[7] By 'multi-local', I mean the 'global' concerns of several localities from one region (e.g. the Southern Cone, the Antilles). My use of 'multi-local' here has some points of contact with Greenwood's use of 'omni-local' in her article on Reception Studies and the cultural mobility of classics (2016: 41–9).

[8] This second aim is already part the project of excellent reception studies in postcolonial and decolonial, Anglophone Africa and the Caribbean, in particular. See note 4 for examples.

[9] For a discussion of classical fragmentation in Modernism, see Goldschmidt (forthcoming 2018), whose formative ideas were first delivered at the *Deep Classics* conference at Bristol in 2014 and who recently discussed them in her keynote for the 'Modernist Fragmentation and After' Postclassicisms conference at Princeton, September 29–30, 2016 (www.postclassicisms.org/public-events/previous/modernist-fragmentation-and-after). For a full-scale study of Greek fragments in critical debates on and meta-theatrical performances of Greek tragedy, amongst other issues, between 1970 and 2005, see Ionnidou (2017).

reception is typically in tension with the impulse to recuperate antiquity fully, an aspiration which, Borges believes, can never be satisfied since the distant past is mostly buried, lacunose, ruinous, entangled and corrupted in its complex transmission. But all is not lost. Borges appeals to the notion of the *version*, that uniquely Borgesian paradigm for plotting the classical past (and all past cultures) as it re-emerges in our present, rather than as an incomplete part of a 'better whole'. To view the classics as a version, Borges insists, is a powerful experience, especially if it allows us to alter our perspective and bring antiquity into creative interaction with our imagination. Thus, Borges is fond of recreating memories for the lost classics, or the classics that exist as a minimal reference. Here, he exercises a form of reception that reinvigorates our memory of past culture, above all when the materials of this culture fail to survive and give us concrete reconstructions of its past.

Borges' conception of classical antiquity as a version constantly renewing itself in time raises an important question for the understanding of what the study of global Classics entails: as it emerges in Borges' work, global classics *is not* the study of antiquity as a universal phenomenon. It is a field that acknowledges the multiple, fragmentary and transcultural character of the classical past as it circulates and takes specific forms in different regions around the globe. It is also a field that, as has been argued above, transcends the pervading model of original and copy, so dominant in Western cultural history, to promote instead the idea that the classical tradition is ubiquitous yet uniquely manifests itself as a version through the generations. This suggests several implications about processes such as textual editing, authenticity of authorship and translation, which Borges would identify as a 'version in flux'. It is interesting that the discipline of Classics, which often deals with the mostly profoundly mediated of materials (e.g. texts transmitted in countless copies over the centuries), continues to be a discipline profoundly invested in distinguishing copy from original, in tracing back to the 'source', whether this is the lost Hellenistic source of a literary topos, the true data of an author's life or the 'original' manuscript at the bottom of the textual editor's stemma. Borges' interventions unsettle all these origin-seeking projects. We have seen that Borges' classics partake in constellations and cultural geographies in which the version-as-a process functions transculturally, as well as in tandem with a myriad of memories of other past cultures. Furthermore, his constellations invite consideration of the specifically fragmentary character of the classical object as it acquires a global impact and dimension.

Borges' Global Classicism and 'World' Literature

However fully or minimally the classics emerge before us in Borges' global thought, his classicism broadens our understanding of the place the classical canon has in 'world' literature. This is the point at which Borges' classical receptions enter in dynamic dialogue with Comparative Literature, a field that, as has been outlined in Chapter 1, has recently undergone a series of conceptual and methodological revisions as to the question of *what* world literature is and *who* gets to say what it means. In Borges' transcultural receptions, which blend the concerns of 'Western' and 'Peripheral' Classics, the classical canon coexists with other literary cultures that operate, rather mystically, on the 'world' and 'universal' level. This leads us to one of Borges' most innovative ideas: the classics not only are presences but also crucially they are *absences*.[10] It has been argued that the idea of the absent classic opens up questions about the territory of antiquity, which potentially challenge our more restrictive notions of 'world' literature. Perhaps the best example of this question is Borges' Homer, who may be interpreted as a universal version of Joyce's *Ulysses*. While Stephen Daedalus wanders the city of Dublin for a day on the stage of Joyce's experimental narrative, Borges' Homer becomes an ever-expansive canon that travels erratically through countries and centuries, acquiring multiple identities, until he reaches the climactic turning point of oblivion outside his place in history (an atemporal space which I have identified as his cultural 'post-history'). Borges' placing of the classics between world and universal categories transcends some of the reductive dimensions that many critics have attributed to world and global literature, as observed in Chapter 2.[11]

It seems doubtful that Borges ever explores these ideas to develop an intellectual preoccupation with Global Classics (or indeed the possibility of the global in any other literary cultures he includes in his work). His goal is less explicitly theoretical and more poetic: he rethinks the classics in a literary space whose landscape is no more and no less than the endless human imagination. In turn, this global project challenges the more conventional conceptions of the interplay of space and time and history and fiction. As has been shown, this idea materializes in his appeal to tragic

---

[10] In this sense, Borges' classicism prompts us to conceive of a putative companion to Lorna Hardwick and James Porter's seminal series, *Classical Presences*. 'Classical Absences' would productively emerge as an example of the possible directions that Global Classics can take when this field enters in interdisciplinary dialogue with Reception Studies and Comparative Literature, since Borges' ontology of absence betrays preoccupations shared by both disciplines.

[11] For which, see chapter 2, 36–7.

and liminal figures in Graeco-Roman myth. Here, Borges opens up his global readings to a disorienting degree at which all literature, including classical literature, has no beginning and no end. This is where antiquity becomes truly 'atopic' for Borges and can complement recent reformulations by those working at the intersection of Reception and Comparative Literature.[12] I have termed this Borgesian idea the 'Möbius effect of literature', a literature whose territorial boundaries are constantly blurred and reclaimed, whether these boundaries relate to the Western canon, or the re-appropriation of this literature on the edge of the West. While Borges never ignores these issues, he rethinks his favourite classics further and beyond these 'local' preoccupations to make his idea of literature inhabit a cultural space that blends life and the imagination, memory and oblivion. In the next, final chapter, we shall see that these formulations are innovatively reread by the successors of Borges' classicism, twentieth- and twenty-first-century writers who, like Borges, are also concerned with what the classics are, how we read them and what place they may claim as they enter the realm of 'the literatures of our world'.[13]

Global Classics vs World Studies

One last point worth discussing at this juncture is the interplay of Global Classics and the study of Classics as a discipline. Perhaps the most pressing issue with regard to the aims and scope of global Classics is that this field should not be interpreted as 'taking the classics out of Classics'. There has been some recent concern, even from the most progressive students of Classical Reception, that Classics with a global dimension could run the risk of becoming a 'World Studies' where 'Classics goes to die'.[14] My hope is to have illustrated as fully as possible that Borges' global approach does not render the classical canon moribund. Rather, it enables some of the most overstudied classical authors in the canon to thrive once more by revealing them in a light rarely observed before. A significant illustration of this practice in his oeuvre is, for instance, his reimagining of Heraclitus as an almost forgotten writer of epigrams whose collective memory exists in

---

[12] The best example of this endeavour is Brooke Holmes' Postclassicisms Network. See the public event on 'Atopia' held at the Boghossian Foundation, Brussels, on May 12–3, 2017, in which Borges' classical atopia was part of the discussion: www.postclassicisms.org/public-events/forthcoming/atopia/

[13] This contested term has emerged in recent debates, for which see Pettersson (2008).

[14] See Martindale (2010), where he reviews Page duBois' *Out of Athens: The New Ancient Greeks*, and his 'Response to Forum Debate' on the twenty years since the publication of his *Redeeming the Text* (2013).

a constellation of other cultural memories that draw coordinates between East and West, past and present, our world and oblivion. This is hardly killing the classics. It is reaching out to the classics by intimate appeal to their own culture, ideas and messages. In fact, a crucial goal of the present study of Borges' global encounters with the Graeco-Roman past has been 'to bring reception back into Classics in an integral manner'.[15] This aim involves a rethinking of the interplay of place and space, a key element in Borges' unique brand of global classicism, together with the concept of time. While Borges may present his classics predominantly in an unfamiliar, even bizarre manner, he is not interested in displacing the classics from their classical setting and context. His claim is more profound. He is not arguing that the classics do not belong to the classical world, rather that this world may be reinterpreted and equally relocated elsewhere as our memories of it become inevitably distant and fragmentary. The spatial integration of the classics in Borgesian reception is also evident in Borges' love and admiration for the Latin language, its etymologies and meanings. As he often tells his readers, he never learned Greek. Yet, for instance, his cultural geographies of the Virgilian oeuvre have a deeply philological basis. His innovation is to put Virgilian Latin in creative dialogue with elements of modernist literature, such as highly experimental narrative landscapes that combine sensory modes of recalling Virgil's classicism. The pursuit of global Classics should bear this Borgesian lesson in mind, as the field explores 'distant' classicisms that span classical philology and knowledge and the specific concerns of local adaptations of antiquity.

---

[15] As formulated by James Porter, for which see Martindale (2013: 249).

CHAPTER 7

Successors of Borges' Classicism

To a potential reader,
If the pages from this book allow an opportunity for some apt verse,
forgive me, reader, for the discourtesy of having seized it in advance
myself. Little do we differ. The circumstances that make you the
reader of these exercises and me their scribe are trivial and fortuitous.

J. L. Borges, Prologue to *Fervor de Buenos Aires* (1923)
(trans. L. Jansen and A. Laird)

Borges' modality of recalling antiquity in his oeuvre, his stances vis-à-vis
the classical past, as well as his technique for plotting the classical tradition
in space and time, have had an impact on a series of writers whose
authorships display the global quality and vision that we have found thus
far in Borges' classicism. Three names offer excellent illustrations of this
Borgesian influence: Italo Calvino (Cuba 1923–Italy 1985), Umberto Eco
(Italy 1932–2016) and Derek Walcott (Santa Lucia 1930–2017).[1] Of course,
my list could have been more extensive. Indeed, a more exhaustive survey
of the successors of Borges' classicism could fill in the pages of an entirely
new book, one that would include an understanding of the classics beyond
ancient Greece and Rome, as well as a group of internationally less known,
yet equally important, readers of Borges and antiquity worldwide.[2] I have
chosen Calvino, Eco and Walcott because, in their own distinctive ways,
and through contrasting levels of engagement with Graeco-Roman literature and culture, they offer a template for capturing the impact of Borges'
global approach to the classical past during and immediately after Borges'
life and literary career. Yet these three successors could already be studied

---

[1] For Calvino's life and literary career, see Weiss (1993: 1–8) and Perella (1999). For an excellent
introduction to Eco's career in the context of postmodern Italian writing, see Bondanella (2006). For
Walcott, I have found King (2000) and Baugh (2006) useful guides.
[2] One can think of the (literary and geo-cultural) impact of Borges' classicism on writers such as
Alberto Manguel, Ricardo Piglia, Roberto Calasso and Roberto Bolaño, amongst many other authors
whose encounters with antiquity engage with Borges' global approach.

for their own impact on subsequent writing since they offer powerful re-readings not only of Borges' classical vision, but also of mid–late twentieth-century global classicism itself.[3] Moreover, these authors are amongst the most adept readers of Borges' cultural system, bringing to light aspects of Borges' encounters with the classical past that may not be immediately apparent in our reading of Borges.[4] Furthermore, the authors selected for discussion have produced groundbreaking interpretations of both Borges' writings and the classical canon itself, in addition to their experimentation with the boundaries of fiction and criticism, for which Borges offers a generic model.[5] In considering these three successors, however, this chapter will continue to bear in mind Borges' radical revision of the notion of literary influence from antiquity to modernity, as Borges presents it in 'Kafka and his Precursors': 'The fact is that each writer *creates* his precursors. His work modifies our conception of the past, as it will modify the future' (1951: *CF* 365). If Calvino, Eco and Walcott can be considered successors of Borges' classics, Borges would remind us that they can equally be explored as writers who *re*create Borges himself, to the extent that one may be able to view his authorship and his engagement with ancient Greece and Rome in a new light, namely, one that invites us to reread Borges' classics *after* his successors.

This Borgesian notion can be taken even further by appeal to the epigraph heading this chapter. Borges writes this prefatory note in 1923 for 'a potential reader' of *Fervor de Buenos Aires*, his first publication of poems, which can be collectively explored as a foundational mythology for nineteenth-century Buenos Aires, one prior to the first wave of Southern European immigration.[6] The note betrays the kind of rhetoric of persuasion that find in Roman authors such as, for instance, the young Ovid of the *Amores*. In this collection, Ovid cleverly confounds the expectations of the readers of his edition of elegiac poems by suggesting that what they are about

[3] To my knowledge, this is an unexplored topic that could offer much food for thought in future studies of Borges and his successors. The first study of this kind, dealing with the impact of Borges in twentieth-century literature, philosophy, theory and the visual arts, is the now seminal volume by Aizenberg (1990), published soon after Borges' death in 1986.

[4] Of course, there are equally adept readers of Borges and the classics, if we take 'classics' to mean something more encompassing than the Greek and Latin canon. For instance, Alberto Manguel touches ubiquitously on Borges' 'world' classics from antiquity to modernity, and from East to West (1997, 2007 and 2010). Ricardo Piglia is to my mind the best reader of Borges and the Argentine classics, such as Domingo Faustino Sarmiento's *Facundo*, a text that Piglia reads by close reference to Borges. See Piglia (2005: 26–36).

[5] For the interplay of fiction and criticism in Borges, see Piglia (2001: 73–86 and 149–70).

[6] For the blend of modernism and local genres in this Borgesian mythology, see Olea Franco (2013: 172–8). For an excellent introduction to this collection, see Bernès (2010: 1257–70) in *ŒC*.

to read is, in fact (or fiction!), a 'second edition' of a first edition that they have never read, and possibly does not exist (*qui modo Nasonis fueramos quinque libelli | tres sumus; hoc illi praetulit actor opus | ut iam nulla tibi nos sit legisse uoluptas | at leuior demptis poena duobus erit,* 'We who were five booklets of Naso now are three; the author preferred the work this way. Now, if it is no joy to you to read us, it still is a lighter pain with two books taken away').[7] In his prefatory note, Borges is using a similar rhetorical mechanism vis-à-vis the reader – one that appeals to the reader's curiosity and desire to read the pages that follow – but with a different effect in mind. For his readers are invited to consider their roles, not simply as active audiences of *Fervor de Buenos Aires*, but also as the collection's *potential authors*. The fact that they find themselves in the role of readers instead is purely circumstantial, Borges claims. In this sense (and even if, for some of us, this gesture reads like false modesty and/or convention), Borges presents his authorial page as a locus for contestation in which poetic ideas and literature more broadly do not belong exclusively to writers who 'note them down' at a particular point in time, but also to readers who can potentially conceive of those ideas as writers. One can appreciate from the strategies found in 'Kafka and his Successors' and 'A quien leyere' (the original title of Borges' prefatory note in Spanish) Borges' innovative revision of the role of authors and readers with regard to their writings and, by implication, of the notions of precursors and successors: readers, who can also be writers, here are offered the possibility to become *co-creators* of literature and the memory of the cultural past, as well as partake in a complex inverted ontology and temporality of 'before' and 'after'.[8] The sections that follow explore Calvino, Eco and Walcott in this light, as these successors expand on Borges' approach to reading literary influence and the makings of readers and writers in space and time, and continue to develop their own, post-Borgesian engagement with Graeco-Roman antiquity.

This chapter considers these and other relevant themes from the perspective of a selection of materials in the oeuvres of the three successors. Its aim is

---

[7] Generations of scholars have been keen to read Ovid's epigram for its documentary value, and to try to reconstruct from its contents a chronological and structural reality for an *Amores* 1–5 as well as an editorial history of the *Amores* as a whole. Representative of this line of research are Cameron (1968: 320–33); Jacobson (1974: 300f.); Syme (1978: 1ff.); Murgia (1986a: 74–94) and (1986b: 203–20); della Corte (1986: 70–8); Holzberg (2006: 58–9), though see note 4. For a discussion of the absence of documentary evidence that may adequately substantiate the editorial history of the *Amores*, see McKeown (1987: 74–89). See also Hutchinson (2008: 176 and n.1) for some further thoughts on the subject.

[8] Not dissimilar to the way allusion and intertext operate in Roman poetry, as argued by Hinds (1998), for which see especially 1–16.

to focus predominantly on their literary and cultural criticism, as well as on works that blend criticism with fiction. The first part of the discussion will engage with Italo Calvino's superb essays in *Why Read the Classics?* and *Six Memos for the Next Millennium*, together with references to his *Invisible Cities* and *Mr Palomar*. It will be argued that Calvino is a close, if not perhaps the closest, successor of Borges' 'physics of reading' classical antiquity, and that certain aspects of this Borgesian mode of reading become more revealing once we approach Borges from the perspective of the Italian writer. The second section explores Umberto Eco's engagement with Borges, as well as with Borges' approach to reading the classical past and its tradition. A major point of contact between Eco and Borges is their poetics of 'everything and etcetera' which potentially situates the classics in a constellation that spans 'world' and 'universal' literature. The third and last section deals with Derek Walcott's *The Muse of History*, an outstanding piece of cultural criticism in which the author of *Omeros* (1990) interprets Borges as a sublime reader of both classical civilization and the classical tradition as a phenomenon that renews itself fragmentarily through our history. It is with Walcott that one obtains a grand image of Borges not only as a 'global classicist', but also as a 'deep reader' of the classical past.

Italo Calvino

In *Why Read the Classics?*, a collection of short essays that ranges from canonical authors from Homer, Xenophon, Ovid and Pliny the Younger, to modern 'world' classics such as Tolstoy (Russia 1828–1910), Hemingway (United States 1899–1961) and Cesare Pavese (Italy 1908–50), Calvino devotes an entire chapter to Borges, his one chosen author outside North America and Europe. While the collection is illustrative of Calvino's multiple influences, its overall feel is very Borgesian. This is evident to the avid reader of Borges, who detects in Calvino's canonical list various allusions to Borges' choice of ancient and modern writers in his *Capsule Biographies* (*SNF* 163–74), *Book Reviews and Notes* (*SNF* 175–96), *Prologues* (*SNF* 243–7; 411–8; 437–49) and *Prologues to a Personal Library* (*SNF* 511–22). Calvino's collection furthermore betrays a personal taste for and understanding of the canon,[9] as well as a vision of literature which, like Borges', is not organized by principles of originality and imitation, or

---

[9] As García Jurado rightly notes, Calvino's selection 'places Homer's *Odyssey* before the *Iliad*, Xenophon before Thucydides, and Virgil and Pliny the Elder before Cicero'. See García Jurado (2016: 201–2).

a desire to situate certain texts, typically considered 'foundational', at the heart of Western literary culture. As he moves from author to author, and from antiquity to modernity, Calvino instead is keen to disclose a series of qualities – or values – that offer thoroughly fresh insights into his classics, ancient and modern, insights that he tends to present as a constellation, rather than a genealogy of literature. The most salient of these qualities are multi-directionality and superimposed form, depths of time, mnemonics, absent presences, repetition and renewal, as well as the interplay of the senses, all of which powerfully evoke Borges' physics of reading antiquity explored in the present book.[10] By way of illustration, we need to look no further than the thematic titles of Calvino's *Six Memos for the Next Millennium*, originally written for the 1985–86 Charles Eliot Norton Lectures at Harvard, to detect a strong point of contact with Borges.[11] The five lectures included in this collection are entitled: 'Lightness'; 'Quickness'; 'Exactitude'; 'Visibility' and 'Multiplicity'.[12] They each offer highly innovative readings of the ancient and modern canon, including Calvino's outstanding observations about Lucretius' *De rerum natura*, worth citing in full:

> The *De rerum natura* of Lucretius is the first great work of poetry in which knowledge of the world tends to dissolve the solidity of the world, leading to a perception of all that is infinitely minute, light, and mobile. Lucretius set out to write the poem of physical matter, but he warns us at the outset that this matter is made up of invisible particles. He is the poet of physical concreteness, viewed in its permanent and immutable substance, but the first thing he tells us is that emptiness is just as concrete as solid bodies. Lucretius' chief concern is to prevent the weight of matter crushing us. Even while laying down the rigorous mechanical laws that determine every event, he feels the need to allow atoms to make unpredictable deviations from the straight line, thereby ensuring freedom both to atoms and to human beings. The *poetry of the invisible, of infinite unexpected possibilities – even the poetry of nothingness* – issues from a poet who had no doubts whatever about the physical reality of the world. (I. Calvino, 'Lightness', *Six Memos for the Next Millennium* (1996: 8–9) (my emphasis))

It would not be far-fetched to imagine that Borges, who died a year after Calvino and possibly never read this lecture, would have taken great delight

---

[10] For the four aspects of Borges' physics of reading, see Chapter 1, 23–6.

[11] In turn, this is another point of contact between the two authors, since Borges gave the Charles Eliot Norton Lectures at Harvard in 1967–8.

[12] Calvino managed to prepare five out of the six lectures before his death in September 1985, when his visiting lectureship was due to commence. He planned to write the last lecture on 'Consistency' at Harvard. See Esther Calvino's 'A Note on the Text' in Calvino (1996).

in every word of this passage, which stresses the light, fluid character of our material world, as it emerges in Lucretius' Epicurean reading of φύσις, or *natura*. Here, Calvino shows us not only a novel way of reading Lucretius' physics of reading the cosmos through the concept of 'lightness', but also a way of grasping his own physics of reading a classical text, one that would be of profound appeal to Borges. It has been noted that Borges feels intellectually closer to Lucretius than to Virgil ('Virgil', *Conversations* II, 2015: 241). In this instance, one can also envisage an intellectual closeness to Calvino,[13] and by implication to Calvino's Lucretius, especially when it comes to Calvino's vision of the *De rerum natura* as 'the poetry of the invisible, of infinite unexpected possibilities – even the poetry of nothingness'. For, throughout his writings, as we have seen, Borges constantly emphasizes exactly this intellectual vision of Lucretius from a contrasting yet complementary viewpoint, i.e. the partial visibility and the partial absence of the Lucretian text in historical time, as Virgil and other authors, in addition to readers' preferences, keep eclipsing its canonical presence, its *weight* as a classic. Thus, while Borges reads a spectrum of invisibility and ontological absence in the cultural history of Lucretius, Calvino plots this spectrum in the central message of Lucretius' text as 'a poetry of nothingness'. They both read the *De rerum natura* through semantic shades of the *inane*, or 'void', and through its levels of absence, invisibility and *lightness*, against the 'gravity' of other canonical texts.

The close correspondence between Calvino's and Borges's intellectual vision of the canon is also traceable in Calvino's essay on Borges in *Why Read the Classics?*, mentioned above. In this piece, seven pages long in English, Calvino touches on Borges' innovative readings of the Italian tradition, especially of Dante Alighieri (ca. 1265–1321) and Ludovico Ariosto (1474–1533). Yet the essay is more intimately concerned with the impact that Borges has on Calvino himself after the *Fictions* and *Artifices* appear in Italian and for the first time in a foreign language.[14] As Calvino describes this impact on his authorial persona, he outlines what he understands to be Borges' 'idea of literature':

> I recognize in Borges an idea of literature as a world constructed and governed by the intellect ... the discovery of Borges was for me like seeing a potentiality that had always been toyed with now being realized: seeing the

---

[13] This seems powerfully illustrated in a famous photograph of Borges and Calvino usually titled 'Calvino and Borges in Rome in 1983'. For the image, see https://bluelabyrinths.com/2015/02/25/borges-and-calvino-invisible-cities-and-dreams-invisible-cities-review/.
[14] Calvino (2009: 237).

world being formed in the image and shape of the spaces of the intellect, and inhabited by the constellation of signs that obey a rigorous geometry. (I. Calvino, 'Jorge Luis Borges', *Why Read the Classics?* (2009: 238))

This passage discloses key aspects of Calvino's globalizing vision of both Borges and his own poetics of (meta)fiction.[15] Of course, the Borges that Calvino recalls in his essay in the early 1980s, and that he first reads in the 1950s and 60s,[16] is predominantly the Borges of 'The Library of Babel', 'The Garden of Forking Paths' and other celebrated titles that begin to circulate worldwide and gain critical acclaim in the 1950s in Europe.[17] Thus Calvino's discovery of Borges is the discovery of a Borges who already is undergoing a process of globalization as a modern classic, and the reason why Calvino innovatively includes him in his list of classics already worth reading as canonical, even when Borges is still alive. It is also this version of Borges' authorship that Calvino recognizes as a potentiality in him, in Calvino the writer: 'the discovery of Borges was for me like seeing a potentiality that had always been toyed with now being realized'.[18] It is in this recognition that we can view Calvino as a powerful successor of Borges' classicism. We could perhaps take this point further by recalling Borges' note to a potential reader of *Fervor de Buenos Aires*. It is *as a reader* of Borges that Calvino detects the global qualities already at work in his vision *as a writer*.

This Borgesian vision already is at play in Calvino's first essay in *Why Read the Classics?*, entitled 'The Odysseys Within *The Odyssey*'. In this piece, Calvino explores the *nostos* to Ithaca as an approach to reading (and rereading) the multiple stories of return embedded in the *Odyssey*. With magnificent brevity, he touches on several characters in the epic who (1) know and retell the *'nostoi* to Troy', tales presented in the *Odyssey* as predating its narrative beginning, such as, for instance, the bard Phemius in the palace at Ithaca, the Proteus that Menelaus captures after disguising as a seal, and the sirens who sing to Odysseus; (2) set off in search for the

---

[15] For the generic and epistemological aspects of Calvino's 'metafiction', rather than 'fiction' (in the Borgesian sense), see Krysinski (2002: 185–204). For Calvino's emulation of Borges' narrative journeys, or 'odysseys', see Varsava (1990: 182–99).

[16] For this and other dates of production of the essays in *Why Read the Classics?*, Calvino (2009: viii).

[17] This is no mere detail. The Borges of *Fervor de Buenos Aires* and other earlier works would have not had the same qualities Calvino finds in the global Borges. We know that Borges heavily revised that publication in 1974, two years after Calvino compiles *Why Read the Classics*, as his complete works were being translated and collected for international consumption. See Bernès (2010: 1257) in *ŒC*.

[18] This experience is not unique to Calvino, but can be found in other twentieth- and twenty-first-century writers, such as the Australian novelist Peter Carey: 'You are quite right when you suggest that it might be difficult to say exactly how Borges may have influenced me, also right to suggest that the influence is/was there . . . It is there, it cannot not be there', see Ross (1990: 44).

story of *nostos* (e.g. Telemachus); and (3) are themselves experiencing the return which is being narrated to us in multiple ways, as one moves from beginning to end (i.e. Odysseus). For Calvino, recollection, or 'not forget-ting', is the principle that holds this complex narrative structure of *nostoi* in Homer's poem together, as well as the guiding principle to reading Odysseus' final return to Ithaca:

> The return must be sought out and thought and remembered: the danger is that it can be forgotten before it happens . . . Ulysses must take care [as he faces the risk of forgetting (e.g. the Lotus eaters; Circe's drugs; the Sirens' songs) in books 9–12] if he does not want to forget in an instant . . . his home, his return voyage, the whole point of his journey . . . Ulysses must not forget the road he has to travel, the shape of his destiny: in short, he must not forget *The Odyssey*. But even the bard who composes an improvised poem . . . must not forget if they want to 'tell of the return': for someone who sings poems without the support of the written text, 'to forget' is the most negative verb in existence; and for them 'to forget the return' means forgetting the epic poems called *nostoi*, the highlight of the repertoire. (I. Calvino, *Why Read the Classics?* (1999: 12–3))

A central question explored in this book is that of our collective memory of antiquity, a memory that Borges plots through the idea that the past can be either partially or fully lost, buried and eclipsed to us. Forgetting texts, and forgetting the stories they tell, is also at the heart of Borges' preoccupation with how we recuperate the memory of our past. In Borges' reworking of the *Odyssey*, for instance, Homer forgets not only his authorship, but also the story of his preclassical past, which he finally begins to remember, however faintly, after a tormenting, labyrinthine journey through errant geographies and temporalities that lead him to the moment just before his own extinction. It is on this moment when he becomes pointedly aware of his narrative past and his fame, as well as the spatio-temporal impact of his authorship, as he turns to his future in 'eternity', which paradoxically will be the location of his oblivion. In the passage cited above, Calvino stresses the importance of memory in the *Odyssey*, but from a contrasting perspec-tive: if Odysseus does not want his (literary) memory to elapse, he must keep remembering the story of his return to Ithaca – he must keep rehearsing what Calvino calls the art of not 'forgetting the future':

> On [the] theme of 'forgetting the future', I wrote a few thoughts some years ago . . . which ended: '. . . memory truly counts – for an individual, a society, a culture – only if it holds together the imprint of the past and the plan for the future, if it allows one to do things without forgetting what one wanted

to do, and to become without ceasing to be, to be without ceasing to become.' (I. Calvino, *Why Read the Classics?* (1999: 12–3))

Borges' Homer manages in the end not to 'forget the future', which ultimately means an obliteration of his past, as well as the knowledge of his imminent 'ceasing to be', as Calvino puts it. By exploring the interplay of memory and forgetfulness, Borges and Calvino thus not only elaborate on an interpretative idiom for reading themes such as the Homeric return, but also construct a cultural paradigm for thinking about the way narratives and traditions are *re*collected in time.

To return to his essay on Borges, where he explores a Borgesian potential in his authorship, Calvino considers 'the spaces of the intellect' and 'the constellation of signs that obey a rigorous geometry' as the intrinsic features that make Borges 'a classic'. These are equally dominant features in Calvino's own literary poetics, which is prone to global systems, or 'pan-globalisms', in the sense we have considered them in Borges. Perhaps the most representative example of this Borgesian influence in Calvino emerges in *Invisible Cities* (first published in Italian in 1972), a masterpiece of Italian postmodernism.[19] This text explores the imaginary geographies and complex temporalities of fifty-five cities, many of them called after classical mythological names (e.g. Isidora, Chloe, Phyllis, Berenice), and all of them ultimately alluding to the city of Venice. Calvino's overall structural organization is mathematical and follows a certain geometrical form. *Invisible Cities* is divided into nine chapters. Chapters one and nine contain ten cities each, while the rest of the chapters in between contain five cities. Each chapter begins and ends with a dialogue between Marco Polo, who describes his voyages to cities he supposedly has visited, and the emperor Kublai Khan, the first emperor of China of the Yuan Dynasty in the thirteenth century, who is keen to believe Marco Polo's 'fictions'. Each invisible city is an intellectual feast, of the kind experienced in Borges' fantastic fiction. As he moves from one imaginary city to another, the Italian merchant retells his journeys through forgotten, convoluted, multi-structured and multi-temporal urban and topographical spaces in and out of our physical world to an ageing emperor mostly interested in knowing how far his empire expands *sine fine*. This recalls Borges' own engagement with Marco Polo explored in Chapter 4. There Borges appeals to the *Travels of Marco Polo*, the thirteenth-century travelogue that records the merchant's journeys to Central Asia and China,

---

[19] Bondanella (2006).

to map out the 'Silk Road' that leads to the haptic influences of Virgil's *Georgics* and, eventually, to the emotional impact of the Virgilian oeuvre on Borges' own Buenos Aires. Similar fictional global roads, or paths, can be traced in Calvino's appeal to Marco Polo in his *Invisible Cities*, whose bizarre narrative structures and appearances powerfully resound in our memory of Borges' 'Library of Babel':

> *The library is unlimited but periodic.* If an eternal traveller should journey in any direction, he would find after untold centuries that the same volumes are repeated. (J. L. Borges, 'The Library of Babel' (1944: *CF* 118))

> The catalogue of forms is endless: until every shape has found its city, new cities will continue to be born. When the forms exhaust their variety and come apart, the end of cities begins. (I. Calvino, *Invisible Cities* (1997: 139))

In these passages, one can appreciate the deepest connections between Borges and Calvino's global vision of the space of textuality, which, as Calvino puts it, makes up a 'constellation of signs that obey a rigorous geometry'. In the case of Borges, literature, including the classics, operates in infinite spaces, though its stories are periodically repeated (hence Borges' Odyssean Homer roams the endless literary landscapes of cosmos and chaos, but his story is basically the same as Odysseus' in different forms: he is someone in search of the past to recuperate his present and understand his future). Calvino also makes use of a Platonic-inspired 'catalogue of forms which is endless', but whose stories are versions of the same idea: invisible cities that may resemble the Graeco-Roman world and other civilizations, but ultimately are about one 'ideal' city – Venice.

One final dimension in which we can consider Calvino as a successor of Borges' physics of reading antiquity emerges in Calvino's provocative reflections in *Why Read the Classics?* (1999: 3–9),[20] the essay introducing the collection under the same name and featuring important points of contact with Borges' essay 'On the Classics'. One may approach these connections either from the perspective of Calvino or Borges, as both their views on the question of the classics constantly complement each other in highly enriching ways. I begin with Borges and then follow with Calvino:

> A classic is the kind of book which a nation, a group of nations or the length of time has decided is to be read as if everything in its pages was as deliberate, fatal and profound as the cosmos, with endless room for interpretations. . . .
> A classic is not (I repeat) a book that inevitably has these or those worthy qualities: it is a book different generations of human beings, under different

---

[20] Originally published in Italian in 1981, Calvino (1999: 9).

pressures, read on a long-established impulse and with mysterious loyalty. (J. L. Borges, 'On the Classics' (1980: *OC* II: 151) (trans. L. Jansen and A. Laird))

Rarely do we encounter an attempt to define what a classic is and how it is subsequently received from such a truly universal perspective. Borges compares a classic to the cosmos and, in doing so, remains faithful to his hypothesis that the universe is like his library of Babel, the literary cosmos that contains the 'Total Book', *the* classic of all classics containing the knowledge of all, and that moves between time and no time, like Tacitus, the minor Hellenistic poets whose epigrams are lost to us, in addition to many other Babelian texts, discussed in Chapters 1 and 2. Furthermore, for Borges, 'the classic as a cosmos' is open to unpredictable interpretation and peculiar followings, as generations of readers follow this phenomenon with a quasi-religious, almost unquestionable trust ('read on a long-established impulse and with mysterious loyalty'). In this sense, Borges represents the classics as texts open to fluid interpretation, perhaps recalling Umberto Eco's notion of the *opera aperta*, the 'open work', which he develops from the viewpoint of semiotics.[21] But we can also bring a Calvinean perspective to this vision of the classics as a cosmos. It is hard not to think of each one of Calvino's own novels as micro-performances of the 'classic as a cosmos' that Borges evokes (and Eco theorizes). We can think of *Cosmicomics* (1965), which records memories of the history of the universe, and whose original book cover features Escher's famous lithographical piece 'Another World' (1947), an artist who, as it has been noted, also can be plotted as having important intellectual associations with Borges' idea of textuality and literature. Calvino's *Mr Palomar* (1983), arguably a close intertext to Borges' 'The Aleph' (*CF* 274–86), is also a telling example of a mini-classic as a cosmos. In this short novel, a man called Palomar keeps attempting the impossible – to view the totality of the cosmos as if it were a text to be read from multiple perspectives, one that includes Palomar's own vision of the self (e.g. 'Reading a Wave'; 'The Infinite Lawn'; 'The Eye of the Planets'; 'The Contemplation of the Stars'). In this sense, just as Calvino recognizes Borges as a 'classic' in his essays on canonical authors, we could envisage a Borges who may well interpret Calvino's oeuvre as a particular case study of his vision of what a classic is and how it performs in the flux of tradition.

Calvino's classics become differently globalized such that they extend, and even further define, Borges' presentation of a classic.

---

[21] Eco (1989) and originally published in Italian in 1962. For a discussion of Borges ideas of textuality and interpretation and Eco's *The Open Work* (1984), see Capozzi (2002: 165–84).

In his introductory essay in *Why Read the Classics?*, Calvino once more appeals to memory as an important factor explaining why a classic remains 'alive' in our collective consciousness:

> The classics are books that exercise a particular influence, both when they imprint themselves on our imagination as unforgettable, and when they hide in the layers of memory disguised as the individual's collective unconscious. (I. Calvino, *Why Read the Classics?* (1999: 4))

Yet it is in his final conclusions that one can trace a more powerful Borgesian presence. In a passage that recalls Borges' dialogue with Ferrari about the 'scattered conjectures' of the ancient peripheral Greeks resounding in their own conversations about literature and culture (Chapter 1), Calvino offers an outstanding vision of how a classic echoes in the distance in our modernity. In particular, Calvino invites us to view modernity also as a sound, or 'noise', that intervenes in our understanding of a classic, including the four Graeco-Roman classics (Homer, Xenophon, Ovid and Pliny the Elder) that the author includes in his *Why Read the Classics?*:

> Perhaps the ideal would be to hear the present as a noise outside our window, warning us of the traffic jams and weather changes outside, while we continue to follow the discourse of the classics which resounds clearly and articulately inside our room. But it is already an achievement for most people to *hear the classics as a distant echo*, outside the room which is pervaded by the present as if it were a television set on at full volume. We should therefore add: 13. A classic is a work which relegates the noise of the present to a background hum, which at the same time the classics cannot exist without. (I. Calvino, *Why Read the Classics?* (1999: 8))

In his *Conversations* with Ferrari, Borges makes groundbreaking statements about the manner in which antiquity, in this case ancient peripheral Greece, resounds from the distance in our present. The imagery used by Borges to describe the cultural impact of this phenomenon is suitably Lucretian:

> These scattered conjectures were the first root of what we call today, perhaps pretentiously, metaphysics. Western culture is inconceivable without these few Greeks. Remote in space and time, this volume (the *Conversations with Ferrari*) *is a muffled echo* of those ancient conversations. ('Prologue', *Conversations* I (2014: ix) (trans. J. Wilson with minor alterations) (My emphasis))

Borges here appeals to the figure of a 'muffled echo' to describe the way he and Ferrari somehow hear the Greek past. Elsewhere, Borges' classics take the shape of a 'rumour', as was Homer's experience in 'The Maker', when the old, blind poet of the *Iliad* and the *Odyssey* eventually hears distant memories of his preclassical existence. With equally Borgesian sensibility and innovation, Calvino explores the interplay of sound and the classics in his modernity. Yet, while for Calvino the classics may be heard as a 'distant echo' in the way Borges hears them, they also have the power to relegate the noise of modernity to a 'background hum'. Most creatively, Calvino invites us to visualize the 'sounds of the classics' by imagining their sonority as a phenomenon that is 'diffused', or played on a TV set. In this Calvinean sense, the Graeco-Roman classics that he engages with in *Why Read the Classics?* become 'episodes' we 'tune in' to hear, as we attempt to lower the noises of modernity that may block those of the past, but without which the classics paradoxically 'cannot exist', or emerge, as Calvino concludes. Once more, viewed as a successor, Calvino implicitly points to ways of rereading and expanding on aspects of Borges' classicism through a deeply Borgesian sensibility, one that constantly encourages us to consider the presence of the past in our own time from eccentric modes of perception.

Umberto Eco

In the work of Umberto Eco, the encyclopaedia and the catalogue become the two interrelated paradigmatic forms in his thinking about the classics and their tradition, as well as the two main dimensions in which Eco can be identified more fully as a successor of Borges' global classicism.[22] In his essay, 'Borges and My Anxiety of Influence', published in English in 2006, Eco situates his authorship in close, albeit complex, relation to Borges:

> Saying that there is no idea in Borges that did not exist before is like saying there is not a single note in Beethoven that had not already been produced before. What remains fundamental in Borges is his ability to use *the most valid debris of the encyclopaedia* to make *the music of ideas*. I certainly tried to imitate this example … What can I say? Compared with Borges' divine melodies, so instantly singable, memorable, I feel as if I blow into an ocarina. But I hope that still someone will be found after my death who is even less skillful than me, *someone for whom I will be recognized as the precursor*. (U. Eco, 'Borges and My Anxiety of Influence' (2006: 134–5) (My emphasis))

---

[22] Eco's engagement with Borgesian figures, such as mirrors and labyrinths, is extensive and may arguably be plotted as elements in Eco's classicism, though not as closely, in my opinion, as the encyclopaedia and the catalogue. For a discussion of Borgesian figures in Eco, see Capozzi (2002: 165–84), Krysinski (2002: 185–204) and Farronato (2003: 111–17). For Eco's cultural and political appropriation of the figure of Borges, see Parker (1990: 842–49).

Here, Eco's rhetoric of authorial modesty is not dissimilar to Borges' in his note to a potential reader that prefaces this chapter. The idea behind Eco's rhetoric is to play with, as Borges does, the notions of successors and predecessors and before and after. Eco presents his authorial persona as a 'less skillful' follower of Borges and his literary poetics, while simultaneously signalling his putative status as a future predecessor of an author 'less skilled' than himself. Technically, the idea behind this rhetoric is to contend that even authors of 'divine melodies', like Borges, are not original models by default, but part of the complex flow of tradition and innovation. In other words, they each become a *version* of the notion of 'successors who once were predecessors', just as someone seemingly unique like Beethoven is part of an ongoing flow of tradition in the world of classical music, and emphatically not an isolated genius. Yet Eco notes something distinctive in Borges and, by implication, in his own image as a successor of Borges. This is Borges' ability to make literature out of a clever recycling of the 'valid debris' that makes up the encyclopaedia. For Borges, the encyclopaedia is that cyclical form of ordering all disparate knowledge that exists in our tangible world, as well as notionally a structure that could potentially encompass the knowledge of all that ultimately exists but that we cannot possibly know. It is by appeal to this dual encyclopaedic structure and vision that Borges' classics operate both in and out of our space and time as 'world' and universal' literature, respectively. For Eco, this is *the* element that makes Borges' (and presumably Eco's) literary art resemble 'a music of ideas', even if Borges' music sounds like a Beethoven symphony and Eco's a tune played on 'an ocarina'. It is also this distinctive dimension of Borges' poetics that explains Eco's self-positioning in the tradition of global authors after Borges, especially in the sense that we have studied the notion of globality and global visions in the previous chapters. It will be argued that Eco's idiosyncratic classicism engages substantially with this aspect of Borges' authorship. Furthermore, like Borges, Eco appeals to the catalogue to articulate a poetics of 'everything and other things', as Eco explains it in his *Infinity of Lists*, a work that takes Homer's Catalogue of Ships in the *Iliad* as its central, though not exclusive, cue.[23]

It is worth pausing momentarily at this point to argue that Eco's Borges is predominantly the 'late Borges'. In the case of Calvino's Borges, one finds that the Borges who exerts an influence on the author of *Invisible*

---

[23] Eco (2009: 7). Other classical models explored by Eco are, amongst many others, the Shield of Achilles in Homer, *Iliad* 8, which Eco explores as a model attempting to represent the structure of 'everything' in our cosmos, Virgil's attempt to list all the types of grapes that exist in *Georgics* 2.157, and Aristotle's classifications of the physical world by appeal to the telescope.

Cities is the writer who is undergoing a process of globalization as a modern classic during the 1950s and 60s. While this version of Borges is present in Eco, Eco tends to engage much more with the image of the blind, consecrated author in his late seventies and early eighties.[24] This is the Borges who has become truly global and now is critically acclaimed world-wide as a 'literary philosopher'. In other words, Eco's Borges is a more idealistic, in the Platonic sense, version of Calvino's globalizing Borges.[25] The early pages of Eco's celebrated novel *The Name of the Rose* feature a mildly burlesque version of this Borgesian image. Here, one of the two central characters, the Franciscan friar William of Baskerville, sees for the first time an old, blind monk in charge of the monastery's library. His name is Jorge of Burgos:

> We turned. The speaker was a monk bent under the weight of his years, an old man white as snow, not only his skin, but also his face and his pupils. I saw he was blind. The voice was still majestic and the limbs powerful, even if the body was withered by age. He stared at us as if he could see us, and always thereafter I saw him move and speak as if he still possessed the gift of sight. But the tone of his voice was that of one possessing only the gift of prophecy.
>
> 'The man whom you see, venerable in age and wisdom,' Malachi said to William, pointing out the newcomer, 'is Jorge of Burgos. Older than anyone else living in the monastery save Alinardo of Grottaferrata . . .' (U. Eco, *The Name of the Rose* (2014: 85))

Eco's Burgos has been interpreted as a 'mirror inversion' of Eco's Borges.[26] This is partly right. For, on a basic level of interpretation, Borges cannot possibly be the equivalent of the fictional Burgos, a lone, medieval librarian who turns out to be a villain and the murderer in the complex plot of Eco's crime novel. On another level, however, both Borges and Burgos feature a series of interesting similarities. Aside from a physical likeness to Borges,

---

[24] In fact, this is predominantly the Borges who appeals to late twentieth- and twentieth-first-century writers worldwide. See, for instance, Don DeLillo's conception of Borges as a source of inspiration in his daily writing routine: 'A writer takes earnest measures to secure his solitude and then finds endless ways to squander it. Looking out the window, readings random entries in the dictionary. To break the spell, I look at the photograph of Borges, a great picture sent to me by Irish writer Colm Tóibín. The face of Borges against a dark background – Borges fierce, blind, his nostrils gaping, his mouth amazingly vivid . . . he's like a shaman painted for visions, for the whole face has a kind of steely rapture. I've read Borges of course, although not nearly all of it, and I don't know anything about the way he worked – but the photograph shows us a writer who did not waste time at the window or anywhere else. So I've tried to make him my guide out of lethargy and drift, into the otherworld of magic, art and divination', Begley (1993: 128).

[25] For Borges and Eco (and Calvino) as 'literary philosophers', see Gracia, Korsmeyer and Gasché (eds. 2002: 1–14).

[26] de Lailhacar (1990: 155–6).

as well as the Borgesian sense of intellectual aura that Eco gives to his
Burgos, one particular connection between the two is biographical, since
Borges was director of the National Library in Buenos Aires from the mid-
1950s to the early to mid-70s. Characterization also shows a point of
contact between Eco's Burgos and Borges' 'global' librarians. One can
think of Eco's enigmatic Burgos as an allusive reference to the librarians in
the hexagons in Babel. As is the case with those librarians, Burgos is not
portrayed as holding the key that unlocks total textuality. Yet, he nevertheless is presented as a character equipped with the methodologies that
would allow him to tackle global readings of Babel's 'Total Book', which
contains knowledge of all. As a lover of a genre that blends the philosophical and fantastic with the detective novel, Borges would have enjoyed
Eco's humorous, dark version of his own image deeply. Yet in his postscript
to *The Name of the Rose*, Eco prefers not to make too meaningful an
association between Borges and his Burgos, especially when it comes to
the central plot of his novel:

> Everyone asks me why my Jorge, with his name, suggests Borges, and why
> Borges is so wicked. But I cannot say. I wanted a blind man who guarded
> a library (it seemed a good narrative idea to me), and a library plus blind
> man can only equal Borges, also because debts must be paid ... But when
> I put Borges in the library I did not yet know he was the murderer. He
> acted on his own, so to speak. (U. Eco, *Reflections on The Name of the Rose*
> (1994: 27–8))

Narratologically speaking, this surely is the case. However, it would be
hard for the author of *Opera aperta* to deny his readers the possibility of
plotting a more intimate connection between Borges and Burgos, even if
the same readers do not forget that Burgos belongs to the sphere of fiction.
It has been suggested that one way of plotting Burgos in connection with
Borges is as a global reader. Namely, a reader with a deep understanding of
cultural phenomena spanning space and time. As in Borges' parable of
Cervantes' *Quixote*, this Burgos betrays knowledge of 'the tissue of the
whole plot', i.e. the Borgesian vision of 'world' literature through the lens
of the Möbius strip, which blends together the lives of authors with their
myths, as well as the physical with the metaphysical to project totalizing
moments in which we may catch a (disorienting) glimpse of 'universal
literature' (cf. Chapter 5, 107–110). On a narrative and character level,
Burgos knows from the outset the whole plot that forms Eco's narrative
cosmos, since he is represented as the internal 'Ecoean' author of the grand
crime that organizes the story as a whole. On another level, and when one

focuses on Burgos as the monastery's librarian, the associations with Borges are powerful.

One can imagine Burgos as a reader of the classics in the Babelian cosmos in which his medieval library is situated. Like the librarians of Borges' Babel dwelling in hexagonal libraries, Burgos putatively has a global understanding of textuality that allows him to deduce that lost texts *per excellence*, like Tacitus', or the forgotten Heraclitus of *The Greek Anthology*, exist somewhere in the utopian shelves of the eternal library. Like Borges, the fictional Burgos very possibly has no access to these forever-lost texts. At least not in the way the 'Man of the Book' does as 'director' of the Eternal Babel. What he has is an *encyclopaedic perspective* of what that universal literature may be like or contain, i.e. a potential vision of the whole plot in which the ancient Graeco-Roman world coexists in and out of our world as a constellation of extant materials and lost cultural memories. The key difference between Borges and Burgos must be what they would make of this global vision, what uses they would give to it, since one is a murderer in fiction and the other a modern world classic, as announced by Calvino. What seems attractive about this series of speculations is that Eco's Burgos can be understood as a successor of Borges' global approach, even though Burgos makes use of this approach to commit a crime in Eco's novel. Borges would have made a great short fiction out of this diabolic idea.

Borges' encyclopaedic approach continues to be a constant presence and guiding principle in the organization of Eco's late, non-fictional works such as *On Beauty* (2004) and *On Ugliness* (2007), two interrelated volumes that represent Eco's core aesthetics and cultural poetics. *On Beauty* and *On Ugliness* ubiquitously situate the Graeco-Roman classics in a network that marks various coordinates between the present and the past. Both books are highly visual, encouraging readers to trace an understanding of how beauty and ugliness are conceived in the history of Western ideas, in the way Borges does, for instance, in his treatment of the canonical Virgil and his cultural impact on Western history and aesthetics. It would require more than a chapter to explore these works by Eco alone, as well as the substantial inspiration they draw from Borges and his classicism. Yet one example from *On Beauty* offers a powerful illustration of how Eco's modality of plotting the classics exhibits important points of contact with Borges'.

In this book, Eco introduces a series of 'Comparative Tables' prefacing the seventeen chapters that follow, many of which engage with classical aesthetics, philosophy and science (e.g. Chapter 1, 'The Aesthetic Ideal in

Ancient Greece'; Chapter 2, 'Apollonian and Dionysiac'; Chapter 3, 'Beauty as Proportion and Harmony').[27] Eco's comparative tables invite us to appreciate manifestations of beauty in visual art as versions that cyclically renew themselves from preclassical antiquity to Eco's modernity. These manifestations of beauty include Venus, Adonis, the Madonna, Jesus, Kings and Queens. One comparative table follows 'Venus Nude', from a miniature statue from the thirteenth millennium BC ('Venus of *Willendorf*) and the 'Venus of Milo' dating back to the second century BC, through the Venus of Botticelli ('The Birth of Venus', circa 1482) and Manet ('Olympia', 1863), to photographs of Brigitte Bardott in 1965 and a nude Monica Bellucci in 1997 for a *Pirelli Calendar*. While the beauty of 'Venus Nude' is represented in chronological order for the viewer, the intention behind the display of Aphrodite's beauty is not to mark a beginning and end in the cultural history of the naked goddess, nor to contend that the calendar image of Monica Bellucci is a popular 'copy' of the 'original' eroticism found in the small figure of the 'Venus of Willendorf' from the thirteenth millennium BC. On the contrary, the tables of the naked Venuses are emphatically comparative in their visual arrangement, inviting viewers to draw connections freely, and to add further examples to the temporal layout that organizes Eco's presentation at whichever point they wish.[28] Eco's idea is to represent the beauty of naked Venus in visual art as an *ongoing version* that potentially strives towards – but cannot possibly achieve – an encyclopaedic vision of this phenomenon, which Eco can only possibly represent as a fragment. In Eco's case, the cultural fragment of a putative 'Venus Nude Whole' that he presents in his table is but a chapter, or a mini-cosmos of its Western manifestation and impact. Namely, his 'Venus Nude' is an instantiation of a cultural list whose very logic is open-ended. This idea evokes Borges' *ad infinitum* poetics of reading cultural systems, as well as his open attitude towards the global character and reach of his classical examples.

The catalogue, another paradigmatic mode of structuring knowledge that fascinates Borges for its infinite character and possibilities, is a constituent element in Eco's conceptualization of the encyclopaedia and its scope. As with his study of beauty and ugliness, Eco's exploration of the catalogue includes – and is substantially informed by – classical antiquity, as well as by Eco's understanding of the place of the classics in

---

[27] Eco (2004: 16–35).
[28] As we shall see below, Eco's encourages this kind of participation in his treatment of lists.

Borgesian poetics (one needs to think no further than Borges' attempt to a universal catalogue from 'the detailed history of the future', through 'the translation of every book in every language', to 'the lost books of Tacitus' in 'the Library of Babel', *CF* 115). In his preface to *The Infinity of Lists* (2009), Eco reads the classics as part of a cultural history that could potentially develop *ad infinitum* and thus out of control, at least within the graspable sphere of historical time. As with other prefaces and post-scripts by Eco, Borges emerges as an important example and influence when it comes to this topic. It is worth citing Eco's prefatory remarks almost in full, since they articulate a final point worth stressing about Eco as a successor of Borges' classicism. Namely, the manner in which Borges inspires Eco's global vision of classical literature by appeal to a 'poetics of everything included' and of 'etcetera':

> If anyone were to read my novels he would see that they abound with lists ... between litanies and the list of things contained in the drawer of Leopold Blooms' kitchen in the penultimate chapter of (Joyce's) *Ulysses* there stand a good number of centuries, and many more centuries again stand between medieval lists and the model list par excellence: the catalogue of ships in Homer's *Iliad*, from which this book takes its cue. It is also in Homer that we find the celebration of another descriptive model: the one ordered and inspired by the criteria of harmonious completion and closure represented by Achilles' shield. In other words, already in Homer it seems that there is a swing between a poetics of 'everything included' and a poetics of 'etcetera'.
>
> While this was already clear to me, I had never set myself the task of making a meticulous record of the infinite cases in which the history of literature (from Homer to Joyce to the present day) offers examples of lists, even though names such as Perec, Prévert, Whitman and Borges all come to my mind straight away. The result of this hunt was prodigious, enough to make your head spin, and I already know that a great number of people will write to ask me why this or that author is not mentioned in this book. The fact is that not only am I not omniscient and do not know a multitude of texts in which lists appear, but even had I wished to include in the anthology all the lists I gradually encountered in the course of my explora-tion, this book would be at least one thousand pages long, and maybe even more.
>
> In conclusion, the search for lists was a most exciting experience not so much for what we managed to include in this volume as for all those things that had to be left out. What I mean to say, in other words, is that this is a book that cannot but end with an etcetera. (U. Eco, *The Infinity of Lists* (2009: 7))

One can appreciate from these remarks the degree to which Eco's study of the list is both classicizing and Borgesian. Eco's formulation of the catalogue subscribes closely to Borges', especially in terms of how it operates structurally and to what effects. Chapter 2 and passim discussed how Borges catalogues the classics and other literatures as cultural items illustrating certain phenomena, and how, while his listings have their own narrative beginnings and ends, he presents their dimensions as potentially incalculable. This was the case of Borges' 'infinite catalogue of authorities' dealing with the philosophical notion of eternal repetition, a list that gravitated heavily around antiquity, from Heraclitus and Hesiod, to early Virgil, Seneca and Marcus Aurelius (Chapter 2, 37–40). In *The Infinity of Lists*, Eco's 'gravitating classic' is the *Iliad* and its Catalogue of Ships in Book 2. In this narrative Homer aims to give a sense of the enormous scope of the Greek army in relation to the increasingly terrified Trojans coming under external attack. Yet Eco does not exactly appeal to Homer's catalogue as *the* foundational model for his study of all catalogues. In his preface, Eco points out that this is where he takes his 'cue', since the phenomenon of listing is 'already' an idea in practice in Homeric literature. What interests Eco is the structural character of the Homeric catalogue. The catalogue, Eco argues, offers a classical example of a physical infinity, one that 'in fact ... does not end, nor does it conclude', but that can continue to increase to unimaginable proportions.[29]

Eco's exploration of the list is furthermore represented as a 'hunt', i.e. a search that ultimately is open to chance and circumstances outside his knowledge and calculation ('The fact is that not only am I not omniscient and do not know a multitude of texts in which lists appear'). In fact, and in connection to this image of wilderness, one can envisage Eco's study of the infinity of lists, and especially of their complex proliferation, by appeal to the image of *silvae* that Borges uses to characterize the compilation of his poetry, an eclectic cosmos that owes much to his engagement with Graeco-Roman myth (Chapter 5). This conceptualization of the interplay of clear enumeration and an increasing blurring sense of infinity is not dissimilar, one may add, to Catullus' attempt to count the endless number of kisses that he will give Lesbia as they both become confused in their passion in Catullus 5 (*dein, cum milia multa fecerimus | conturbabimus illa, ne sciamus* 10–1, 'Then, when we have made many thousands, we will mix them all up, so that we don't know'). Eco, like Borges and Catullus, also articulates the

---

[29] Eco (2009: 17).

tension between infinite potential and mathematical impossibility in his understanding of the catalogue: 'the result of this hunt was prodigious, enough to make your head spin ... even had I wished to include in the anthology all the lists ... this book would be at least one thousand pages long, and maybe even more', as Eco puts it. What fascinates Eco is also a source of fascination for Borges. For both authors, it is not exactly what can be included in their lists – or in the encyclopaedic debris that form their literatures – but what cannot be included (cf. 'the search for lists was a most exciting experience not so much for what we managed to include in this volume as for all those things that had to be left out'). Perhaps this is *the* place where Eco's classicism blends with Borges' in highly complementary ways, namely, in the appeal to the classics to expound a poetics of 'all and more'. Compare, as a way of final illustration, both authors' use of Homer to express their aesthetics of enumeration and infinity as they come to a narrative closure in their own texts:

> Already in Homer it seems that there is a swing between a poetics of 'everything included' and a poetics of 'etcetera'. (U. Eco, *The Infinity of Lists* (2009: 7))

> I have been Homer; soon like Ulysses, I shall be Nobody; soon, I shall be all men. (J. L. Borges, 'The Immortal', *The Aleph* (1949: *CF* 194))

> Perhaps there was no single Homer; perhaps there were many Greeks whom we conceal under the name of Homer. (J. L. Borges, 'Blindness' (1977: *SNF* 479))

For Eco and his Argentine predecessor, all our literature, all our knowledge, whether it be conveniently identified as 'classical', 'medieval' or 'modern', is but a fragmentary list that cannot but follow the logic of 'etcetera'. It is through this logic, Borges would add, that both the cultural 'stories' of literature can be plotted and envisaged in terms of world presences and universal absences, recuperation and loss, knowledge and ignorance. Homer's distinctive status within this plotting of literature's histories suggests why his catalogue of ships serves as a paradigmatic matrix for grasping Eco's classicism and for rethinking Borges' classics from the perspective of his successor.

Derek Walcott

The last author in this chapter's catalogue of successors of Borges' classicism is Derek Walcott. Walcott's case as a successor is quite different from Calvino's and Eco's. Like Borges, Walcott appeals to antiquity, and especially to Homer (*Omeros*, 1990 and *The Odyssey: A Stage Version*, 1993),[30] to articulate questions such as how notions of historical temporality, hybridity and innovation have played a culturally defining role in the tradition and reception of the Western European canon in his national literature.[31] Yet Walcott's 'Caribbean Classics'[32] do not distinctively, or more immediately, betray a Borgesian poetics, not at least in the way they do in Calvino and Eco. When it comes to Walcott, it is rather in his profile as a critic of postcolonial literature of the New World that he emerges as a follower of Borges' global classicism or, more precisely, as a keen observer of how Borges' engagement with ancient Greece and Rome forms part of the network and intellectual power of Borges' cultural system.

One way to begin thinking about these issues is to trace Walcott's connections with Borges in Walcott's literary career, as well as the extent to which Walcott's vision can be understood to be Borgesian. We know that Walcott met Borges on public occasions, and it is striking that Borges was in the audience when Walcott delivered his 1971 lecture on 'The Muse of History', which considers the Argentine author's mode of experiencing history and past civilizations, including the classical.[33] Details of Walcott's biography and career furthermore indicate that he became increasingly interested in the literature of South America,[34] and that he felt an urgent sense of 'fraternity' with poets such as Borges and Neruda, as he began to distance himself

[30] Beyond Homer, Walcott's classical presences variously emerge throughout his poetic oeuvre, from *Origins* (1964) to *White Egrets* (2010). For discussions of Walcott and Rome and Walcott's translation of empire, see Greenwood (2009: 255–74) and (2010: 165–82), respectively. I am grateful to Emily Greenwood for discussing Walcott's oeuvre and classicism with me.

[31] As we have seen in our discussion of Borges' 'The Argentine Writer and his Tradition' (1951: *SNF* 425–26) in Chapters 1, 15 and 3, 72–3. For a discussion of these issues in Walcott, see McConnell (2013: 107–54).

[32] I look forward to Justine McConnell's forthcoming study of Walcott's classics, provisionally entitled 'Derek Walcott: A Caribbean Classical World', for Bloomsbury's *Classical Receptions in Twentieth-Century Writing* series. For a discussion of Caribbean Classics and the postcolonial canon, see Greenwood (2010).

[33] E.g. at the International Congress of Poets in Berlin, September 22–27, 1964, where Walcott talked with J. P. Clark, Wole Soyinka, Césaire, as well as meeting Auden and Borges, and at a 1971 conference at Columbia University on April 12–14, which Borges attended and at which Walcott delivered the lecture which was subsequently published as 'The Muse of History'. See King (2000: 202 and 269, respectively).

[34] E.g. in his meeting with Walcott in Trinidad in December in 1966, Selden Rodman gave Walcott a copy of *South America of the Poets*, which includes conversations with Borges and Neruda. See King (2000: 230).

from 'the great tradition' of English literature.[35] One telling example of Walcott's affinity with both Borges and his poetic sensibility can be found in 'Poem VI' of Walcott's *Midsummer* collection, published in 1984, whose contents blend politics with geography, geopoetics and the data of senses in a manner that recalls elements of Borges' haptic poetics and transcultural classicism discussed in Chapter 4 and Chapter 5, respectively.[36] In 'Poem VI', Borges, Buenos Aires and the allusive background of popular revolution and military coups in the Argentina of the mid-50s and 70s[37] inform Walcott's experience of both Port of Spain in Trinidad, where he moved in 1953,[38] and his city's turbulent times:[39]

> The Capitol has been repainted rose, the rails
> round Woodford Square the colour of rusting blood.   5[40]
> Casa Rosada, the Argentine mood,
> croons from the balcony.[41] Monotonous lurid bushes
> [. . .]
> In Belmont, mournful tailors peer over the old machines,   10

[35] 'Claiming these common archetypal forms facilitated a dialectic of abrogation and reincorporation in the 1970s when [Walcott] strategically distanced himself from the "Great Tradition" of English literature as the unique influence on his artistic sensibility and laid claims to a nascent literary fraternity which he called in the Sunday Guardian Magazine "the comradeship of Guillen, Borges and Neruda."' Derek Walcott, 'West Indian Art Today', *Sunday Guardian Magazine*, May 8, 1966, 8, cited by McDermott (2013: 57).

[36] *Midsummer* started as an epistolary collection, in dialogue with Joseph Brodsky, and comprises 54 poems – one for each year of Walcott's life, written at the midlife (midsummer point). It is interesting that the dense classical allusions in many of the poems in *Midsummer* and the poems' wide geographical range are subordinated to this private chronological scheme. See, especially, 'Poem II', with the references to Rome and Brodsky's Roman Elegies ('like those of Ovid'). See Breslin (2001: 224–31).

[37] It is not certain to which Argentine revolutionary climate Walcott may be alluding. His references to the Casa Rosada, the 'Argentine mood' and 'croons from the balcony' could refer to either the Revolución Libertadora of 1955 in Argentina, in which a military and civilians uprising ended Juan Domingo Perón's second government on September 16, or the role Montoneros played as an armed revolutionary in the early- and mid-1970s during Perón's last government and the military junta formed in March 1976.

[38] For an overview of Trinidad as Walcott's 'second home' and the place where he develops his career as a professional writer, see King (2000: 161–264).

[39] Walcott's allusions to violence, blood, horror and mourning are politically oblique and generalized references to the Black power movement and waves of social unrest in Trinidad in 1970, which resonated throughout the 70s.

[40] These lines correspond to the line number in the whole poem.

[41] Poem VI is a revised version of an earlier poem in *The Fortunate Teller* (1981) entitled 'Port of Spain'. While the earlier version refers to Borges and Buenos Aires in the last lines, it does not refer explicitly to Argentine politics and the Casa Rosada but, rather, to the revolutions of Latin American politics. Compare lines 4–7 in 'Port of Spain' with the equivalent lines in 'Poem VI' cited above: the capitol has been repainted rose, the rails round the parks the colour of rusting blood; *junta* and *coup d'état*, the newest Latino mood, broods on the balcony.

stitching June and July together seamlessly.
[. . .]   I can understand   25
Borges's blind love for Buenos Aires,
how a man feels the streets of a city swell in his hand.
                    'Poem VI', *Midsummer* (1984: 16) (trans. Farrar, Straus and Giroux)

These lines can be plotted further beyond Walcott's explicit association
of the Red House in Port of Spain's Woodford Square, where parliament
is situated near the Trinidad Cathedral, with the 'Casa Rosada' (6), the
executive office of Argentine government, located in Plaza de Mayo and
facing to its right the Catedral Metropolitana de Buenos Aires. On closer
inspection, the poem points to deeper connections between the two
authors and their poetic expression which are suggestive of how
Borgesian Walcott can be, even if Walcott tends to emerge as a more
explicitly political writer than Borges. It is significant that in this piece
Walcott primarily interprets the world around him in a manner that is
close to Borges' approach explored throughout the present book, especially when it comes to the topic of time and the senses. Note, for
instance, the following Borgesian traits in Walcott's vision of Port of
Spain: (1) as if he were a blind Borges ('I can understand | Borges' blind
love for Buenos Aires', 25–6); (2) through his insistence on sound as an
alternative vehicle to grasping his experience of Trinidad (and Buenos
Aires) by senses other than ocular vision ('croons from the balcony', 7;
'the barks of a revolution's crying wolf', 20); (3) during a summer period
that is articulated as a continuous, even monotonous, phenomenon, with
no clear temporal separation of the month of June from the month of July
('stitching June and July together seamlessly', 11); and (4) through the
symbolic significance of colour (red and rose [4 and 5]; orange [16 in the
complete poem]; and yellow, so predominant in Borges' oeuvre [22 in the
complete poem]) in the poem's visualization of power, violence, mood
and extreme heat.

Perhaps most significantly, 'Poem VI' closes with an explicit reference
to Borges and the streets of Buenos Aires as analogues for the metaphorically haptic experience of a 'blind Walcott' and the streets of Port
of Spain swelling in his hand. Here, Walcott's representation of his
'hand touch' in tandem with a geographical location powerfully evokes
Borges' haptic readings of Virgil's hand and its role in Borges' transcultural geographies of Virgil's cultural memory. Indeed, Walcott's appeal
to Buenos Aires, a city not immediately known for its exchanges with
Port of Spain and Trinidad more widely, recalls the type of syncretism
practised by Borges in his comparisons of literatures and cultures with

limited or no connections at all. Furthermore, Walcott's syncretic comparison of Port of Spain with Buenos Aires can be understood as a constituent aspect of his decentred vision of Trinidad and Tobago's capital, its culture and political history, one that recalls Borges' readings of, for instance, Buenos Aires and Geneva. One could argue that the poetics of 'Poem VI' is representative of Walcott's Caribbean and New World postcolonial modernism.[42] Yet the specific Argentine allusions are pointed in the piece, and support an explicit engagement with the work, poetic thought and situation of Borges, as evoked at the end of the poem.

The fragmentary character of the past, the forms of disclosure of antiquity in our present and the deep, lateral understandings of history that are found in Borges' global classicism also are central to Walcott's cultural system. These facets of Walcott's poetics run through Walcott's oeuvre, from *Origins* (1964), through *Omeros* (1990) to *White Egrets* (2010), yet they emerge more explicitly in two pieces of cultural criticism: his 1971 lecture at Columbia University, entitled 'The Muse of History' and his 1992 Noble lecture, entitled 'The Antilles: Fragments of Epic Memory', both of which are included in *What the Twilight Says.*[43] In his Heraclitean receptions of Caesar (Chapter 2), Borges shows a keen interest in how antiquity renews itself in modernity, and how the plots of literature and life that keep recurring in different, often unexpected, forms put antiquity and modernity into fruitful dialogue. It is precisely this facet of Borges' intellectual vision that Walcott understood perfectly well and thought to be revolutionary, if one takes this attribute to mean something more inclusive than its usual socio-political dimensions and implications, in his literary criticism. This is one of the central themes in Walcott's 'The Muse of History', a deeply personal essay concerned with the question of how colonized nations in America have reacted to, and even rejected, the literatures of their European colonizers. In response to this question, Walcott appeals to another sense of history and the literary tradition, one typically found in the artists and thinkers of the New World. This includes seemingly isolated literary figures like St-John Perse, Whitman, Neruda and, of course, Borges, who prefer to plot their modernity, not in terms of the

[42] For this aspect of Walcott's poetics and its contrasts with Kamau Brathwaite's (Barbados, 1930–), see Pollard (2004: 30–7).
[43] For which see www.nobelprize.org/nobel_prizes/literature/laureates/1992/walcott-lecture.html. The lecture has also been included in *What the Twilight Says* (Walcott 1998: 65–84).

oppressive perpetuation of colonial ideals (though their oeuvres show a deep awareness of this question), but as a complex reconfiguration of the past and its traditions:

> The great poets of the New World, from Whitman to Neruda, reject this sense of History [which posits that New World history is a tragedy and the New World a form of perpetuation of colonial ideals]. Their vision of man in the New World is Adamic. In their exuberance, he (sc. the Adamic figure) is still capable of enormous wonder. He has paid his accounts to Greece and Rome and walks in a world without monuments and ruins. They exhort him against the fearful magnet of older civilizations. Even for Borges, where the genius seems secretive, immured from change, it celebrates an elation that is vulgar and abrupt, the life of the plains given an instant archaism by the hieratic style. Violence is felt with the simultaneity of history. So the death of a gaucho does not merely repeat, but is, the death of Caesar. This is not jaded cynicism which sees nothing new under the sun, it is an elation that sees everything as renewed. Like Borges, too, the poet St.-John Perse conducts us from the mythology of the past to the present without a tremor of adjustment. This is the revolutionary spirit at its deepest [...] What Perse glorifies is not veneration but the perennial freedom; his hero remains a wanderer, the man who moves through the ruins of great civilizations [...] the poet carrying entire cultures in his head [...] His are poems of massive or solitary migrations through the elements. (D. Walcott, 'The Muse of History' (1998: 37–8))

Perhaps with the exception of authors such as Alberto Manguel,[44] rarely has a reader of Borges been so incisive in their understanding of the role that the Graeco-Roman classics play in Borges' cultural outlook as Walcott has. There are various aspects to Walcott's interpretation, all of which point to Borges (and Walcott) as practitioners of a 'deep reading' of classical antiquity, of the kind that has been recently explored in *Deep Classics*, a volume fully dedicated to rethinking reception as a *lateral*, rather than a chronologically linear, process of reading the cultural past.[45] In the passage cited above, Walcott plots Borges as an Adamic reader of civilizations, who wanders through the history of our cultures paying homage to them, while never fully gravitating too closely to any one of them in particular ('They exhort him against the fearful magnet of older civilizations'). It is in this

---

[44] Manguel is a complex example of a successor of Borges' classicism since, despite dealing with Homer in his books about the history of reading, his idea of the classics is more broadly defined to include 'word' classics. This is the subject of my next project on Borges. See note X in this chapter.

[45] Butler (ed. 2016: 1–3) prompted by Manguel's approach to reading Homer (2007).

context that ancient Greece and Rome emerge in Walcott's portrayal of Borges – as an Adamic reader who privileges a vision of antiquity as universal yet centreless and non-gravitational ('He has paid his accounts to Greece and Rome and walks in a world without monuments and ruins'). This kind of reader does not attempt to plot ancient Greece and Rome by focusing on their 'monuments and ruins', i.e. by recalling a nostalgic sense of loss of an 'original' classical world now eroded or lost. Instead, Walcott understands Borges (and Neruda and St-John Perse) to view cultural phenomena as ongoing versions that present us with stories of the past that have no beginning or end, and that constantly retell themselves through the generations and across geographies in an inconstant form and manner. Here lies the revolutionary logic of Borges' global encounters with the classical past, as acutely identified by Walcott: for Borges, antiquity is no more and no less than an ongoing part of a whole that one can imagine and reimagine, but that one will never get to know in its full scope. The alternative to this impossibility of acquiring full knowledge may be to reposition ourselves in such a(n Adamic) way that we witness its renewal in multiple combinations.

Walcott captures this Borgesian logic perfectly. As he puts it in his essay, while Borges may appear as a 'secretive [genius], immured from change', his outlook is by no means the result of a 'jaded cynicism'. Like Perse, Borges betrays a 'revolutionary spirit at its deepest', one that opens up the classical world to a radical revision. Hence, Walcott tells us, Borges' recasting of a gaucho as a near-contemporary, Argentine Caesar is emphatically not the product of a dispassionate form of reception, but the celebration of 'an elation that is vulgar and abrupt' and by which 'the life of the plains [is] given an instant archaism by the hieratic style'. It is in this sense that Walcott presents Borges as a reader who wanders through great civilizations while bearing 'entire cultures' in his literary imagination. This is how the author of 'The Library of Babel' keeps 'see[ing] everything as renewed', including ancient Greece and Rome, through an oblique, albeit highly complex, vision of the whole. Yet, for Borges, such a world-vision can be no more than partial – a version of multiple recurring phenomena that forms our cultural memory and presences.

Indeed, Walcott's Adamic world-perspective bears in mind the tensions at the heart of the interplay of whole and fragmentation, as well as centre and periphery that constantly preoccupy Borges. In 'The Antilles: Fragments of Epic Memory', one notices Walcott's keen concern with fragments and how his take on classical and epic pasts at the intersection of different global cultures is relevant for the study of Borges' classical absent-presences, as well as geopoetical and geopolitical traditions that decentre Europe, and which are central to Borges' approach to the classical world. Walcott opens his discussion with a description of Felicity, a village with a mostly East Indian population in Trinidad. At the time that the author visits Felicity, the village was preparing the performance of *Ramleela*, an 'epic dramatization of the Hindu epic the *Ramayana*':[46]

> I had no idea what the epic story was, who its hero was, what enemies he fought, yet I had recently adapted the *Odyssey* for a theatre in England, presuming that the audience knew the trials of Odysseus, hero of another Asia Minor epic, while nobody in Trinidad knew any more than I did about Rome, Kali, Shiva, Vishnu, apart from the Indians, a phrase I use pervertedly because this is the kind of remark you can still hear in Trinidad: 'apart from the Indians'. (D. Walcott, 'The Antilles: Fragments of Epic Memory' (1998: 66))

This passage opens up at least two perspectives on this performance. On the one hand, it is about individuals' knowledge and ignorance of each other's cultures, its (epic) traditions and influences: 'I had no idea what the epic story was'; '[N]obody in Trinidad knew any more than I did about Rome, Kali, Shiva, Vishnu, apart from the Indians'. On the other hand, it presents us with a cultural event that betrays multiple influences known to some and ignored by others and vice versa. This is what Walcott means by 'fragments of epic memory', the subtitle of his lecture. *Ramleela* is a site in which disparate fragments of the epic past that we know and do not know converge with one another and create a *new transcultural memory* that competes with, even transcends received ideas about the epic tradition of the European West and its adaptations in other regions. This latter notion is at the forefront of Walcott's postcolonial thought on epic memory and the classical past, more broadly. Note how he criticizes his own initial outlook on *Ramleela*:

> They (the performers) believed in what they were playing . . . while I, out of the writer's habit, searched for some sense of elegy, of loss . . . I was polluting the afternoon with doubt and with patronage of admiration. I misread the event through a visual echo of History – the cane fields, indenture, the evocation of vanished armies, temples, and trumpeting elephants – when all around me there was quite the opposite: elation . . . a delight

[46] Walcott (1998: 65).

of conviction, not loss. (D. Walcott, 'The Antilles: Fragments of Epic
Memory' (1998: 67))

'I misread the event through a visual echo of History': in this instance,
'the echo of History' comes to represent the influence of a traditional
Western European outlook on the cultural production of the postcolonial world. It is a perspective that tends to be guided by a nostalgic,
'elegiac' sense of loss of a past that is understood to offer an authoritative model for the cultural appropriations of the present. It is also an
outlook informed by a 'memory that yearns to join the centre', like 'a
limb remembering a body from which it was severed' (1988: 67). Those
persuaded by 'the echo of History' observe an epic phenomenon like
Ramleela in the same way that 'grammarians look at a dialect ... cities
look on provinces and empires on their colonies' (1988: 67). For
Walcott, it is this sense of cultural history that initially offered him
what he believes was a misguiding paradigm for understanding *Ramleela*
in the context of his knowledge of the Homeric epic tradition and
particularly of the *Odyssey*. The alternative must be a reconsideration of
how we position ourselves to visualize such cultural events. At this
point, we reach one of the most inspiring moments in Walcott's
lecture – the metaphorical description of the culture of the Antilles as
a broken vase:

> Break a vase, and the love that reassembles the fragments is stronger than
> that love which took its symmetry for granted when it was whole. The glue
> that fits the pieces is the sealing of its original shape. It is such a love that
> reassembles our African and Asiatic fragments, the cracked heirlooms
> whose restoration shows its white scars. This gathering of broken pieces
> is the care and pain of the Antilles, and if the pieces are disparate, ill-
> fitting, they contain more pain than their original sculpture, those icons
> and sacred vessels taken for granted in their ancestral places. Antillean art
> is this restoration of our shattered histories, our shards of vocabulary, our
> archipelago becoming a synonym for pieces broken off from the original
> continent. (D. Walcott, 'The Antilles: Fragments of Epic Memory'
> (1998: 69))

With this metaphor, Walcott once more practises a lateral reading of
transcultural phenomena that is informed by the disparate fragments of
past memory, like the performance of *Ramleela* and the histories that
make up the art and culture of the Antilles. Instead of concentrating on
the 'wholeness' of the original vase, or on the sense of loss that its
restoration may recall, Walcott directs his attention to the substance
that reassembles the shattered piece, as well as the cracks that now

populate its renewed surface. 'Break a vase, and the love that reassembles the fragments is stronger than that love which took its symmetry for granted when it was whole': 'love' in this instance is nearly synonymous with 'glue' ('The glue that fits the pieces . . .'), but it also comes to signify the force of attraction that keeps reassembling fragments of the cultural past in unexpected combinations. In being such a force of attraction, Walcott's 'love' brings out the semantic sense of desire, but also of absence that, as we have seen, animates Borges' reading of eclipsed, lost, or partially known texts of classical antiquity. Walcott's use of 'love' and 'glue' has furthermore points of contact with Borges' appeal to sounds, like whispers and echoes, that explain the mnemonic recollection of the fragmentary past in the present, as exemplified by Borges' postclassical Homer. For Walcott and Borges, love, glue and sound offer alternative, indeed enduring metaphors for conceiving the processes that make up the history of transcultural phenomena. For it is not the original (in the sense that Walcott uses the word three times in the above passage to mean 'whole' or 'continent'), or the fragment that explains the restored vase, *Ramleela*, and the archipelago of the Antilles. Rather, it is the 'cracks' and the 'scars' and the sea that curves around islands that hold their 'shattered histories' together and offer a map for reading their complex cultural reassembling. Like the 'patient labyrinth of lines' that make up the face of the old man and tell of his life experience in the epilogue of Borges' *The Maker* (1960: *SP* 142), the scars in Walcott's vase speak of this artefact's cultural amalgamation through its blemished surface.

'Antillean art is this restoration of our shattered histories, our shards of vocabulary, our archipelago becoming a synonym for pieces broken off from the original continent': Walcott's broken vase draws attention to yet another crucial aspect of Walcott's cultural system. Namely, his archipelagic thinking, which he shares with authors like Édouard Glissant,[47] and which calls on the sea that contains a chain of scattered islands as a geographical metaphor for the specific cultural restoration that he sees at the heart of the Antilles and their continental fragments ('It is such a love that reassembles our African and Asiatic fragments'). Walcott's archipelagic cosmos in turn opens up a fresh understanding of Borges' constellation thinking about the classics. As we have seen throughout this book, Borges also builds his classical networks on (atopic) geographical

---

[47] Glissant (1997). For a recent discussion of Glissant's archipelagic thought vs continent thought, see Obrist and Raza (2017).

patterns and figures. Like Walcott's archipelago, the classical constellations found in Borges can be equally understood to restore the sense of cultural fractures and dislocations that Western and peripheral readings of the classics produce, while drawing attention to their renewal as global forms.

For readers of Borges' global classicism, Walcott's shattered-vase metaphor powerfully evokes Borges' approach to reading Graeco-Roman antiquity. We have seen that this approach seeks to understand the classical past from a perspective that moves beyond the interplay of original and reconstruction that persistently organizes the cultural history of the West. Instead it locates elements that explain how the fragmentary past comes together to make up our cultural memory, whoever and wherever we are. Like Walcott's love, this element functions as an agency that operates between past and present in Borges' oeuvre, joining these tenses as if they were broken pieces which, when put together, reveal new images and untold narratives. In Borges' classics, this sense of in-between may take the form of an absent-presence, a distant-yet-familiar rumour, a touch or a disorienting spot. Examples of this process abound Borges' oeuvre, as we have seen. Some of the most revealing are the Mobius effects of literature which mysteriously blend history and myth and allow a mythical character like Oedipus to glimpse the 'tissue of [the] whole plot', however momentarily. Other examples are the touch of Virgil's hand which innovatively charts Borges' memory of the Virgilian oeuvre from China to Buenos Aires, and the untold intertextual paths that guide us, not without difficulty, through the unknown landscape of oblivion, where Heraclitus sings his 'Nightingale' poem. The catalogue of these Borgesian readings seems as infinitely possible as Eco's lists, and as multidirectional and superimposed as Calvino's invisible cities, once we consider them from this in-between perspective. Yet, it is through Walcott's broken-vase metaphor that this perspective emerges as the most apt way of encapsulating Borges' classicism. When viewed from Walcott's own global readings, Borges' classics take the intriguing form of a gathering of cultural shards that momentarily reveals the fragmentary or lost images of the Graeco-Roman past on the scarred surface of the present. This is precisely the kind of image invoked by Scianna's photograph of Borges facing the Temple of Hera at Selinunte, which illustrates the opening pages and discussion of the present book. There, standing in front of the ruined temple, the almost-blind Borges does not feel a nostalgia of a lost world in ruins which he can no longer see in its former glory. Instead he is reinvigorated by the distant echoes and whispers that he hears, the touches he feels and the paths he follows as he rethinks the fragments of the classical past in the landscapes of his global imagination.

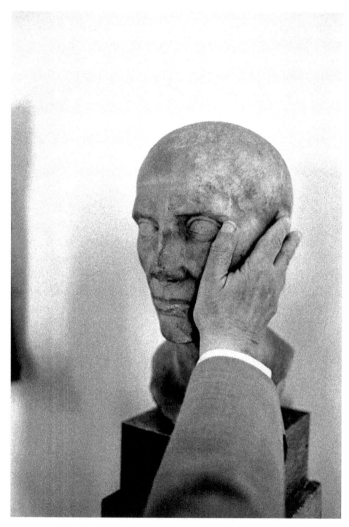

Argentinian writer, Jorge Luis Borges, in Palermo touching a sculpture of Julius Caesar in the Archaeological Museum, 1984. Photo by Ferdinando Scianna.

Bibliography

Aizenberg, E. (ed.) (1990), *Borges and His Successors: The Borgesian Impact on Literature and the Arts*. Columbia and London: University of Missouri Press.

Aizenberg, E. (ed.) (1990), 'Introduction', in *Borges and His Successors: The Borgesian Impact on Literature and the Arts*. Columbia and London: University of Missouri Press, 1–16.

Alazraki, J. (1990), 'Borges's Modernism and the New Critical Idiom', in E. Aizenberg (ed.), *Borges and His Successors: The Borgesian Impact on Literature and the Arts*. Columbia and London: University of Missouri Press, 99–108.

Alexopoulou, M. (2009), *The Theme of Returning Home in Ancient Greek Literature: The Nostos of the Epic Heroes*. Lewiston, NY and Lampeter, Wales.

Almeida, I. and Parodi, C. (2005), 'Borges en diálogo sobre el Budismo', *Variaciones Borges*, 20, 101–24.

Anderson, W. S. (2005), *The Art of the Aeneid*. Mundelein, IL: Bolchazy-Carducci Publishers.

Apter, E. (2013), *Against World Literature: On the Politics of Untranslatability*. London: Verso Books.

Assman, J. (1995), 'Collective Memory and Cultural Identity', in J. Assman and J. Czaplicka (eds.), *New German Critique*, 65, 125–33.

Bagnall, R. S., Brodersen, K., Champion, C. B., Erskine, A. and Huebner, S. R. (eds.) (2013), *The Encyclopedia of Ancient History*. Malden, MA and Oxford: Wiley-Blackwell.

Bailey, C. (1947), *Titi Lucreti Cari De Rerum Natura Libri Sex*, Vol. I. Oxford: Oxford University Press.

Balderstone, D. (2008), 'Borges, las sucesivas rupturas', in R. Olea Franco (ed.), *'In memoriam' Jorge Luis Borges*. Mexico: Colegio de México, Centro de Estudios Lingüísticos y Literarios, 19–36.

Bär, N. (2010), 'Borges se anticipó medio siglo a las neurociencias', *La Nación*, February 4.

Barchiesi, A. (1988), 'Ovid the Censor', *AJAH* 13: 96–105.

Barrenechea, A. M. (1965), *Borges the Labyrinth Maker*, translated by R. Lima. New York, NY: New York University Press.

Barthes, R. (1991), *Essais critiques*. Paris: Seuil.

Bartoloni, P. (1997), 'Spatialised Time and Circular Time: A Note on Time in the Work of Gerald Murnane and Jorge Luis Borges', *Australian Literary Studies*, 185–90.

(2004), 'The Problem of Time in the Critical Writings of Jorge Luis Borges', *Modern Greek Studies: Australia and New Zealand*, 11(12), 317–33.

Baugh, E. (2009), *Derek Walcott*. Cambridge: Cambridge University Press.

Beecroft, A. (2008), 'World Literature without a Hyphen: Towards a Typology of Literary Systems', *New Left Review* 54, 87–100.

(2013), 'Greek, Latin, and the Origins of "World Literature"', *Comparative Literature and Culture* 15.5 https://doi.org/10.7771/1481-4374.2334

(2015), *An Ecology of World Literature: From Antiquity to the Present Day*. London and New York, NY: Verso Books.

Begley, A. (1993), 'Don De Lillo, The Art of Fiction No. 135', *The Paris Review*, 128.

Benario, H. W. (2012), 'The *Annals*', in V. E. Pagán (ed.), *A Companion to Tacitus*. Malden, MA and Oxford: Wiley-Blackwell, 101–22.

Billings, J. (2016), 'The Sighs of Hellenism', in S. Butler (ed.), *Deep Classics. Rethinking Classical Reception*. London: Bloomsbury Publishing.

Bloom, H. (1975), *A Map of Misreading*. Oxford and New York, NY: Oxford University Press.

Bondanella, P. (2006), 'Italo Calvino and Umberto Eco: Postmodern Masters', in P. Bondanella and A. Ciccarelli (eds.), *Cambridge Companion to the Italian Novel*. Cambridge: Cambridge University Press, 168–81.

Borges, J. L. (1923–49), *Obras Completas I, Edición crítica anotada por Rolando Costa Picazo e Irma Zangara*, Buenos Aires: Emecé.

(1952–72), *Obras Completas II, Edición crítica anotada por Rolando Costa Picazo e Irma Zangara*. Buenos Aires: Emecé.

(1975–85), *Obras Completas III, Edición crítica anotada por Rolando Costa Picazo e Irma Zangara*. Buenos Aires: Emecé.

(1975–88), *Obras Completas IV, Edición crítica anotada por Rolando Costa Picazo e Irma Zangara*. Buenos Aires: Emecé.

(2010), *Oeuvres completes I, Préface de L'Auteur et edition établie, présentée et annotée par J. P. B.* Paris: Gallimard.

(2010), *Oeuvres completes II, Préface de L'Auteur et edition établie, présentée et annotée par J. P. B.* Paris: Gallimard.

(1984), *Seven Nights*, translated by E. Weinberger. New York: New Directions Publishing.

(1998), *Collected Fictions*, translated by A. Hurley. New York: Penguin.

(1999), *Selected Non-Fictions*, edited by E. Weinberger. New York: Penguin.

(1999), *Selected Poems*, edited by A. Coleman. New York: Penguin.

(2002), This Craft of Verse, *The Charles Eliot Norton Lectures 1967–1968*. Cambridge, MA: Harvard University Press.

Borges, J. L. and Carrizo, A. (1983), *Jorge Luis Borges, Borges el memorioso, Conversaciones Jorge Luis Borges con Antonio Carrizo*. Mexico: Fondo de Cultura Económica.

Borges, J. L. and Ferrari, O. (2014), *Jorge Luis Borges, Osvaldo Ferrari Conversations I*, translated by J. Wilson. London and New York, NY: The University of Chicago Press.

Borges, J. L. and Ferrari, O. (2015), *Jorge Luis Borges, Osvaldo Ferrari Conversations II*, translated by T. Boll. London and New York, NY: The University of Chicago Press.

Borges, J. L. and Ferrari, O. (2012), *Jorge Luis Borges, Osvaldo Ferrari Dialogues I: Borges en dialogues. Nouveaux dialogues*, translated by René Pons. Paris: Pocket Publishing.

Bossart, W. H. (2003), *Borges and Philosophy: Self, Time, and Metaphysics*. New York, NY: Peter Lang.

Bough, E. (2006), *Derek Walcott*. Cambridge Studies in African and Caribbean Literature. Cambridge: Cambridge University Press.

Breslin, P. (2001), *Nobody's Nation: Reading Derek Walcott*. Chicago: The University of Chicago Press.

Brodersen, K. and Talbert, T. (eds.) (2004), *Space in the Roman World: Its Perception and Presentation*. Münster: Lit ag.

Butler, S. (2011), *The Matter of the Page: Essays in Search of Ancient and Medieval Authors*. Madison, WI: The University of Wisconsin Press.

Butler, S. (ed.) (2016), *Deep Classics: Rethinking Classical Reception*. London, Oxford, New York, New Delhi, Sydney: Bloomsbury Publishing.

Butterfield, D. (2016), 'Some Problems in the Text and Transmission of Lucretius', in R. Hunter and S. Oakley (eds.), *Latin Literature and Its Transmission*. Cambridge: Cambridge University Press, 22–53.

Cajero, A. (2006), '"A quien leyere": La poética de Fervor de Buenos Aires', *Variaciones Borges* 22, 101–28.

Caldwell, T. M. (2008), *Virgil Made English: The Decline of Classical Authority*. New York, NY: Palgrave Macmillan.

Calvino, I. (1996), *Six Memos for the Next Millennium*. London: Penguin.

(1997), *Invisible Cities*. London: Penguin.

(2009), *Why Read the Classics?* London: Penguin.

Cameron, A. (1968), 'The First Edition of the *Amores*', *CQ* 62, 320–33.

Capozzi, R. (2002), 'Knowledge and Cognitive Practices in Eco's Labyrinths of Intertextuality', in J. J. E. Gracia, C. Korsmeyer and R. Gasché (eds.), *Literary Philosophers: Borges, Calvino, Eco*. New York, NY and London: Routledge, 164–84.

Carricaburo, N. (2011), 'Los enciclopedistas y el enciclopedismo de Jorge Luis Borges', in M. Cámpora and J. R. González (eds.), *Borges – Francia*, Buenos Aires: Universidad Católica Argentina, 461–73.

Casanova, P. (2004), *The World Republic of Letters*, translated by M. B. Debevoise. Cambridge, MA: Harvard University Press.

Cassin, B. (ed.) (2004), *Vocabulaire européen des philosophies: Dictionnaire des intraduisibles*, Vol. 26, No. 2, Paris: Seuil.

Cédola, E. (1994), 'Borges et la ferveur de Buenos Aires', in B. Melançon et P. Popovic (eds.), *Montréal 1642–1992. Le grand passage*, Montréal: XYZ, 169–89.

Charbonnier, G. (1967), *Entretiens avec Jorge Luis Borges*. Paris: Gallimard.

Cheah, P. (2008), 'What Is a world? On World Literature as World-Making Activity', *Daedalus*, 167, 26-38.

(2016), *What Is a World? On Postcolonial Literature as World Literature*. Durham, NC: Duke University Press.della Corte, F. (1986), 'Gli Amores di Ovidio ripidiati', in U. J. Stache, W. Maaz and F. Wagner (eds.), *Kontinuität und Wandel. Lateinische Poesie von Naevius bis Baudelaire. Franco Munarizum 65. Geburtstag*. Hildesheim: Weidmann, 70–8.

Damrosch, D. (2013), *What Is World Literature?* Princeton, NJ: Princeton University Press.

Derrida, J. (1981), *Dissemination*, translated by B. Johnson. London and New York, NY: The University of Chicago Press.

Deufert, M. (2016), 'Overlooked Manuscript Evidence for Interpolations in Lucretius', in R. Hunter and S. Oakley (eds.), *Latin Literature and Its Transmission*. Cambridge: Cambridge University Press, 68–87.

Dupont, F. (2013), *L'Antiquité, territoire des écarts. Entretiens avec Pauline Colonna d'Istria et Sylvie Taussig*. Paris: Broché.

Fraenkel, E. (1950), *Aeschylus: Agamemnon*, edited with commentary. Oxford: Oxford University Press.

Earle, P. G. (2003), 'In and Out of Time (Cervantes, Dostoevsky, Borges)', *Hispanic Review*, 71, 1–13.

(1989), *The Open Work*. Cambridge, MA: Harvard University Press.

(1994), *Reflections on The Name of the Rose*. London: Minerva.

(2004), *On Beauty: A History of a Western Idea*. London: Secker & Warburg.

(2006), *On Literature*. London: Harcourt.

(2007), *On Ugliness*. New York, NY: Rizzoli.

(2009), *The Infinity of Lists: From Homer to Joyce*. London: Rizzoli.

(2014), *The Name of the Rose*. Translated by W. Weaver. Boston and New York: Houghon Mifflin Harcourt.

Eliot, T. S. (1944), *What Is a Classic? An Address Delivered Before the Virgil Society on the 16th of October 1944*. London: The Virgil Society.

Enguídanos, M. (1986), 'Seventeen Notes towards Deciphering Borges (Glosses)', in C. Cortínez (ed.), *Borges the Poet*. Fayetteville, 315–21.

Farrell, J. (1991), *Vergil's* Georgics *and the Traditions of Ancient Epic: The Art of Allusion in Literary History*. Oxford: Oxford University Press.

Farronato, C. (2003), *Eco's Chaosmos: From the Middle Ages to Postmodernity*. Toronto: University of Toronto Press.

Fiddian, R. (2013), 'Post-Colonial Borges', in E. Williamson (ed.), *The Cambridge Companion to Jorge Luis Borges*. Cambridge: Cambridge University Press.

Fine, R. (2003), 'Borges y Cervantes: Perspectivas estéticas', in M. Solotorevsky and R. Fine (eds.), *Borges en Jerusalén*. Veruvert: Iberoamericana, 117–25.

Fishburn, E. (2013), 'Jewish, Christian, and Gnostic themes', in E. Williamson (ed.), *The Cambridge Companion to Jorge Luis Borges*. Cambridge: Cambridge University Press, 56–67.

Fitzgerald, W. (2016), *Variety: The Life of a Roman Concept*. Chicago: The University of Chicago Press.

Forero, M. T. and Garabieta, L. (2013), *Borges y oriente*, Buenos Aires: Diseño.

Foucault, M. (1970), *The Order of Things: An Archaeology of the Human Sciences*. London: Tavistock Publications.

(1984), 'Of Other Spaces, Heterotopias', *Architecture, Mouvement, Continuité*: 46–9.

Fowler, R. (2004), 'The Homeric Question', in R. Fowler (ed.), *The Cambridge Companion to Homer*. Cambridge: Cambridge University Press, 220–32.

Fry, P. (2000), 'Classical Standards in Romantic Period', in M. Brown (ed.), *The Cambridge History of Literary Criticism. Vol. 5: Romanticism*. Cambridge: Cambridge University Press, 7–28.

García Jurado, F. and Salazar Morales, R. (2014), *La traducción y sus palimpsestos: Borges, Homero y Virgilio*. Madrid: Escolar y Mayo.

García Jurado, F. (2016), *Teoría de la tradición clásica: Conceptos, historia y métodos*. México: Universidad Autónoma de México.

García Martin, E. (2005), 'The Dangers of Abstraction in Borges's "The Immortal"', *Variaciones Borges*, 20, 87–100.

Genette, G. (1997), *Paratexts: Thresholds of Interpretation*, translated by J. E. Lewin. Cambridge: Cambridge University Press.

Giskin, H. (2005), 'Borges' Revisioning of Reading in "Pierre Menard, Author of the Quixote"', *Variaciones Borges* 19, 103–23.

Glissant, E. (1997), *The Poetics of Relation*, translated by B. Wing. Ann Arbor, MI: University of Michigan Press.

Goff, B. and Simpson, M. (2007), *Crossroads in the Black Aegean: Oedipus, Antigone and Dramas of the African Diaspora*. Oxford: Oxford University Press.

Goldschmidt, N. (forthcoming 2018), 'Orts, scraps, and fragments', in J. Harding and J. Nash, *Modernism and Non-Translation*. Oxford: Oxford University Press.

González Echevarría, R. (2013), 'The Aleph', in E. Williamson (ed.), *The Cambridge Companion to Jorge Luis Borges*. Cambridge: Cambridge University Press, 123–36.

Gow, A. S. F. and Page, D. L. (eds.) (1965), *The Greek Anthology 1: Hellenistic Epigrams*. Cambridge: Cambridge University Press.

Gracia, J. J. E., Korsmeyer, C. and Gasché, R. (eds.) (2002), *Literary Philosophers: Borges, Calvino, Eco*. New York, NY and London: Routledge.

Graziosi, B. (2002), *Inventing Homer: The Early Reception of Epic*. Cambridge: Cambridge University Press.

Graziosi, B. and Greenwood, E. (eds.) (2007), *Homer in the Twentieth Century: Between World Literature and the Western Canon*. Oxford: Oxford University Press.

Greenblatt, S. (2011), *The Swerve: How the World Became Modern*. New York, NY and London: W. W. Norton & Company.

Greenwood, E. (2009), 'Shades of Rome in the Poetry of Derek Walcott', in S. Harrison (ed.), *Living Classics: Greece and Rome in Contemporary Poetry in English*. Oxford: Oxford University Press, 255–74.

(2010), *Afro-Greeks: Dialogues between Anglophone Caribbean Literature and Classics in the Twentieth Century*. Oxford: Oxford University Press.

(2016), 'Reception Studies: The Cultural Mobility of Classics', *Daedalus Journal of the American Academy of Arts and Sciences* 145(2), 41–9.

Griffin, C. (2013), 'Philosophy and Fiction', in E. Williamson (ed.), *The Cambridge Companion to Jorge Luis Borges*. Cambridge: Cambridge University Press, 5–15.

Güthenke, C. (2008), *BMCR* Review of *Homer in the Twentieth Century: Between World Literature and the Western Canon*. Oxford: Oxford University Press.

Hardie, P. (2009), *Lucretian Receptions: History, the Sublime, Knowledge*. Cambridge: Cambridge University Press.

Hardwick, L. (2007), 'Introduction', in L. Hardwick and C. Gillespie (eds.), *Classics in Post-Colonial Worlds*. Oxford: Oxford University Press, 1–14.

Haubold, J. (2007). 'Homer after Parry: Tradition, Reception and the Timeless Text', in B. Graziosi and E. Greenwood (eds.), *Homer in the Twentieth Century: Between World Literature and the Western Canon*. Oxford: Oxford University Press.

Heubeck, A., West, S. and Hainsworth, J. B. (1988), *A Commentary on Homer's Odyssey, Vol. I*. Oxford: Oxford University Press.

(1989), *A Commentary on Homer's Odyssey, Vol. II*. Oxford: Oxford University Press.

Hinds, S. (1998), *Allusion and Intertext: Dynamics of Appropriation in Roman Poetry*. Cambridge: Cambridge University Press.

Holzberg, N. (2006), 'Playing with his Life: Ovid's "Autobiographical" References', in P. E. Knox (ed.), *Oxford Readings in Ovid*. Oxford: Oxford University Press, 51–68.

Huggan, G. (2011), 'The Trouble with World Literature', in A. Behdad and D. Thomas (eds.), *A Companion to Comparative Literature*. Oxford: Wiley-Blackwell, 490–506.

Hunter, R. (1992), 'Callimachus and Heraclitus', *MD* 28, 113–23.

Hutchinson, G. O. (1985), *Aeschylus, Septem Contra Thebas*. Oxford: Oxford University Press.

(2006), *Propertius: Elegies Book IV*. Cambridge: Cambridge University Press.

(2008), *Talking Books: Readings in Hellenistic and Roman Books of Poetry*. Oxford: Oxford University Press.

Ioannidou, E. (2017), *Greek Fragments in Postmodern Frames: Rewriting Tragedy 1970–2005*. Oxford: Oxford University Press.

Jacobson, H. (1974), *Ovid's Heroides*. Princeton: Princeton University Press.

Jansen, L. (2012), 'On the Edge of the Text: Preface and Reader in Ovid's Amores', *Helios* 39(1), 1–19.

(2014), *The Roman Paratext: Frame, Texts, Readers*. Cambridge: Cambridge University Press, 1–18.

(2016), 'Borges and the Disclosure of Antiquity', in S. Butler (ed.), *Deep Classics: Rethinking Classical Reception*. London: Bloomsbury Publishing, 291–309.

(2018), 'Extreme Classicisms: Jorge Luis Borges', in E. Richardson (ed.), *Classics in Extremis*. London: Bloomsbury Publishing.

Johnson, D. E. (2009), 'Time. For Borges', *CR: The New Centennial Review* 9(1), 209–26.

de Jong, I. (2001), *A Narratological Commentary on the Odyssey*. Cambridge: Cambridge University Press.

de Lailhacar, C. (1990), 'The Mirror and the Encyclopaedia: Borgesian Codes in U. Eco's The Name of the Rose', in E. Aizenberg (ed.), *Borges and His Successors: The Borgesian Impact on Literature and the Arts*. Columbia and London: University of Missouri Press, 155–79.

Kahn, C. H. (1979), *The Art and Thought of Heraclitus: An Edition with Fragments with Translation and Commentary*. Cambridge: Cambridge University Press.

Kefala, E. (2007), *Peripheral (post) Modernity: The Syncretist Aesthetics of Borges, Piglia, Kalokyris and Kyriakidis*. New York: Peter Lang.

Kennedy, D. F. (2002), *Rethinking Reality: Lucretius and the Textualization of Nature*. Ann Arbor, MI: University of Michigan Press.

(2007), 'Making a Text of the Universe: Perspectives on Discursive Order in *De rerum natura*', in M. R. Gale (ed.), *Oxford Readings in Lucretius*. Oxford: Oxford University Press, 276–96.

King, B. (2000), *Derek Walcott: A Caribbean Life*. Oxford: Oxford University Press.

Klaeber, F. (2008), *Klaeber's Beowulf and The Fight at Finnsburg*, edited by R. D. Fulk, R. E. Bork and J. D. Niles. Toronto: Toronto University Press.

Kristal, E. (2002), *Invisible Work: Borges and Translation*. Vanderbilt and Nashville: Vanderbilt University Press.

Krysinski, W. (2002), 'Borges, Calvino, Eco: The Philosophies of Metafiction', in J. E. Gracia, C. Korsmeyer and R. Gasché (eds.), *Literary Philosophers: Borges, Calvino, Eco*. New York, NY: Routledge.

Laín Corona, G. (2009), 'Borges and Cervantes: Truth and Falsehood in the Narration', *Neophilologus* 93(3), 421–37.

Lapidot, E. (1991), 'Borges y Escher: artistas contemporáneos', *Revista Iberoamericana*, Vol. LVII, No. 155–56, 607–15.

Lazarus, N. (2004), 'Introducing Postcolonial Studies', in N. Lazarus (ed.), *The Cambridge Companion to Postcolonial Studies*. Cambridge: Cambridge University Press, 1–16.

Levine, S. J. (2013), 'Borges on Translation', in E. Williamson (ed.), *The Cambridge Companion to Jorge Luis Borges*. Cambridge: Cambridge University Press, 43–55.

Loeb, P. S. (2013), 'Eternal Recurrence', in K. Gemes and J. Richardson (eds.), *The Oxford Handbook of Nietzsche*. Oxford: Oxford University Press.

López-Baralt, L. (2013), 'Islamic Themes', in E. Williamson (ed.), *The Cambridge Companion to Jorge Luis Borges*. Cambridge: Cambridge University Press, 68–80.

Macadam, A. (2013), 'The Maker', in E. Williamson (ed.), *The Cambridge Companion to Jorge Luis Borges*. Cambridge: Cambridge University Press, 137–45.

Madrid, L. (1987), *Cervantes y Borges: La inversión de los signos*. Madrid: Pliegos.

Manguel, A. (1997), *A History of Reading*. London: Flamingo.

(2006), *With Borges*. London: Telegram.

(2007) *Homer's the Iliad and the Odyssey: A Bibliography*. New York, NY: Atlantic Monthly Press.

(2010), *A Reading on Reading*. New Haven, CT and London: Yale University Press.

(2012), 'Translating Borges', *Biblioasis International Translations Blog*, http://biblioasistranslation.blogspot.com/2012/04/alberto-manguel-translating-borges.html.

Martin, R. H. (2010), 'From Manuscript to Print', in A. J. Woodman (ed.), *The Cambridge Companion to Tacitus*. Cambridge: Cambridge University Press, 241–52.

Martindale, C. (1993), *Redeeming the Text: Latin Poetry and the Hermeneutics of Reception*. Cambridge: Cambridge University Press.

(1997), 'Introduction: The Classic of Europe', in C. Martindale (ed.), *The Cambridge Companion to Virgil*. Cambridge: Cambridge University Press, 1–18.

(2010), 'Leaving Athens: Classics for a New Century?', Review of Page duBois, Out of Athens: The New Ancient Greeks, *Arion* 18(1), 135–48.

(2013), 'Response to Forum Debate', *Classical Receptions Journal* 5(2), 246–51.

Martínez Pérsico, M. (2010), 'Analogías de la invención: M. C. Escher y Jorge Luis Borges', *Cartaphilus* 7(8), 112–8.

Marx, J. (2004), 'Postcolonial Literature and the Western Literary Canon', in N. Lazarus (ed.), *The Cambridge Companion to Postcolonial Studies*. Cambridge: Cambridge University Press, 83–96.

Master, J. (2012), 'The Histories', in V. E. Pagán (ed.), *A Companion to Tacitus*. Malden, MA, Oxford and Chichester: Wiley-Blackwell, 84–100.

McConnell, J. (2013), *Black Odysseys: The Homeric Odyssey in the African Dispora*. Oxford: Oxford University Press.

McDermott, H. (2013), 'The Mulatto of Criticism: Walcott and Literary Criticism', in J. Antoine-Dunne (ed.), *Interlocking Basins of a Globe: Essays on Derek Walcott*. Leeds: Peepal Tree Press, 51–70.

McKeown, J. C. (1987), *Ovid: Amores. Text, Prolegomena and Commentary*. Volume I (Arca 20). Liverpool: ARCA 20.

Moretti, F. (2004), 'Conjectures on World Literature', in C. Prendergast (ed.), *Debating World Literature*. London: Verso.

Morgan, L. (1999), *Patterns of Redemption in Virgil's* Georgics. Cambridge: Cambridge University Press.

Mosher, M. (1994), 'Atemporal Labyrinths in Time: J. L. Borges and the New Physicists', *Symposium* 48(1), 51–61.

Mualem, S. (2012), *Borges and Plato: A Game with Shifting Mirrors*. Madrid: Iberoamericana/Vervuert Verlag.

Murgia, C. E. (1986a), 'The date of Ovid's Ars Amatoria 3', *AJPh*, 107, 74–94.
  (1986b), 'Influence of Ovid's Remedia Amoris on Ars Amatoria 3 and Amores 3', *CPh* 81, 203–20.
  (2012), 'The Textual Transmission', in V. E. Pagán (ed.), *A Companion to Tacitus*. Malden, MA, Oxford and Chichester: Wiley-Blackwell, 15–22.

Nagy, G. (2010), *Homer The Preclassic*. Berkeley, CA, Los Angeles, CA and London: University of California Press.

Neer, R. (2012), *Greek Archaeology: A New History, c. 2500 – c. 150 BCE*. New York, NY: Thames & Hudson.

Obrist, H. U. and Raza, A. (2017), *Mondialité or the Archipelagos of Édouard Glissant*. Villa Empain, Brussels: Boghossian Foundation.

Olea Franco, R. (1993), *El otro Borges, el primer Borges*. Mexico: El Colegio de México – Fondo de Cultura Económica.
  (2013), 'The early poetry (1923–1929)', in E. Williamson (ed.), *The Cambridge Companion to Jorge Luis Borges*. Cambridge: Cambridge University Press, 172–85.

O'Sullivan, G. (1990), 'The Library Is on Fire: Intertextuality in Borges and Foucault', in E. Aizenberg (ed.), *Borges and His Successors: The Borgesian Impact on Literature and the Arts*. Columbia and London: University of Missouri Press, 109–21.

Palmer (2014), *Reading Lucretius in the Renaissance*. Cambridge, MA: Harvard University Press.

Parker, D. (1990), 'The Literature of Appropriation: Eco's Use of Borges in Il Nome della Rosa', *Modern Language Review* 85, 842–9.

Perella, S. (1999), *Calvino*. Roma.

Petrovic, I. (2014), 'Posidippus and Achaemenid Royal Propaganda', in R. Hunter, A. Rengakos and E. Sistakou (eds.), *Hellenistic Studies at a Crossroads: Exploring Texts, Contexts and Metatexts*. Berlin: De Gruyter, 273–300.

Pettersson, A. (2008), 'Transcultural Literary History: Beyond Constricting Notions of World Literature', *New Literary History* 39, 463–479.

Piglia, R. (2001), *Crítica y ficción*. Barcelona: Anagrama.
  (2005), *El último lector*. Barcelona: Anagrama.
  (2013), Clase 3: 'La biblioteca y el lector en Borges', *Borges por Piglia*, www .tvpublica.com.ar/programa/borges-por-piglia.

Pollard, C. W. (2004), *New Worlds of Modernisms: T. S Eliot, Derek Walcott and Kamau Brathwaite*. Charlottesville, VA and London: The University of Virginia Press.

Porter, J. (2004), 'Homer: The History of an Idea', in R. Fowler (ed.), *The Cambridge Companion to Homer*. Cambridge: Cambridge University Press, 324–43.

(2008), 'Reception Studies: Future Prospects', in L. Hardwick and C. Gillespie (eds.), *Classics in Post-Colonial Worlds*. Oxford: Oxford University Press, 469–81.

Prosperi, V. (2010), 'Lucretius in the Italian Renaissance', in S. Gillespie and P. Hardie (eds.), *The Cambridge Companion to Lucretius*. Cambridge: Cambridge University Press, 214–26.

Purves, A. (2017), *Touch and the Ancient Senses*. Abingdon and New York, NY: Routledge.

Rabau, S. (2012), *Quinze (brèves) rencontres avec Homère, L'Antiquité au present*. Paris and Berlin: Fabula.

Reeve, M. (2010), 'Lucretius in the Middle Ages and the Renaissance: Transmission and Scholarship', in S. Gillespie and P. Hardie (eds.), *The Cambridge Companion to Lucretius*. Cambridge: Cambridge University Press, 205–13.

Reynolds, L. D. and Wilson, N. G. (eds.) (1983), *Texts and Transmission: A Survey of the Latin Classics*. Oxford: Oxford University Press.

Richardson, B. (2012), *Borges and Space*. Bern: Peter Lang.

Robinson, T. M. (1987), *Heraclitus: Fragments. A Text and Translation with a Commentary*. Toronto: University of Toronto Press.

Rodriguez Monegal, E. (1983), *Jorge Luis Borges: Biographie Littéraire*. Paris: Gallimard.

Roman, L. (2015), 'Statius and Martial: Post-Vatic Self-Fashioning in Flavian Rome', in W. J. Dominik, C. E. Newlands and K. Gervais (eds.), *Brill's Companion to Statius*. Leiden: Brill, 444–61.

Rosato, L. and Álvarez, G. (2010), *Borges, libros y lecturas: catálogo de la colección Jorge Luis Borges*. Buenos Aires: Ediciones Biblioteca Nacional.

Ross, R. (1990), 'It Cannot Not Be There: Borges and Australia's Peter Carey', in E. Aizenberg (ed.), *Borges and His Successors: The Borgesian Impact on Literature and the Arts*. Columbia and London: University of Missouri Press, 44–58.

Sagastume, J. R. and Martínez-Sáenz, M. (2005), 'Desmantelamiento y reconstrucción textual: Borges, «Pierre Menard, autor del Quijote y la traducción»'. *Bulletin of Spanish Studies* 82(6), 815–29.

Salazar Morales, R. (2011), *Homerus redivivus: Borges et ses 'Vies imaginaires' d'Homère*. Paris: Université de Paris IV.

(2015), 'Homère dans la Cité des Immortels: de la "vie imaginaire" à l'imaginaire philosophique dans "El inmortal" de Jorge Luis Borges', *Comparatismes en Sorbonne (Les Classiques aux Amériques)* 6, 1–15, www.crlc.paris-sorbonne.fr/FR/Page_revue_num.php?P1=6.

Sarlo, B. (1988), *Una modernidad peripherica: Buenos Aires, 1920 y 1930*. Buenos Aires: Ediciones Nueva Visión.

(1993), *A Writer on the Edge*. London and New York, NY: Verso.

Saunders, T., Martindale, C., Pite, R. and Skoie, M. (eds.) (2012), *Romans and Romantics*. Oxford: Oxford University Press.

Schwob, M. (2004), *Vies imaginaires. Présentation par Jean-Pierre Bertrand et Gérald Purnelle*. Paris: Klincksieck.

Scianna, F. (1999), *Portraits of Jorge Luis Borges*. Italy: Franco Sciardelli.

Skempis, M. and Ziogas, I. (eds.) (2014), *Geography, Topography, Landscape: Configurations of Space in Greek and Roman Epic*. Berlin: De Gruyter.

Stead, E. (ed.) (2009), *Seconde Odyssée: Ulysse de Tennyson à Borges, textes réunis, commentés et en partie traduits par Evanghélia Stead*. Grenoble: Jérôme Millon. Nomina, essais et documents.

Syme, R. (1978), *History in Ovid*. Oxford: Oxford University Press.

Tcherepashenets, N. (2008), *Place and Displacement in the Narrative Worlds of Jorge Luis Borges and Julio Cortázar*. New York, NY: Peter Lang.

de Toro, A. (1995), 'Post-Coloniality and Post-Modernity: Jorge Luis Borges: The Periphery in the Centre, the Periphery as the Centre, the Centre of the Periphery', in F. de Toro and A. de Toro (eds.), *Borders and Margins: Postcolonialism and Post-Modernism*. Frankfurt and Madrid: Vervuert Verlag, 11–43.

Varsava, J. (1990), 'The Last Fictions: Calvino's Borgesian Odysseys', in E. Aizenberg (ed.), *Borges and His Successors: The Borgesian Impact on Literature and the Arts*. Columbia and London: University of Missouri Press, 183–99.

Walcott, D. (1981), *The Fortunate Traveller*, New York, NY: Farrar, Straus & Giroux.

(1984), *Midsummer*. New York, NY: Farrar, Straus & Giroux.

(1998), *What the Twilight Says. Essays*. New York, NY: Farrar, Straus & Giroux.

Webb, T. (1982), *English Romantic Hellenism: 1700–1824*. Manchester: Manchester University Press.

Weiss, B. (1993), *Understanding Italo Calvino*. Columbia, SC: University of South California.

Widzisz, M. A. (2012), *Chronos on the Threshold: Time, Ritual, and Agency in the Oresteia*. Lanham, MD and Plymouth: Lexington Books.

Williamson, E. (1994), 'The Question of Influence', in E. Williamson (ed.), *Cervantes and the Modernists: The Question of Influence*. London: Tamesis, 1–8.

(2004), *Borges: A Life*. New York, NY and London: Penguin.

(2013), 'Borges in Context: The Autobiographical Dimension', in E. Williamson (ed.), *The Cambridge Companion to Jorge Luis Borges*. Cambridge: Cambridge University Press, 201–25.

Wilson, J. (2013), 'The Late Poetry', in E. Williamson (ed.), *The Cambridge Companion to Jorge Luis Borges*. Cambridge: Cambridge University Press, 186–200.

Wood, M. (1994), 'Cervantes reads Borges and Nabokov', in E. Williamson (ed.), *Cervantes and the Modernists: The Question of Influence*. London: Tamesis, 29–41.

(2013), 'Borges and theory', in E. Williamson (ed.), *The Cambridge Companion to Jorge Luis Borges*. Cambridge: Cambridge University Press, 29–42.

Ziolkowski, J. M. and Putnam, M. C. J. (eds.) (2008), *The Virgilian Tradition: The First Fifteen Hundred Years*. New Haven, CT and London: Yale University Press.

Zonana, V. G. (2006), 'Memoria del mundo clásico en "Funes el memorioso"', *Revista de Literaturas Modernas* 36, 207–33.

Index

Milton Keynes UK
Ingram Content Group UK Ltd.
UKHW021942280124
436877UK00018B/81